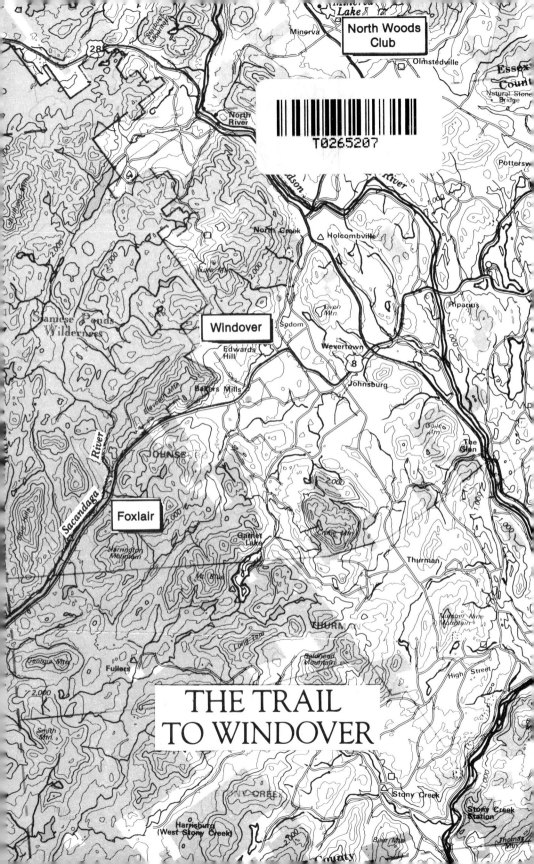

North Woods
Club

T0265207

Windover

Foxlair

THE TRAIL
TO WINDOVER

AN
ADIRONDACK
ARCHIVE:
THE TRAIL TO WINDOVER

ELISABETH HUDNUT CLARKSON

North Country Books, Inc.
Utica, New York

An Adirondack Archive
The Trail to Windover

Copyright © 1993
by Elisabeth Hudnut Clarkson

ISBN 0-925168-17-3

Library of Congress Cataloging-in-Publication Data

Clarkson, Elisabeth Hudnut.
    An Adirondack archive : the trail to Windover / by Elisabeth
Hudnut Clarkson.
        p. cm.
    Includes bibliographical references.
    ISBN 0-925168-17-3
    1. Hudnut family.   2. Adirondack Mountain Region
(N.Y.) — Biography.   I. Title.
CT274.H82C53   1993
929'.2'0973 — dc20   93-8211
                                                                CIP

Published by
North Country Books, Inc.
PUBLISHER — DISTRIBUTOR
18 Irving Place
Utica, New York 13501

Contents

	Preface		v
	Acknowledgements		viii
Chapter	1	The Alexander Hudnut Family	1
Chapter	2	The Earliest Adirondack Visits of William Hudnut	13
Chapter	3	The Beechers of Fish House	23
Chapter	4	The Fish House of Sir William Johnson	25
Chapter	5	Godfrey Shew and the Settlement of Fish House	30
Chapter	6	Further Adventures of the Fish House Settlers	41
Chapter	7	The Fish House Summer of 1889	47
Chapter	8	Overture to a Fish House Wedding	68
Chapter	9	The Golden Age of Fish House	82
Chapter	10	The Sacandaga Reservoir: Changing Times	94
Chapter	11	The Lake Pleasant Years: Prologue	99
Chapter	12	The Family of Camp Perkins	108
Chapter	13	The Hudnut Family at Speculator	119
Chapter	14	Speculator Farewell	138
Chapter	15	Oregon	145
Chapter	16	Richard Hudnut	147
Chapter	17	The Early Days of Foxlair	155
Chapter	18	The Estate	170
Chapter	19	The People	178
Chapter	20	The Valentino Summer	182
Chapter	21	The Last Days of Foxlair	200
Chapter	22	Windover	218
		Appendixes	239
		Bibliography	261

Preface

Whoever made me think our family's history in the Adirondacks could be material for a book?

It was Warder Cadbury. Warder is a history professor at SUNY Albany, an Adirondack historian and writer of note, and one day in the early 1960s he set out, from his camp at Indian Lake, to search out possible manuscripts for the Adirondack Museum in Blue Mountain Lake to publish. He appeared that afternoon at my parent's beach, where a small group of us were sitting around, basking in the sun and watching our tiny children swim and build sandcastles.

My father got up and went to greet this stranger, who introduced himself and said, "I'm looking for the Hudnut who writes."

At that time I was the only Hudnut who had had a book published and so I roused myself and joined their discussion. Warder explained his connection to the Museum, and that he was looking for people who could write about little-known parts of the Adirondacks, for potential publication under their name. Someone had suggested that he come to our family, and he had evidently heard of my book, published several years back.

Quite naturally, I was intrigued. Our family knew the Adirondack Museum and delighted in visits to it. It was smaller by far in those days, also less known and celebrated than it is now. It was the creation of one ardent lover of the Adirondacks, Harold Hochschild, and master-minded still by its brilliant creator, with a small staff and no outside board of directors or membership.

The Museum published wonderful books including the fascinating series by Mr. Hochschild himself, and at least one by Cadbury, which I owned.

Professor Cadbury may have been prompted to come to Windover by William Wessels' paperback collection called *Adirondack Profiles*, which had a chapter on my great-uncle Richard Hudnut, and on Fox-lair, his summer home, written largely from an interview with Father and Grandfather. Mr. Wessels had felt the spell of Grandfather's charm and noted him to be "the most alert man of ninety-five years that I have ever met." He ended his brief profile of our family with a sweeping accolade: "The Hudnuts have made a great contribution to American life, and they sojourn each summer on their estate in Peace-ful Valley, each having his own home, fronting on a private lake, and are truly lovers of the Adirondack country." Grandfather was embar-rassed by Mr. Wessels' effusions, not the least of which was his having called "Windover," our beloved family camp, an "estate." But perhaps that little book brought Warder Cadbury to us and, hence, this book to you.

Since my childhood, my mother had reminded me of our Beecher family connections, as if to motivate my love of writing. My Grand-father, William H. Hudnut, called me his "amanuensis," and I could often be found recording question-and-answer sessions with him on the Big House porch.

He died at 98 in 1963 and was buried, with all the honors and cere-monials due a beloved patriarch, in the family cemetery at Windover, next to our Grandmother, Harriet Beecher Hudnut.

The following summer an enormous box was delivered to me. It was marked, "For Nannie," and it was a legacy for his amanuensis, con-taining a wealth of archival things in yellowed envelopes — packets of letters, memorabilia of a long life. Most important, it contained the manuscript of his *Memoirs*, written at Uncle Bill's encouragement, in the lonely early years after Grandmother's death. Much of what was in that box is contained in this book.

By the time my first manuscript was more or less complete, the Adi-rondack Museum had changed directors, and the new one had no knowledge or previous interest in this book. However, a few summers later we became acquainted with Mary and Harold Hochschild; Mary, a Marquand, had grown up in Princeton and knew Father when in his undergraduate days he had come to call on her sister. She urged me to bring my work to the new Director of Publications at the Museum; Mary Hochschild had read my manuscript and enjoyed it.

So I spent time with the late William Vernor, a vivid Adirondack writer from Long Lake, and he was very helpful. He told me that it was entirely too long to be published economically. He also told me something else: "What is really compelling in your family story is the contrast between the two brothers, and between their two places. Here you've got Richard and his grand Foxlair—gone now, and your grandfather—William—founding your place that's still going strong!" He leaned back, as I remember, pleased with his insight. "*There's* your story!" he said.

Almost a quarter of a century later now, I have taken my manuscript out of its back shelf in my study and revised it. I want my Windover family to have it; I want the children who are Will and Harriet's great-great grandchildren to know their Adirondack roots. And, in the same way that I have eagerly read many another Adirondack story, there are perhaps others who will read this, finding in it something of their own.

—E.H.C.

Acknowledgments

In addition to the members of the older generations of my family, who shared valuable memories and materials with me, as well as giving trustworthy critical and evaluative readings of various chapters, I need to thank some others whose help I have so much appreciated. Many are no longer living, but they are very much alive in my memory and gratitude.

In the Fish House chapters I am indebted to the Fish House Historian, Kathryn Roosevelt Sleezer; to Mrs. Bovee, lately of the Johnstown Public Library; to Mignonette Riker of Fish House, Genealogist of the Beecher and Marvin families and to Mrs. Frank Sinclaire of Rosslyn House. In their various ways they enlarged the love of Fish House which was so early planted in me by my great-aunt "Nan," H. Emily Beecher.

Rose Perkins Gallup, daughter of Isaiah and Susan Lawrence Perkins, was able to authenticate and clarify Grandfather's and Father's romantic tales of Camp Perkins; she gave me some rare photographs of the family at Perkins' Clearing as well.

In writing the Foxlair chapters I was helped by Mrs. Betty Bowman, Sophronia Dunkley Montena, Roy Dunkley, Dan Nevins, Willett Randall, John Robbins, and, most of all, one who lived at Foxlair so many years, Katherine Armstrong.

The expert editing assistance of my cousin, Holly Hudnut Halliday, and the clerical help of Rose Sury and Janice R. Conner, have been crucial to the completion of this work. My gratitude to all.

CHAPTER 1

THE ALEXANDER HUDNUT FAMILY

The central figure in this story—its hero and patriarch—is William Herbert Hudnut. There is a heroine as well, but though she is at the heart of our tale, she doesn't enter it until our hero has found his way to Fish House, that idyllic village of old in the Adirondack foothills, founded by her ancestors in the eighteenth century. So we begin our story with Will Hudnut, fourth eldest son of the Alexander Hudnut family of New York and West Orange, New Jersey.

Alexander Hudnut, born in 1830, came of an old New Jersey line which had emigrated from England in 1740. The first to come was Titus Hudnut, of whom we know nothing save that two of his grandsons were General Lafayette's guides through the New Jersey wilderness, and that another grandson, Richard II, was a Fife Major in the American Revolution. By the middle of the nineteenth century a branch of the family was well established in the town of Princeton. Alexander Malieu Hudnut, for whom young Alexander was named, had served several terms as mayor. Of the mayor's brother, Robert Savage Hudnut, and his wife, Elizabeth, we know very little. Both died when Alexander was very young, and their children were left with relatives in Princeton.

A little later, Alexander was sent to live with his married sister,

1

Carrie Adams, in Philadelphia, where she had a thriving business in seashells in nearby Atlantic City. She soon found the young lad a job with a local pharmacist, washing bottles. Thus were the beginnings of one who was to make his fortune as a druggist.

In marriage young Hudnut "bettered himself," for his wife came from the Parker family of Long Branch, New Jersey, which, though modestly reduced in circumstance from the great land-owning days of the seventeenth century, still was numbered among the first families of New Jersey. By the time Alexander Hudnut came courting, Peter Parker had lost most of his inherited property. All that was left was his father's farm that spread along a beautiful stretch of seashore, and the handsome farmhouse where he and his wife, the former Rebecca Herbert, lived with their six daughters and two sons. We do not know how Alexander came to know the Parkers. But once they met, it was a lifelong attraction.

His first wife was the second eldest daughter, Margaret Parker. She was reportedly bright and capable, and she bore three children: Edgar Lamartine, Richard Alexander, and Nellie Julie Florence Grace. However, Margaret died of typhoid fever while the children were very young. Alexander returned in less than a year to the family he had come to know and trust, in search of a second wife.

The Parkers must have thought well of him; in fact, he must have seemed a worthy suitor. His pharmacy in Brooklyn was expanding rapidly, but of more interest to the Parker daughters, he was a brilliant and strangely striking man, tall, slight of build, darkly handsome, with a single blue eye—the other having been put out in early childhood. He dressed with singluar distinction, more like an English gentleman than a Brooklyn shopkeeper. And he had found the family he desired in the Parkers of Long Branch.

In March 1861, Alexander married Maria Louise, the next eldest Parker daughter, barely twenty-one years of age, shy, reserved and beautiful—a very different person from the self-possessed Margaret, her predecessor. The image of her large brown eyes, unusually expressive and responsive, may be recognized here and there in later generations, an unacknowledged legacy from this gentle forbear, who, lovely as she was, was no match for the passionate nature of Alexander Hudnut.

It is hard to imagine Maria, the young bride, moving from the big farm home at Long Branch to the rather crowded family quarters over Alexander's drug store in Brooklyn, with three young children and a dominating, fiercely ambitious husband to cope with. The next few years saw the birth of three more sons: Frank Parker, William Herbert (our grandfather), and Paul Albert. A thriving business kept Alexander preoccupied; Maria's health began to be noticed as "delicate."

Imagined scenarios rarely give the flavor of a family life as well as a primary source, and so, even though his *Memoirs* were written very many years after those early days in Brooklyn, we use William's own recollection to advance our tale:

> While the family lived in Brooklyn the terrible Civil War was fought. But it did not invade our home, because Father was able to pay for a substitute. His older brother, Richard, a veteran of the Mexican War, enlisted and attained the rank of Captain. While the horrors of war did not reach Brooklyn, I heard Mother describe a time of terror when the draft riots were raging and she watched all night in a panic of fear. Towards morning there came the tread of marching troops and from her window she saw the soldiers — the city was saved. She was very young, very beautiful and that night there were sleeping in her home four small children.
>
> I was a very little boy when Father decided to move his drug business from Court Street to 218 Broadway, under the Herald building, where he rented of James Gordon Bennett. As we had been living over his store, the family had to be moved too. So for short periods we lived in Montrose and East Orange, N.J.
>
> My boyhood life, however, really began when Father purchased "Arcadia" in the centre of Llewellyn Park, West Orange. His move to New York was very timely and immediately the family fortunes were greatly enhanced, making it possible to purchase an estate of some twelve acres with lovely lawns and pine groves and a pasture lot.

Another child, Maude Louise, had been born to Maria and Alexander, so that when the Hudnuts moved into their home in Llewellyn Park there were seven children in Maria's care. There was also a house and a garden staff of seven or more. Added to this considerable number were several retainers who were supported by Alexander and had rooms in the servants quarters. One was a seamstress; another was an aged uncle who served as household carpenter and handyman, and who, in his spare time invented marvelous contraptions to intrigue the children. The supervision of this establishment, with its complex demands, was a heavy responsibility for its gentle mistress.

A building program soon added its dislocations to this domestic picture, for with such a resident population, Alexander was inspired to design a new addition to Arcadia, which more than doubled its size. It transformed the house into a handsome Italianate villa, with a fine Tuscan tower and long arched cloisters. It was the background for a period which my grandfather, the young William, remembered with lyric intensity.

The whole green world of Llewellyn Park was his to enjoy with his brothers. There was winter sledding on the Orange Mountain, and they belonged to the Essex County Hunt and loved to ride. Will sang in the boy's choir at St. Mark's Episcopal Church, where he was confirmed, and he went to dancing school, where he often was chosen to lead the German, a popular reel of the times, with his first love, Miss Fanny Curtis.

Alexander also had a summer home at Sea Bright, later at Monmouth Beach, where Will and his brothers were ardent sailors. And it is entirely possible that in all the distractions and activities of this privileged family life, the young ones didn't notice that their parents were becoming estranged. Years later, Grandfather wrote:

> Mother was in very frail health during most of our life in Arcadia. I can recall a year when she was in bed practically the whole time. During the summer they had to hang wet sheets in her room to cool the air. Her invalidism was not only hard on her but on the whole family. She could not thus mother us children nor attend to the housekeeping, which consequently fell to the lot of her younger sister, Lydia Frances, who came to live with us.
>
> Aunt Fanny was younger than Mother by eight or nine years. She was very young and beautiful when she came, in the prime of her womanhood, and, as I remember her, handsome and alluring. She was a decided brunette with very fair skin, large brown eyes, beautiful hair, a rather sensuous mouth, and the best nose in the family. Her manners and her speech were very affected and her simpering, airy ways made us boys sick. Sometimes in the evenings, Father would ask her to recite poetry and when it came to "The Curfew Shall Not Ring Tonight," the agony she piled on would reduce any bell to silence.
>
> Father fell in love with her, desired and coveted her. More and more she had her way in everything, was petted and pampered. She was flattered by his attentions, lured by his admiration, and dazzled by his success and wealth. In every way she catered to him. She had a good mind and shared his intellectual interests.

Alexander at thirty-five

Maria at thirty-six

"Arcadia," Llewellyn Park, newly built c. 1863 by Alexander Hudnut.

Maude in England

Paul Hudnut, schoolboy in England

"Edgemont," East Orange, NJ, home of Alexander Hudnut, c. 1880

Alexander and coachman at Edgemont.

Maria in middle age.

Evening after evening they were together in the library with the door closed, whether in pursuit of literature or love was never definitely settled.

In this way the disintegration of the Hudnut family began. Maria could not, or would not, endure the scandal of a divorce. And so the family's life shaped itself to mask and accommodate a Victorian drama, an explosive intimacy. Maria and the younger children spent the winters abroad, mostly in England. In the summer she would take up residence at home in Llewellyn Park, as Alexander and the older boys left for the house at Monmouth Beach. Everyone maintained the fiction of a marriage, and, indeed, Alexander felt free to live with them, whether at home or in London. Young Will was sent off to boarding school at Exeter, specifically because he could not get along with his imperious Aunt Fanny. Paul was at school in England, and more and more they were what would today be called a dysfunctional family.

It was the summer of 1882 at Monmouth, when William made the final break with his father, as he wrote:

One day that summer, after my return from Exeter, I had some altercation with Aunt Fannie during which I became so infuriated that I slapped her. Of course she told Father as soon as he came home from New York. He was enraged and sought me out at once where I was walking on the beach. It was an appropriate setting for such a passionate interview, the evening sky darkening over the sea and the waves breaking at our feet. I was still very angry over what had occurred and not prepared under any circumstances to ask her forgiveness. Then for the first and last time I upbraided him for his treatment of Mother and for putting Aunt Fannie in Mother's place. I had always been afraid of him until that hour and then all fear left me as I championed Mother's cause. Finally he told me that I would have to leave home at once. I think I was too angry to care, too ignorant to foresee what this exile would mean. Anyway, with Mother away, home had ceased to be home to me. There was no one there to advise me or give me a sympathetic hearing. What my future might have been had this crisis not arisen I have never been able to envisage. You may say that I lost my father, and in a sense that is true, but in reality I had lost him already. It must be said that while he exiled me he did not disown me.

He decided to send me to Princeton, and Henry Van Dyke, the Registrar of the College, was engaged as my tutor. I was given an

allowance and thereafter for several years all of my affairs were
carried on through Charles Faber, Father's confidential clerk.

With this backdrop, the resolve to create his own happy family life
was early formed in the young Will Hudnut. And the summers in the
Adirondacks were to be at the center of his intentions.

You will read of his later life in the following pages. As for the others
in this story, Maria received the equivalent of a modern divorce settlement: a home in Wellesley, and an income which provided for her life
and travels. She visited her children, and her grandchildren adored
her. But William believed that she loved Alexander, and grieved for
his loss, to the end of her days.

In 1890, Fanny Parker sailed for England with Alexander and they
never returned. Alexander leased a handsome villa outside of Hove,
then a small resort near Brighton. It was on Palmeira Crescent with a
fine hillside view of the sea. They are buried together in a quaint Victorian cemetery in Hove, beneath a sober red granite tomb with — and
finally chaperoned by — yet another Parker sister, Dolly, the youngest,
who went over to live with Fanny after Alexander's death.

Important to our story is the fact that in these years of the Hudnut
family's diaspora, both William and his elder brother Richard were
making their first trips to the Adirondacks. They followed very different trails — in the mountains as in life — but each in his own way and
his own time would find a destination there, not far apart, in the
remote valley that curved its way from what was then called Oregon,
through Bakers Mills to the Sodom Crossroads and on to North Creek.

CHAPTER 2

THE EARLIEST ADIRONDACK VISITS OF WILLIAM HUDNUT

Fixing a date upon William's first journey into the mountains he would come to love so well is not possible, for he did not note it on any calendar we have available to us. However, we can venture an accurate guess for it was before he was sent off to Exeter in 1880, and he was still spending summers with the family by the ocean at Sea Bright. So this seems to point to the summer of 1879, when he was not yet fifteen.

An editorial in the *New York Times*, August 9, 1864, heralded the coming of a railroad from Saratoga, "running north from that town toward the Upper Hudson and aiming directly at the heart of the wilderness" which the writer referred to as "still a realm of mystery."

At the times of these earliest of Will Hudnut's visits, the wilderness had opened up considerably, thanks to the railroad's coming. But access to the more remote regions was still punishing, and accommodations for the traveler, primitive. This, doubtless, was part of its charm. And these mountains, with their much-reported crystalline air and healing pine essences, had become a mecca for those in search of better health. Alexander Hudnut chose an Adirondack visit as a cure for his wife, Maria, who during this period in the family life was much of the time an invalid. In happier days they had gone to Saratoga, to the United States Hotel, taking the waters of the famous Saratoga Springs along with the high summer culture. It now seemed to him that she could journey farther into the mountain region which the railroad penetrated. When he chose young Willy to accompany Maria, who could know that he was sending the lad on an adventure of a lifetime?

From the Hudnut *Memoirs,* we have a description of this early journey:

> The seashore did not agree with Mother and for several years
> she went to Lake Placid in the Adirondacks. To my unspeakable
> delight I was appointed her companion. We went by train to
> Westport on Lake Champlain, and thence by stage through Eliza-
> bethtown and North Elba, a long day's ride over a rough, hilly
> dirt road. At Lake Placid there was one hotel, the Stephens'
> House, kept by two brothers. It had a very fine location, com-
> manding an uninterrupted view of the lake, beyond whose farthest
> shore towered the mile-high peak of White Face [sic] Mountain.
> In every direction the lake was girdled with unbroken reaches of
> forest. It was indeed a wild and beautiful prospect. I guess that I
> was born to be an Indian but too late for the age of scalps and
> feathers. I have a passionate love for nature. I should never have
> lived in cities. The changeful splendor of variegated sunsets; frosty
> nights of blazing stars; moonlight on moving waters; the gorgeous
> tapestry of October forests; the serrated skyline of mountain
> ranges; the roaring, on-sweeping rush of mighty waves at sea; a
> wood thrush singing across the lake at evening; the unexpected
> sight of deer, or ruffled grouse or purple gentian in the woods —
> such aspects of nature move me profoundly.
>
> The Lake Placid region in those days offered abundant scope
> for the development of these nascent tastes, and forthwith I must
> into the forests go. The trails that led to the Elysian fields of sport
> were then unmarked save for the mystic blazes of the woodman's
> axe. There were no lean-tos on those dim forest trails. To hunt or
> fish those mountain lakes or streams the tenderfoot must have a
> guide, a Charlie Stevens, or a Jim Sturges, who had a shack on the
> Racquet River or at Pillsbury Pond, a boat securely hidden behind
> some old moss-covered log, and was able to carry in his pack
> basket sixty pounds of duffle, or mayhap he called it "calamity,"
> to that far away lodge at the end of the trail.
>
> One of my earliest fishing adventures was to Ray Brook, on the
> road to Saranac, where Duncan Cameron kept a primitive road
> house, so far removed from civilization that his son and daughter
> had never seen a railway train. There an ideal trout stream flowed
> deep and still through a little meadow, which only his guests were

allowed to fish.

I soon acquired the rudiments of trout-fishing and took some nice fish as the least barefoot boy can do, who is commonly pictured with crooked alder pole over his shoulder and a lovely string of trout dangling from his other hand, passing with triumphant whistles an up-to-date sportsman's tent from between whose flaps peer out two curious, amazed faces. You can go even so far as that with garden hackle and a bent pin.

However—when you essay fly-casting you enter a field of sport so different and highly technical that comparatively few of the followers of Izaac Walton ever attained professional standing. The mastery of the art with both wet and dry flies involves the tying of the flies, the knowing whether to use a Parmachene Bell, or a Royal Coachman, or a Montreal, or a Blue Quill, or a Silver Doctor, or any one out of a book filled with all sizes and colors, taking into account the weather, the season, the time of day, the insects upon which the trout are feeding, if they are feeding, "the subjectivity of the fish" and the location of the stream or lake you are fishing, for the same flies will not kill in all waters. And then the length and accuracy of the cast: to know where, in a stream, the trout will be lying—to drop your cast at the exact spot, and, if you are using dry flies, to drop your fly with wings cocked. Then finally, in the thrilling conclusion when the fish rises to the lure, to be able to give the quick stroke that hooks him. Even then he is not yours until you have played him, keeping your line tight through his furious rushes, wearying him until you can bring him to net, until you can drop him into your creel, and gloat over his speckled splendor!

There were other waters in this neighborhood where one might fish. There was that deep hole under the spillway of an old lumber dam. I could see the fine fish in the dark recesses of this pool, but in no way could I entice them. So I determined to get at least one. It was three miles to Saranac Village and I walked there and back bringing with me a gang of hooks. I rigged this on a short, stout pole and, stooping down at the side of the spillway, continued to cast it into the dark boiling water. After repeated futile efforts I hooked one of the largest trout in the back and managed to throw him out on the bank behind me. He was a beauty and I bore him home in triumph. That was the largest fish taken at Ray Brook that season. Of course I should have been deeply ashamed of such unsportsmanlike conduct; but I wasn't. I was more proud than ashamed.

At the Stephens' House I fell under the spell of the guides.

There were always some of them sitting around telling stories of the deer they hunted and the fish they caught. Old Charlie Stevens (no relation of the man who kept the hotel), who had a small place at North Elba, talked with me about the Cold River which was some fifteen miles through the forest at the foot of Santanoni Mountain and which emptied into the Racquet River.

From then on I gave Mother no peace until she consented to finance the trip. A man, whose name I have forgotten, wanted to go too, so we split the expense of guide and provisions.

It was a long, hard trail requiring a woodsman's skill to follow. At five miles we passed Moose Pond where later I night-hunted for deer. Here on the trail we came upon a beautiful fat buck which someone had killed and was going to skin and carry out. This was the first deer I had ever seen. Charlie cut out its heart and brought it along for our supper.

A mile or so farther on the trail skirted a swampy pond which was covered with lily pads and bore no signs of trout. Old Charlie said that he had never fished it, but that he would like to. So he knocked over a few dry stubs and quickly fashioned a crude raft. Upon this he and I embarked, leaving the other man on the shore. Charlie poled the raft around through the lily pads for quite some time before he found a place where there was a very small area of open water. Here he held the raft while I threw in my line. Instantly I had a bite and there for about a half-hour I took fine fish, often two at a cast, as fast as I could play them and Charlie could land them. I never again caught so fine a mess of trout in so short a time. We stopped because we had enough and not because they ceased biting.

Charlie had a small camp and a boat securely hidden at the head of the Cold River still water. Here we fished day after day with excellent success. The fish we caught were kept fresh by packing them in moss and putting them beside the cold spring. O, the zest of the great forest and the dark, winding river!—The camp fire in the evening when we came in hungry and tired; the delicious broiled fish and the flapjacks; the bed of fragrant balsam boughs; the cool air of the evening; the voices of the night,—the deep throated bull frogs, the distant hoot of the great horned owl, the splash of a jumping fish; and then the sweet oblivion of sleep.

On the way out my friend caught another fine mess of trout in the lily pad pond, whilst I sat on the shore watching him pull them in. We packed out over thirty pounds of fish.

My first gun was a Flobert 22 with which I practiced shooting at a target. I used to go down around the head of the lake where there was much dead timber and where the woodpeckers could be heard hammering in loud staccato all day long. Hunting here one day I started up a ruffed grouse. The foolish bird flew up upon a limb and sat there craning its neck. He was such an easy mark that I knocked him off and bore him home to Mother in great pride.

Thus began my acquaintance with the Adirondacks and my initiation in woodcraft. I did not then foresee how many of my summers would be passed amongst those mountains nor how they were to be the scene of much that was most important and sacred in my life.

Between this and the next Adirondack entry in Grandfather's *Memoirs,* he underwent the painful separation from his family as a result of his confrontation with his father over the infidelity with Aunt Fanny. And though he frequently saw his mother and sister, and occasionally visited his older brothers, he was effectively exiled from any relationship with his powerful father.

Will's next trip to the Adirondacks took place in the fall of 1885:

> In September of my senior year [at Princeton] I was not feeling at all well. I longed for a change, for other companionships and scenes. I felt if only I could breathe some Adirondack air I would be whole again. I wrote Mother about my condition and she, who never failed me, sent me a check. Immediately I was off for Lake Placid.
>
> I had made up my mind that to save stage fare I would walk from Elizabethtown to North Elba. It is a long pull up over the height of land and by nightfall when I arrived I was desperately tired. I went at once to see old Charlie's son and engaged him for a trip in to Cold River.
>
> As it was late for fishing we took along an old hound dog to run deer. The listing and buying the duffel for such a trip is always very interesting. The purchases were made at an old country store where they kept a supply of almost everything campers would need. The problem was to buy enough to feed two men for a couple of weeks and not have more than one man could carry. I was not husky enough to carry more than my own clothes and gun.
>
> It was about a six hour carry through the forest.
>
> We had fine weather; the woods were full of fall light and the rustle of fallen leaves. It turned cold and we had a snow[fall] that stripped the trees and opened up the forest. All the conditions

seemed favorable for hunting, but though I watched day after day on different runways I never even *saw* a deer. One location, where I spent many hours, was seated amidst the branches of a great tree that leaned far out over the river rapids. Someone who had there kept watch before me had carved a large coin in relief on the trunk. Sitting by running water it is amazing how many sounds you can hear—ringing bells, baying hounds, people talking.

Our luck was so bad that I blamed the guide for laziness. And what was there to prevent his lying out in the woods after stationing me on my location, there to remain until he came for me late in the day! But though I got no deer, I had a glorious time in the forest.

My appetite for flapjacks and maple syrup, and eggs and bacon was enormous. Our evenings in camp about the roaring fire were very comfortable and companionable. Charlie had some rollicking folk songs he would sing. One of those I recall, and have never heard it sung by anyone else. I set it down here for I think it should be preserved:

> Come, all you roving Belgy boys,
> I pray you, pay attention;
> When love it first began,
> 'Twas the Devil's own invention.
> For when first in love I fell
> O the girls they smiled bewitchin'
> 'Twas to one Miss Susie Belle
> Down in Captain Phoebe's kitchen.
>
> *Chorus:* Tommy rila tu-ra-loo
>   Tommy rila tu-ra-lido
>   Tommy rila tu-ra-loo
>   Tommy rig-fa-lu-fa lido.
>
> At the age of seventeen
> I was bound unto a grocer
> Close by Stephen Green
> Where Missy Belle did go, Sir.
> Her manners were so free
> That she set my heart a-twitchin'
> And she invited me
> To a flare-up in the kitchen.

At the hour of seven o'clock
We sat unto the table,
And there we all did sit
And we ate whiles we were able.
And there we all did sit
'Til our sides began a-stitchin'
Whilst we kicked up high life
Down in Captain Phoebe's kitchen.

As I sat upon her lap
With a kiss she hinted marriage,
And just as that began
Up drove Captain Phoebe's carriage.
Our courtin' then broke up
With no further word of hitchin'
And I wished I'd never come
In to Captain Phoebe's kitchen.

I jumped up off her lap,
I jumped six foot or higher,
And head over heels
She rolled me in the fire.
My brand new coat and nappeals
Which I bought of Mr. Stitchin',
With a thirty shillin' note
Went to blazes 'round the kitchen.

She swore I'd ruined her character
I swore in blank denial;
And there in the court
The case was brought to trial.
The judge would not repeal
The jury's firm conviction,
And six months I trod the wheel
For courtin' in the kitchen.

I returned late for the opening of college, but I had gained
weight and was refreshed and renewed.

Will graduated from Princeton in the Class of 1886. There was a
strong Presbyterian "presence" in the University of those days, and this
had its influence on a young man so cut off from family and essentially

lonely. Some of his friends among his classmates were entering Princeton Seminary, and he decided to join them, although he later found
Union Seminary in New York City more to his liking and transferred
there. In the meantime, during the spring of 1887 at Princeton
Seminary, he became very ill and was sent to a plantation in Thomas-
ville, Georgia to recuperate. A need for further rest and recovery that
summer took him to the north woods he loved so well. He wrote of this
journey:

> I was very much improved by my stay in the South but still had
> what they called intermittent albumenurium. It was thought advis-
> able for me to spend my summer in the Adirondacks. I had heard
> of the Adirondack Fish and Game Preserve [The Adirondack Pre-
> serve Association, later The Northwoods Club], near Minerva, in
> Warren County. The club owned some four thousand acres and
> there were seven lakes on the property. Memberships were selling
> at $100.00. Father was then at home. I had not seen him since
> our break, but as I had no money I decided to go to him, tell him
> of my condition and ask him to buy a membership for me in that
> club. He approved of the plan and gave me the money.
>
> Early in June I took the train for North Creek and from there
> went by stage-coach to Minerva where I arrived in the evening and
> put up at the hotel.
>
> Early in the morning when I came down to breakfast a mist so
> filled the valley that I thought the hotel was on the shore of a
> lake. From there to the club was about a twelve-mile ride in a
> buck-board, ten miles of which was through a great forest over a
> terrible road, much of it corduroy and full of chuck holes. But the
> forest being lovely, and the air stimulating, my spirits rose with
> every mile. I had to walk the last seven miles, in pouring rain.
>
> The club house was a large, two-story log building, surrounded
> by a porch, standing in the midst of a clearing, with a view of
> Mink Pond and a range of hills beyond. The accommodations
> were exceedingly primitive. The rooms were small and bare and
> the fare plain. Our fresh vegetables came out of cans. Every morn-
> ing there were flapjacks with maple syrup. There was plenty of
> milk and fresh eggs, and always as our chef d'oeuvre, trout and
> venison. But any deficiencies in comfort and cuisine were more
> than made good by our appetites and out-of-door life.
>
> I bought a canoe-modeled guide boat with a carrying yoke, in
> which I fished and hunted in the different lakes. The trout fishing
> was pretty good and I took fish in the lakes and streams all
> summer.

*William Herbert Hudnut, with violin, at the North Woods Club, prob-
ably Mr. Bibby and son at right, c. 1886.*

When the deer law came in I went night hunting and got a deer. Later in the season we ran the deer with hounds. I spent hours watching on the run-ways and by the rapids of the Hudson but got nothing. At the time jacking and hounding were both legal.

The superintendent, Bob Bibby, a strapping, big woodsman, capable and kindly, was very helpful to me and we became fast friends.

In a tiny pocket diary that he kept at that time, Will made rudimentary notes, mostly about the number of fish caught and the state of the weather. But there was a list of the members or friends who were there during his summer's stay, and I copied it:

> August 20, Saturday, 1887: Alex [a Hudnut cousin] came up to spend a couple of weeks with me. We had a jolly good time together. The party there during my stay were Mr. and Mrs. Adams & their little girl, Jessie; the Kitchings, Bettie, Yalden. Also Mr. Eliphlet Terry—a jolly nice party of people. We left the Preserve the morning of Sept. 5 & got in New York next morning.

Mr. Terry was the artist of many Adirondack landscapes and convivial camp life scenes. As for the end of this particular experience, the *Memoirs* report that "health improved wonderfully and in September when I returned to Brooklyn [brother] Frank said I was well enough to resume my studies in the Seminary."

We know no more of Grandfather's early Adirondack adventures, though we have reason to believe that he kept his membership in the Adirondack Preserve Association at least through his seminary days. The summer of 1890, when he went as a young seminary intern to preach at the village of Fish House in the foothills of the Adirondacks, is the next recorded tale. His attachment to these mountains had become a pattern to be followed thoughout the summers of his long life. It was here that the young man who had been exiled from his family would create a life for his own family—as he once wrote, "the seat of our greatest happiness together." The pattern was set in the earliest journeys here recorded.

CHAPTER 3
THE
BEECHERS
OF FISH HOUSE

James Fuller Beecher and his family moved to the lovely village of Fish House not many years before the young minister, Will Hudnut, came to preach for the summer at the red brick Presbyterian Church there. For Mr. Beecher it was something of a homecoming, for though he had lived much of his life on a farm high in the hills above Elmira, he had spent his boyhood years and many summer holidays in the little village where his grandparents, Deacon Abraham Beecher and his wife, Lydia Day Fuller, lived. The elder Beechers were now buried in the graveyard beside the church there. In addition to this close tie, Mr. Beecher was directly descended from Godfrey Shew, the first settler of Fish House, as well as many of the other pioneers of that region in the colorful days of the French and Indian War, when Sir William Johnson — acting as King George III's Commissioner of Indian Affairs — had his own fish and game preserve in the wilderness where the village now stood.

Sometime around 1879, when much of the country was in a financial depression, James Beecher suffered his own crisis and lost his farm in Elmira. So it must have seemed the greatest good fortune that one of his close Beecher cousins, Mrs. Frank Sinclaire, who lived in Brooklyn but also had a beautiful big farm in Fish House, asked him to accept employment as Farm Manager. This was a godsend and ever afterward the Beechers felt a special bond of gratitude to the gracious Cousin Lucy who enabled their homecoming. And so they moved to Fish House—James and his wife, Elizabeth Ann Northrup, and their three daughters: Ella Katherine, Harriet, and Hannah Emily, known as "Nan."

The three young Beecher women, unlike their parents, were, by the standards of the day, highly educated. They had attended Miss Dana's School at Morristown, New Jersey, and at the time of our story, Harriet, the middle daughter, had just been graduated. Nan had one year to go and Ella, the eldest, was already making a name as an outstanding scholar and teacher at Miss Mittleberger's School in Cleveland, having apprenticed for a year with Miss Dana after her own graduation. Ella was reportedly gifted in many ways, and was greatly loved by her younger sisters, for whom she was a concerned and generous mentor. She had recently traveled to Europe with the family of Samuel Langhorne Clemens, better known as Mark Twain. She may well have tutored the Clemens daughters, but she was also a close girlhood friend of Mrs. Clemens, the former Olivia Langdon of Elmira.

The Beecher's son, Leman, remained in Elmira where he married, and founded his own family, whom my grandfather always referred to fondly as "the Elmira cousins." As for the three Beecher daughters, they moved to Fish House with their parents, but their lives were already radiating in other directions and they would come to the little village only on holiday. For them, Elmira would always be "home."

James Beecher and his wife, Elizabeth, were soon an active and valued part of the small community. Following the tradition of his Beecher forebears, he was an officer and elder of the Presbyterian Church. He had not been formally educated, but he had the simple dignity and character that was noted in the early New England Beechers. So it was that he and Elizabeth Ann were greatly beloved in Fish House.

For the first year or so, Cousin Lucy gave them the use of the old Marvin House, which had belonged to her father, Dr. Marvin, and stood just behind her own large home on the Village Green. Not the least of the charms of the old Marvin House was that it was said to have been built on the exact spot where the original Fish House of Sir William Johnson had stood. It was there that the Beechers lived when the young minister from New York came for the summer and fell in love with their daughter, Harriet.

CHAPTER 4
THE
FISH HOUSE OF
SIR WILLIAM JOHNSON

In our visits to Fish House each summer we children would hear about the great Sir William Johnson and the fishing lodge he built there long ago, which gave Fish House its name. The original one sat on a nearby spit of land on the Sacandaga River, all now buried beneath the water of the Sacandaga Reservoir, the huge lake just a stone's throw away from Aunt Nan Beecher's home. In images furnished by Father's reading out loud to us from *The Last of the Mohicans*, I would imagine Sir William's birch bark canoe, Indian braves at helm and stern, gliding noiselessly through the rushes and cattails of the Vlaie Creek marshes: red-winged blackbirds skimming the water and trout so abundant they would be jumping to Sir William's line. We were told that coming to the Fish House was his favorite escape from the burden of responsibilities as Commissioner of Indian Affairs in His Majesty's Colonies. We felt a thrill of patriotic pride to know that our ancestor, Godfrey Shew, had fought with Sir William, then Colonel Johnson, at Ticonderoga in The French and Indian War.

In later summers I learned more about Sir William from Aunt Nan's books, and from her Beecher cousin, Mignonette Riker, whose lifelong interest was the history of the Fish House area. The past came to life when my father took us all to see Johnson Hall at Johnstown. We saw the spacious old house and the great circle of lilac bushes on the lawn behind the hall, which marked the Council meeting place. There the sachems of the Six Nations gathered in their ceremonial dress to take part in affairs of state and smoke the peace pipe with Sir William, agent of the King.

Sir William was one of my father's heroes. I always suspected part of it was that Dad, a teetotaller, admired Johnson's legendary refusal to trade with any Indian who had been drinking! What he really admired was Sir William's attitude toward the native peoples: it was an innate respect, as if he was there to serve *them* as much as his monarch. In this he was definitely a radical. Colonists in the frontier settlements were afraid of the Indians and for good reason: memories of such atrocities as the Schenectady Massacre a few years back made them tense and distrustful. They viewed the natives as savages (and I could sympathize, having shivered over the tale of our ancestor, Lodowyck Putman, which is related in the back of this book). But Father said that William Johnson, from his very first dealings with Indians, treated them as fellow human beings. His stagecraft was to study their behavior, their ancient culture, their curiously sophisticated diplomacy. He learned their language, adopted their dress, and played their games. And as the mistress of Johnson Hall and his beloved common-law wife he chose a princess of their people, Molly Brant, who also bore eight of his children. The Mohawk Nation adopted him and gave him an Indian name, "Warraghiaghy," which meant "he who has charge of affairs."

Sir William won the Six Nations as allies for England and this was crucial to the British victory in the French and Indian War. There's a wonderful story about the way he retrieved that support at a critical moment on the eve of the Battle of Ticonderoga. It seems the Six Nations were reluctant to become involved; they were being actively wooed by the French as well as the British. For his part, Johnson was being pressured by the British generals to deliver the Indians immediately; they were desperately needed as guides and scouts for warfare in the forest. But the Mohawks and Johnson's other friends in the Six Nations were against joining the white man's war and were cooling their heels with their confederation. So Johnson hurriedly called a Council of the Six Nations; out of a long loyalty to him they came, one by one, in no great hurry. Hours of oratory around the Council Fire seemed to produce nothing but a stalemate when suddenly Johnson lept into the center and flung down the red-painted wampum, the sign for the drums to begin the war dance. He began to dance, and as the rhythm gathered momentum, one after another of the warriors of the principal tribes joined in. Johnson's biographer wrote:

> This dance, which took place outside the regular orbit of historians and has never been reported by them, signalized what may well have been the turning point in that war which won North America for the English-speaking peoples. The fighting force which controlled the wilderness between Canada and the Colonies had definitely joined the British cause.
>
> (Flexner, *Lord of the Mohawks*)

No story has conveyed quite as vividly to me the extraordinary spirit of that great man. His King, in gratitude after the victory at Ticonderoga, bestowed upon Sir William his hereditary title and a Royal Land Grant of 100,000 acres as well. It was a royal applause for a heroic dance!

Sir William built Johnson Hall at this time. It was an embassy in the wilderness to which "there journeyed from the east, royal governors and colonial statesmen; from the west, sachems who ruled in savannahs no white man had ever seen." When the cares of office weighed too heavily he would escape to his northern hideaway, his Fish House. This was described in the nineteenth-century histories written by Jeptha Simms:

> Traversing the forest in the French war, from Ticonderoga to Fort Johnson, his then residence, no doubt first made Sir William Johnson familiar with the make of the country adjoining the Sacandaga River; and soon after the close of that war he erected a lodge for his convenience, while hunting and fishing, on the south side of the river, nearly 18 miles distant from his own dwelling. The lodge was ever after called the Fish House.
>
> It was an oblong square-framed building, with two rooms below, and walls sufficiently high (one and a half stories) to have afforded pleasant chambers. Its site was on a knoll . . . It fronted the south. Only one room in the building was ever finished; that was in the west end, and had a chimney and fireplace. The house was never painted. The ground from where the building stood, slopes very prettily to the river. No visible trace of this building remains.
>
> (*Trappers of New York*)

Nearby, in the present town of Mayfield, on high ground reaching into the surrounding marshes, Sir William later built a more elaborate dwelling which he called the Summer House, or, sometimes, Castle Cumberland. Here he entertained such visiting dignitaries as General Lafayette, some of whom would remember their trips downriver to the Fish House. Jeptha Simms visited the area with our ancestor, Jacob Shew, whose boyhood memories of those early days brought them alive to Simms:

> There is now along the sides and lower end of Summer House Point, a stunted growth of alder and swamp willow, but when occupied by Sir William Johnson, the bushes were all cut off and the margin of the stream kept clean. He had a beautiful boat there, in which he used to go down to the Fish House, four miles distant, sometimes with company, and at other times attended only by a few servants, or possibly by his faithful Pontioch, who rowed the boat while he sat in the stern and steered it. His greatest time for hunting and fishing was in the spring and fall. When the marsh was flooded, a boat would pass over it anywhere, the water rising at Summer House point from six to eight feet above low water mark. At such times the prospect was grand from the promenade of his cottage. Thousands upon thousands of ducks and wild geese were then floating upon the waters, at which time his double-barreled gun was in almost constant requisition.
>
> (*Ibid.*)

Sir William died just before the beginning of the American Revolution, thus, happily, he did not have to make the hard choice between his king, who had entrusted him with great office, and the country which had truly become his own.

Not so with his autocratic son, Sir John Johnson, who was an ardent Tory. His father's strong influence made it possible for Sir John to retain the loyalty of the Mohawks and a large part of the Indian Nation for England. Sir John and his loyal Indians fled to Canada, but two years later returned to the land of the Sacandaga for a series of raids on their erstwhile homelands that were among the bloodiest sagas of the Revolution. During these raids the Fish House as well as the Summer House, which had been fortified by the British, were burned to the ground. Our ancestors suffered great losses and some were murdered by Indians who had been their friends in earlier times.

At the end of the war the lands that had belonged to Sir William Johnson were confiscated and sold. The land upon which the Fish House had stood was bought, curiously enough, by a Major Nicholas Fish, for one hundred pounds. It changed hands several times in the following years and in the latter half of the nineteenth century was bought by Dr. Langdon Marvin, whose mother was a Beecher. His daughter, Lucy Marvin Sinclaire, inherited the property with its old colonial cottage where her Beecher cousins came to live. The Sinclaire lands were close by the homestead of the Shew family, and the lands given them by Sir William long ago.

CHAPTER 5

GODFREY SHEW
AND THE SETTLEMENT
OF FISH HOUSE

Planning settlements in the wilderness was something Sir William Johnson knew a lot about. As a young man he had come to America to manage his uncle's vast estates in the Mohawk Valley west of Albany. He had planted enough of these small communities to know the work and the leadership needed to clear land and build homes in an untamed forest. He also knew full well the value of these outposts for trading and defense.

The time came when Sir William wanted to have a settlement founded at the Fish House. News had come to him that undesirable squatters had moved in on his land and would be hard to evict unless there were permanent inhabitants to protect the property. But more important, it was a time of unrest, with unfriendly Indian uprisings to the west and insurgent colonists talking revolution to the east. It was time to anchor his vast domain with an outpost at this favorite wilderness haunt by the beautiful Sacandaga.

But Sir William was in no shape to supervise the building of a settlement; he knew what it took in energy and perseverence. Not only was he too busy with affairs of state in those unruly times—he was far from well. Unable, therefore, to be involved in the undertaking, he chose for the task one of the frontiersmen who had fought with him at Ticonderoga, a neighbor who must have been a trusted friend: German immigrant, Godfrey Shew.

Desiring to know more about this Godfrey Shew, who was my great-great-great-great grandfather as well as the hardy ancestor of our Fish House story, I went to the Johnstown Public Library where a kind librarian let me borrow some Shew family papers. I also read the nineteenth-century histories by Jeptha Simms, knowing that the source of many of his tales of Fish House and Sir William Johnson was yet another ancestor, Godfrey's son, Jacob Shew, the first state legislator from Fish House, whom Simms constantly refers to as "the venerable patriot." In 1976, long after I laid all my research aside, a book was written by Donald J. Sawyer entitled *They Came to Sacandaga*, subtitled *Godfrey Shew: Fish House Patriot*. It was published in conjunction with a Bicentennial event and was hailed on its jacket as "an episode in American history well worth remembering."

Sawyer's book is written for young people; he took the facts and family stories about Godfrey Shew's life and enlarged them into a fascinating story which is partly invention and "largely factual." Two of his "inventions" concern aspects of the story which interest and puzzle me, and about which I have done my own share of imagining: namely, the nature of the relationship between Godfrey and Sir William, and secondly, of even greater importance to my family's story, how Godfrey came to meet and marry the young indentured girl, Katherine Frey, in Philadelphia. What follows owes something to Donald Sawyer, and is also the result of my own research and thinking about this "episode in American history."

A Shew genealogy, compiled by Sophie Moore from family records, states that Godfrey Shew was the son of a German nobleman, born in 1710, who set out to visit America at the age of nineteen. He came as a tourist, with adequate funds from a wealthy father, who financed the journey as a part of Godfrey's education. As it was a period when many young men were being forced into military service, the father may have had other motives, but I doubt he would have condoned his going had he known that he would never return to his home and family in Germany. Godfrey could speak a little English, enough to make himself understood. His possessions for the journey were stowed in a large leather-bound and brass-studded trunk, and among them were "leather breeches and a leather jacket, a hunting knife selected for its fine steel and balance, which his father had given him . . . and some trinkets [to use] in bargaining with the Indians." (Sawyer)

If he came only as a student or tourist, why did he stay in America?
An old family record gives us the reason; it was written in 1862 by his
great-granddaughter, Susannah Shew. Her father, Lodowyck Putman
Shew, collaborated with her in writing some notes for a family reunion,
and I found this document in the Johnstown Public Library:

> The subject of this narrative is Godfrey Shew, who embarked
> from Germany about the year 1730 for the purpose of visiting
> America. But, alas, 'ere he completed half his journey, his
> pleasure was clouded with sorrow. The ship was struck with light-
> ning which caused a leak and all on board were in agony, expect-
> ing soon to find a watery grave.
>
> No time was lost in pumping out the water and devising a plan
> to stop the leak, which they succeeded in doing the third day by
> spiking a piece of sole leather over the leak, then placing heavy
> boxes immediately on to close the valve. The exertion of all the
> passengers was so great that the insides of their hands were, in
> some cases, worn through to the bone.

According to Susannah Shew, the voyage was so traumatic that
young Godfrey resolved never to go to sea again.

When Godfrey Shew arrived at the harbor of New York in 1731, the
young Irishman, William Johnson, had been established in the
Mohawk Valley for several years. He was already an accomplished
frontiersman, experienced in the management of his uncle's vast
estates and trading with the settlers. He was skilled in dealing with a
number of different peoples: the Irish families under indenture to his
uncle; the Palatines, impoverished and struggling German refugees,
who had escaped religious persecution in an area known as the
Palatinate of the Rhine; and the Indian population of the adjoining
lands, with whom he conducted his uncle's lucrative fur trade.

Donald Sawyer believes, or perhaps I should say "imagines," that
these two young men, Godfrey Shew and William Johnson, met on that
very day when Godfrey disembarked in New York. It is certainly a
plausible notion that William was delivering a load of furs to a cargo
ship bound for the European market, when he saw the young traveler,
so close to his own age, burdened with a great unwieldy trunk, and
offered to help him. From there it is not hard to accept that the Irish
man liked the German, found that the newcomer had no plans, and
decided to recruit him for the many needed services of the northern
wilderness. So thanks to Donald Sawyer, I imagine young Godfrey

(having accepted the offer of adventure and employment from young Johnson), driving one of William's wagons back to Fort Hunter. As he drove through the beauties of the Hudson Valley to Albany and north, he could not have realized how his future life would be influenced and intersected by the coming fame and fortunes of his new young benefactor.

For many years after that we have no record of Godfrey Shew, but let us assume that he found work in some area of Johnson's enterprises: in settlements, in trading, or in scouting the frontier. All we have from the family records is that he was with Colonel Johnson, based at his camp along the Mohawk River, during the French and Indian War. In the battle of Ticonderoga he fought under Johnson and received a bullet in his right arm, which, according to Susannah Shew, "caused his elbow to remain stiff ever after." He was taken back to Sir William's base camp to recover.

At the time of Godfrey's wounding at Ticonderoga he was forty-eight years of age and still unmarried. His biographer, Donald Sawyer, explains the trip to Philadelphia, where we know that he met Katie Frey, as a business trip for Sir William. As he tells the tale, Godfrey saw a handsome mansion and knocked on its door, asking if he could find accommodations there for the night. The lovely young woman who opened the door was none other than Katie Frey. This was not a boarding house, as Godfrey supposed, but the home of Katie's employer, who, summoned to the door, liked the looks of the weathered frontiersman and bade him welcome. It is a nice picture, built around the simple facts set forth by Simms:

> On arriving in this country, the family [Frey] landed in Philadelphia, at which time Katherine was nine years old, and she was sold into servitude to defray the expense of her passage, for the next nine years.
>
> Not long after this child was thus disposed of, her parents removed to the Wyoming Valley, with the understanding that at the expiration of her time, they would return for her; but as they did not come, she supposed they had been murdered in the French war. Fortunately the little stranger fell into Samaritan hands who appreciated her merits, and from whom she received parental kindness.
>
> (Simms, *Frontiersmen of New York*, 1883)

The period in which the Freys came to America was within the time frame of the Palatine migrations and this name abounds in the records of the Palatine settlements. These German Protestants would often pay for their passage, being penniless, by agreeing to go to such outposts as the Wyoming Valley (where Katie's parents supposedly went); there they were a part of the human barrier to French and Indian invasions. I believe, as Simms suggests, that Margaret and Henry Frey were in all probability killed in just such frontier warfare. All we may be sure of is that Godfrey Shew, veteran of the French and Indian War, on a journey to Philadelphia, met and married Katherine Frey, an indentured girl twenty-five years younger than he.

We know so little of this young woman, but it is a poignant story: indentured at nine; abandoned, however needfully, by her parents; rescued by a kind "Samaritan"; married to a man almost twice her age, with whom she now embarked on a journey into the unknown privations and adventures of a frontier life. I like to believe that in Godfrey Shew she had met a strong and loving husband. In this great-great-great-great-grandmother my imagination finds a woman of strength and spirit to treasure, a real heroine of the Adirondack frontier.

The next record we have of the Shews finds them at home on a farm a mile to the west of Sir William's manor house in Johnstown. I think it quite probable that Godfrey was a tenant of Sir William's, and a participant in the trading and military exercises that were a part of the community life around Johnson Hall. While they surely knew the family at the Hall they were not a part of its social life; their status was altogether more simple. In addition to which, they were increasingly more aligned with the so-called patriots of the valley as tensions escalated between England and its colonists.

Seven children were born to Katie and Godfrey, six in the years in town, and one after their move to the Fish House wilderness. Their three oldest sons, John, Henry, and Jacob (the latter from whom our family is descended), went to school with the children of Sir William and Molly Brant, the Indian mistress of Johnson Hall. The school was the Johnstown Free School, established by Sir William and reportedly the first public school in the state. Walking to school, the Shew boys passed by the Hall each day. Simms reported the following vignette:

> In the vicinity of the Hall were usually to be seen a dozen or more Indians, of whom the [Shew] children were afraid; the fact coming to the knowledge of Sir William, he spoke to a chief in their behalf, and then assured the little urchins, with whom he liked to chat, that they need borrow no more trouble about their red neighbors!
>
> (*Trappers*)

That is the only glimpse we have of young Shew's life in the historic environs of Johnson Hall, except for a footnote which tells us that Schoolmaster Wall "was very severe with most of his pupils, but the Baronet's children were made an exception to his clemancy—they were ever being treated with kind partiality and pointed indulgence." (*Ibid.*)

And so we come to the time when Sir William asked Godfrey Shew to undertake the leadership of his proposed settlement at Fish House. Whether or not Shew wanted to do this, it would have been hard to refuse the man who had been his mentor and benefactor for so many years. Sir William had just two years to live; he was in pain a good deal of the time, plagued with illness and depression, and yet he kept on his feet, dealing with one crisis after another in a country that was ever closer to war. At this downhill time for Sir William, Shew, who was in fact four years older, was in vigorous health. The lives of the two men had been so different, though they had begun with similar endowments of good birth and energy. With all his power and wealth, all his high times and lusty adventures, Sir William was known to cry out towards the end, "Riches, titles, and everything are nothing without health!" (Flexner, p. 336) And so the great man died in 1774 of cirrohsis of the liver at the age of sixty. Godfrey Shew, aged sixty-four, having carried out Sir William's wishes at Fish House, became a father again when Katie produced their seventh child—named Godfrey—the first baby born in the new settlement.

The Shews had moved into the rebuilt and refurbished squatter's house early in 1772. It must have been a sacrifice for even a strong woman like Kate to leave the relative comfort and safety of their home in Johnstown, especially in a time when news of Indian unrest and rumors of demonstrations against the Crown were common. But, said Simms, "the Baronet held out liberal inducements to Mr. Shew, which he accepted." I know that there were "inducements," but I believe Godfrey Shew would have gone in any event; Sir William Johnson was his colonel and his hero—and his friend.

Simms was more specific in the *Frontiersmen* of 1883: Shew was to be given a 100-acre farm, with the promise of a permanent lease. What the terms of a "liberal inducement" might have meant never seemed much of an issue to me until the summer of 1970, when, in a conversation at Johnson Hall, I met a gentleman named Colonel Briggs, who assured me that the land was never *given* to Shew, for the deed of its *sale* to him was recorded in the town records. That it was somehow *given* to him I still believe, since I trust the Shew family records, and would find it hard to imagine that anyone, regardless of loyalty, would undertake such a wilderness venture without adequate incentives. But it seems plausible that Godfrey Shew had to buy back the gift that Sir William gave him, especially if it had been a long lease rather than an outright gift, for after the Revolution all Tory property was confiscated. Since the Johnsons were Loyalists, all the lands of the Fish House would have been taken over by the new American government, and it may have been that the Shew lands, settled by a patriot family, had to go through some sort of re-negotiation. The point that seems important to me is not what Sir William gave or did not give to Godfrey Shew, but that he put faith in his ability to found a settlement in a frontier wilderness.

At first Godfrey and Kate and their children lived in the squatter's hut, but soon they had built their own log house, with logs which the father and sons had cut and seasoned. At this time Jacob was nine years old, the others in their teens. The house stood in the north end of the lot where the Methodist Church of Fish House now stands. Susannah Shew's record tells that "the only method then to obtain the direction of their journey was by marked trees." She continues:

> During the first year after the Shew family settled there, the only method provided to get bread was to go to Johnstown, a distance of about 18 miles and bring sacks of flour on their backs. The second year they raised their own grain, but their labor was doubled, however, as they had to carry the grain to Johnstown, where the nearest grist-mill was located, and then back again. Later, they made a large mortar and apparatus and converted the corn to samp [hominy grits], thus obviating the labor to some degree.

In 1773 Sir William erected a small grist mill at Mayfield. And later, after the Revolution, another mill was erected on the Kennyetto, or Vlaie Creek, which was a mile or two closer to the Fish House settlement. This was at the place now known as Hagedorn Mills.

The little settlement grew, and the tale of its earliest days reads like fiction. Simms tells it all just as Jacob Shew, in turn, told it to him, and as this can scarcely be improved, as primary and secondary sources go, let us repeat the story from the *Frontiersmen of New York*:

> When the struggle for liberty began, the Shew family were numbered among the patriotic ones of Tryon county; and although many of the frontier settlers left their homes for less exposed situations when

Indian depridations began in 1777, still the Shew family chose to remain and brave the dangers of their forest home.

On the south side of the great Vlaie, some two miles westward from Shew, dwelt Robert Martin and Zebulon Alger, occupying the same house; and four or five miles still farther westward lived Solomon Woodworth, who were also men of the times. They, too, remained exposed after the British Indians were let loose.

John and Henry Shew had several times been on militia duty in 1776 and 1777, as had Solomon Woodworth, who was a sergeant. In the afternoon of June 2, 1778, Woodworth, having occasion to call on his neighbor Martin, found to his surprise that his dwelling was tenantless, and conjecturing the family might be prisoners with the enemy and armed with his unerring rifle, he went to Shew's to communicate his suspicions; arriving there early in the evening.

Shew's family were all at home except Henry, who had accompanied Zebulon Alger to Johnstown on an errand. As it was too late and hazardous for Woodworth to return to his own dwelling that evening, he tarried over night at the Shew's, and preparations were made to give the enemy a warm reception, should the house be attacked in the night. As a precautionary measure adopted, a large pile of stones was deposited at the head of the stairway, and Jacob was stationed all night beside it, ready to cast down his cold shot upon the foe.

The inmates of the house were not disturbed during the night, and after breakfast in the morning, Woodworth, Mr. Shew, and his son, John, went out to discover, if possible, what had become of the Martin family. Finding the house still deserted, the three proceeded in the direction of Summer House Point, two miles distant, in the hope of obtaining some trace of the absentees. On the way, John who was a sportsman, and a dead shot, saw a noble buck crossing his path, and forgetting his foes for the moment, he raised his rifle and shot it.

Leaving the animal where it fell, until their return (where it probably rotted) the trio proceeded onward, but in a short distance they were surprised by a dozen Indians who had been encamped near; now drawn to the spot by the young hunter's rifle. Woodworth was about to flee, when the elder Shew, observing the Indians poise their rifles, seized and held him, fearing if he started he would be shot.

It now turned out that about 100 of the enemy, Indians and Tories led by Lieutenant (afterward Major) Ross, had come from Canada by the northern route, many of them to remove their families thither. They were also desirous of taking back some patriots as prisoners, with the plunder their dwellings might afford. That they should not be thwarted in the main object of the expedition, they crossed the Sacondaga two miles below Fish House, where they concealed their canoes, and from thence proceeded with great circumspection to the river settlements near Tribes Hill, where most of their friends resided. They avoided doing any act that might betray their visit to any of the little forts in the neighborhood and elicit pursuit. And, having collected the Indian and Tory families sought, as expeditiously as possible, they were gathering to take their canoes, when fortune gave them the three prisoners named.

On the night of the 2nd of June, the enemy were encamped with their prisoners at a little distance southeast of Summer House Point. After securing (these new prisoners) the enemy proceeded directly to Mr. Shew's dwelling, which they had intended to visit on breaking up their camp in the morning.

When his father left home (that morning) he had charged his son Jacob Shew to keep a good lookout up the river for the foe. Mr. Shew's house was situated in a ravine between two gentle elevations. On the westerly one, Jacob took his station. His vigil had lasted perhaps two hours, when he described a canoe, containing several Indians coming down the creek from Summer House Point. He had not heard the report of his brother's rifle some time before, and on seeing the canoe he ran home to report his discovery; where the party with the prisoners named had already arrived from an opposite direction. Jacob and his brother Stephen now increased the number of prisoners to 16; Jacob was 15 years old when taken.

Several Indians among the invaders, the most of whom were Mohawks, were not only old acquaintances, but long the professed friends of Mr. Shew, from whom they had received numerous favors. The vicinity of his location being a great resort for fishermen and hunters, at times a dozen Indians had slept at the Shew house in a single night, partaking, while there, the hospitality of their table.

He (Godfrey Shew) had been assured by Aaron and David, two of his Indian friends who were brothers, when they followed the Johnson family to Canada, that for the numerous favors they had received from their 'white brother,' as they called him, he should be duly notified of impending danger, and not be injured or captured in his isolated retreat. This promise of the Indians had been heard by young Jacob.

Accordingly, pretending not to consider himself a prisoner upon reaching home, the elder Shew was attentive to the wants of his quondam [former] friends. Observing they were reserved and stoical, he took occasion to remind them of their former promises. David, with a guttural grunt and shrug of his shoulders, replied in his native dialect, 'Yok-tah cock-a-rungkee!' (I do not understand you!). Proving for one, at least, the old adage false, which said an Indian could never forget a favor.

Owing to a combination of circumstances, the enemy were more humane than usual in this invasion, as no women or small children were either killed or carried into captivity. The dwellings of all the captives, except that of Woodworth, which was several miles out of the way, were plundered; and after taking from Godfrey Shew's house whatever they desired, the enemy suffered Mrs. Shew and her three youngest children to remain on the premises, but left them house-less; for now, being out of danger of pursuit, as they so believed, the torch was applied and house mostly consumed before the incendiaries left it. The barn would have escaped destruction as the party had all moved forward, but for William Bowen, a Tory there present, who had also received many favors from the Shew family. Looking back, he exclaimed, 'What, are you going to let the cursed rebel's barn stand?' He then ran back some rods to the burning house, got a fire-brand, set the barn on fire and soon it was in ruins.

Among the plunder made at the Shew home, was about 500 pounds of maple sugar, which the family had made that spring and were husbanding with care to make it last through the year. The Indians' tomahawks were put in use, and soon all the enemy were running about with large cakes, the family not being allowed a morsel of it. This looked cruel, indeed, to the children, whose mouths watered in vain for the saccharine plunder.

Mrs. Shew (Kate), after seeing her husband and two sons led off into the forest, and her buildings and their contents destroyed or carried away, set out for Johnstown, 18 miles distant, with feelings none can justly realize at this late day.

A Tory squatter, an old Irishman named Kennedy, aided Mrs. Shew and her children in crossing the Kennyetto at Summer House Point, from whence they proceeded to the house of Warren Howell, a pioneer settler in Mayfield, eight miles from the ashes of their own home. They were kindly treated at Howell's, considering the bias (Tory) of the family, and remained there over night.

On the following day they set forward, and were met at Philadelphia Bush by Mrs. Amasa Stevens and Miss Hannah Putman, daughters of Lodowyck Putman, on horseback. They had heard of Mrs. Shew's misfortunes, and thus proceeded to meet and assist her in getting to a place of safety. Mrs. Shew tarried all night with the hospitable Putman family and arrived the next day with her children at the Johnstown fort.

(Simms, 1883, Vol. II)

The Putmans were a stalwart pioneer couple, having come from Schenectady to their outpost at Philadelphia Bush, now a part of the town of Mayfield. Lodowyck Putman's grandfather, Jan, was among the first settlers and had perished in the burning and massacre of Schenectada (the old spelling) in 1690. This family was well-established in the area of Tribes Hill; Lodowyck's niece, Clarissa Putman, had for ten years lived at Fort Johnson as mistress and common-law wife to John Johnson, the son of Sir William.

The Putmans enter our family history at this point and in this way: young Hannah Putman, whom we have glimpsed riding to the aid of the Shew family, was then just fourteen. A few years later, after the Revolution, she was to be the bride of Jacob Shew, the fifteen-year-old captive of Lieutenant Ross and the Indians. To complete the link in time to our own day, Hannah and Jacob Shew's daughter Katherine (named for the courageous Katie Frey, wife of Godfrey Shew) would marry a Beecher, and become, in turn, the grandmother of *my* grandmother, Harriet Shew Beecher. In the summer of 1890, in the lovely village of Fish House, a village founded by her ancestors so many years before, and with so much heroic struggle, Harriet Shew Beecher became the bride of William Herbert Hudnut.

CHAPTER 6

FURTHER ADVENTURES OF THE FISH HOUSE SETTLERS

Taken into captivity, Godfrey Shew and his sons did not return for eight long months, but return they did, all but John. The tale of their captivity, told by Jacob Shew to Jeptha Simms, continues:

From Godfrey Shew's place the party proceeded down the river to their canoes. Increased as the party was, by 20 or 30 Indian families from Tribes Hill, and the prisoners, the watercraft (some 20 canoes) was found insufficient, and two large elm trees were cut down, from the bark of which two canoes were made and put afloat in about three hours, each carrying four or five men with their packs. A part of the warriors swam the river with their horses and proceeded along its northern shore, while the remainder, with their prisoners and families, floated down the river in canoes. At the rapids, near the present village of Conklingville, the party halted for the night, the canoes being all drawn on shore.

The prisoners were bound nights, and usually an Indian slept on each side of every captive.

The water party, consisting of part of the enemy, most of the prisoners and the removing families, went down the Sacondaga to the Hudson, crossed that river and transported their canoes to the shore of Lake George. In a carrying place about a mile distant from the lake they found a three-handed bateau, which they took along.

41

They floated down Lakes George and Champlain to St. Johns always encamping on the shore at night.

The party on land with the horses proceeded along the western side of the lakes, and at the south end of Lake Champlain both parties came together. John Shew, known by the enemy to be a good woodsman, was taken with the party on land.

The Alger horse having broken a leg on the uneven ground, was killed and eaten by its new owners. The best horse of the three that had been taken at the Shew's home, was owned by young Stephen. When the parties united Stephen again saw his favorite animal grazing with its fellows, and could not give up the idea of its being his property. Pointing to it, he observed to an Indian who had the care of it,

"That is my horse!"

"Ump, he mine now," replied the Indian by way of comfort to the boy.

The food of the water party and probably that of the other, consisted principally of fresh mutton, beef, poultry, etc., obtained as plunder on the premises of the prisoners. The meat was soon fly-blown [spoiled] but the Indians made soup of it. Jacob Shew carried the saddle of a sheep from the Sacondaga to Lake George. The prisoners generally had food enough, although Indians' fare, but for the two days near the end of their journey, the water party fasted — eating mouldy biscuit, several barrels of which had been left in that neighborhood by a cut-off party of Burgoyne's men the year before.

The captives were 12 days going from Fish House to Montreal, where a British officer paid twelve dollars and a half each for those of them the Indians chose to give up. (John Shew and some others were retained by the Indians.)

At the time of this invasion, the enemy were desirous of getting prisoners for exchange and offered a more liberal bounty for prisoners than for scalps; this probably accounts for there having been no blood shed by Ross's party; believed to have been an unparalleled instance of humanity exercised by Canadian invaders during the war.

The ten captives retained as prisoners of war were kept at Montreal for several weeks and then sent down to Quebec on a sloop, from which they were transferred to the ship, *Maria*, under Captain Max, and remained on board of her at that port two or three months.

While there a British sergeant drew up, at their request, a petition to Sir John Johnson, which the ten Johnstown (Fish House) prisoners signed; proposing that as they were held ready for exchange, they would return home across the lakes and send back an equal number of the enemy, then held prisoners.

To this proposition Sir John would not agree, but went on board the ship and told them in person that "if they would join his corps, they would all return together to possess their lands."

"When the devil will that be?" interrogated the elder Shew in no very good humor.

"The rebels can't hold out much longer," said Sir John, "and at the end of the war, we'll all go back to Johnstown together."

"Never," responded the old patriot with emphasis, "will you go back to inherit your Johnstown possessions again!"

The Tory chieftain was unwilling to believe the war would end so disastrously for his future prospects, and left the ship. A few days after, Sir John sent for Godfrey Shew, to find out if any of the prisoners would enlist in his Majesty's service. Mr. Shew told him he thought they would *not*, but that he would ask them. After a request from Sir John that he would use his influence in that direction, the prisoner was returned to the ship.

The next morning a recruiting officer, Sergeant Hilliard, visited the ship to look for recruits. The prisoners were all on deck and, agreeable to his instructions, he waited upon Mr. Shew. As the young captives gathered around the old gentleman [that is Godfrey Shew, who was then close to 68 years old] he said to them,

"Here is a recruiting officer, come to enlist you into the British service! My lads, if any of you want to sell your country for a green coat with red facings and a cap with a lock of red horse-hair hanging down one side of it, you now have a good chance!"

The reader is aware that the force of an argument depends much on the time and manner of its utterance. That this one of Mr. Shew's had its desired weight may be inferred from the fact after many inducements and golden promises of reward in his Majesty's service, Sergeant Hilliard left the ship without having made a *single* recruit. Thus much for the principles of the back-woods men of western New York in the hour that tried men's souls.

When the *Maria* was moored under the Heights of Abraham, the British on the fortifications would play "Yankee Doodle" to irritate the prisoners. Many of the captives who were in good spirits, however, would throw up their hats, huzza for the cause of Liberty, begin a jig on the ship's deck and shout to the enemy to play away and they would dance for them! Early in September, the *Maria* was ready to sail for England, via New York, where she was to land her prisoners, some 60 in all.

Soon after leaving the Gulf of St. Lawrence, the *Maria* fell in with a privateer, which immediately gave chase. The pursuit lasted for two days, and the British vessel escaped by being a better sailor than her antagonist; but she was driven directly out of her course; after a sail of several weeks, being part of the time nearer Europe than America, and not daring to run down to New York, she returned to Halifax, there landed her captives and sailed directly from thence to England.

Nearly 1,300 captives were then assembled at Halifax, and two ships were fitted out to take them to Boston to be exchanged. Several prisoners had escaped from Halifax, by having good knives; and when the Johnstown prisoners were confined there, their knives were taken from all of them except the elder Shew. They had to cook their own meat in a large kettle set in an arch, and often were allowed but a scanty supply of fuel to do it with. Not infrequently the grease was skimmed off to increase the flame, and at times an old garment was tucked underneath the kettle. If the meat was not half cooked as was frequently the case, it had to be eaten in its raw state, with the peas or beans soaked with it.

Jacob Shew chanced to find a piece of an iron hoop, and with an immense rubbing upon a stone, he made it supply the needs of a knife.

(Simms, 1883, Vol. II)

Many of the Johnstown contingent died before ever reaching Boston, a few others died in Boston and on the way home for there was an outbreak of smallpox. Young Jacob succumbed to the disease in the town of Sudbury, just 20 miles from Boston. He just sat down at the side of the road and said he could go no further. The party found a place that would take him in and nurse him, and they, long gone and panting to get home, left the young lad. Godfrey Shew and his sons Stephen and Henry arrived in the Johnstown Fort on New Year's day, 1779. Mr. Simms concludes his telling of the tale in this way:

Jacob was cured of his loathsome disease, and reached Johnstown on the 17th of March following his capture, it being St. Patrick's day in the morning!

You will remember that John Shew was separated from his father and brothers after the Ross raiders reached Champlain. His grim story is told by Susannah Shew:

You are doubtless anxious to hear more about John, who was retained by the Indians. He was kept a prisoner for 6 months, and having won their confidence by a quick return with plenty of game, was allowed to go alone to hunt. After so long confinement, he resolved to leave them the first opportunity. To prepare for this scheme, he prolonged his stay each time and finally ran away from them.

He subsisted principally on roots and herbs, not daring to shoot his gun, and as often as it became necessary to cross a stream of water, would travel a short distance up and down in order to mislead his pursuers. It was a trial for him to have to part with his gun when he swam across the St. Lawrence River, and yet it must have been torture to him to have it and not be able to shoot it, when starving, for game. At length he arrived home in safety and remained there until peace was proclaimed. About a year from this time when hunting in and around the Town of Milton, Saratoga County, he was suddenly called upon by some eight or ten Indians, to "Surrender" and they would give him quarters.

Seeing no way to escape, he therefore surrendered. They then bound his hands and feet and tortured him to death by shooting arrows into him and mangling him beyond description, as his friends were credibly informed by some two or three who interred his remains.

After their return, Henry, Stephen, and Jacob Shew all enlisted in the American Army, leaving their father to care for the rest of the family. Henry was at the taking of Burgoyne, Stephen was one of the number posted to guard the fort at Johnstown and Jacob was in the Battle of East Canada Creek. In the latter encounter with the Mohawks, the patriots numbered just forty-five men, two-thirds of whom were killed that day.

Jacob rose to the rank of Colonel in the Tryon County militia before the end of the Revolution.

At the end of the war, the Shew family departed from Johnstown once again, this time to rebuild their log house in the Fish House wilderness. In 1784, the Shew family built another house, larger and more handsome, some 40 rods east. Its structure, of the broadly inclusive school later to be known as American Colonial, bears witness to the simple good taste of those early forebears. Still standing, and essentially unchanged, it tells, also, of their building skill. It is on the crest of a knoll overlooking what was then the low-lying valley of the Sacandaga, and is marked by an historical marker as the "Shew House" even though it is no longer owned by the family.

Susannah Shew notes that the elder Shews lived the remainder of their lives in Fish House. Kate died in 1800, Godfrey in 1804, and they were buried there in the community cemetery. However, at the time when the old stones were moved for the flooding of the Sacandaga Reservoir, their headstones were lost. A marker along the winding highway is the only memorial to these pioneers and their heroic struggles to create a settlement in the wilderness.

There is a separate marker for their son, Jacob Shew, the first member of the State Legislature from Fish House. He died in 1853 at the age of 90, the first citizen of a Fish House that had become a handsome and thriving village. In the years before his death, before 1850, as the *Frontiersmen* records, he was often visited by the historian, Simms. Jeptha Simms called the stories of the Fish House settlers which we have quoted in the foregoing chapters, "the narrative of the venerable patriot, Jacob Shew." He concluded the narrative with a tribute to those courageous pioneers and placed them rightly in our country's history:

> The pride of the *old* world has ever been her princes and her nobles, the one inheriting, though seldom meriting, a crown—the others made such by some farcical ceremony, to . . . live on the producing classes of the community.
>
> The pride of the *new* world—particularly that portion which we inherit, is also her princes and her nobles; the former rendered such by the voice of a free and intelligent people—the latter, not by form and court favor, but by true valor and deeds of noble daring. And although it may be said that Americans have no grandfathers, many of her distinguished sons and daughters having risen from obscurity —yet will Americans date an ancestry of real nobility, christened in the blood of freemen, and destined in its moral influence to emancipate the world from oppression.
>
> (*Frontiersmen of New York*)

CHAPTER 7
THE
FISH HOUSE
SUMMER OF 1889

Now that we have explored the earliest times of Fish House and related this history to the Shews and Beechers who are about to enter our family tale, we return to young William Hudnut, who in the spring of 1889 was completing his first year at Theological Seminary at Princeton, and in the act of transferring to Union Seminary in New York. The way in which he came to the Fish House Village for that summer always seemed to him the most extraordinary providence. He wrote in his *Memoirs*:

> Every year one of the main interests of the Seminary students
> was their summer employment. This was due in part to the money
> they would receive, which most of us sorely needed, and in part to
> the opportunity thus afforded for experience in preaching and in
> other forms of church work. Personally I was very keen for
> another summer parish where I could do some fishing. I learned
> that Murray Gardner, a member of the graduating class, had
> spent his last summer in the Adirondacks and I went to him to
> discover how he had secured his place. He told me that he had
> had a double parish, Northampton [N.Y.] and a nearby town,
> Batchellerville. These towns were on the Sacandaga River in the
> southern part of the mountains. He had greatly enjoyed his work

there and desiring a return engagement had written Henry Smith, the Clerk of the Session, several weeks ago but had received no answer. He had in the meantime received an offer from Warrensburg in another part of the Adirondacks, which he had accepted. He could not understand why he had not heard from Mr. Smith and advised me to write him. Thus began a correspondence which resulted in a call to these churches, which I accepted.

I did not know until later upon how tenuous a thread of circumstance my going to Northampton depended. Murray Gardner's letter to Elder Smith was received and, as his ministry the previous summer had been entirely satisfactory, a letter was sent asking him to return, but in addressing this letter Mr. Smith absent-mindedly addressed it to some other Princeton and Gardner never received it. So but for the misdirected letter I would never have seen Northampton.

Mr. Smith's letter, yellowed with age, is a model of Spencerian artistry:

Northampton, N.Y. 4-13-1889

To Mr. W.H. Hudnut, Esq.

I am informed by Rev. I. N. Crockew of Saratoga that your services might be secured by our society for the four months ending about September 15th.

I feel warranted in making you this hasty offer — $160 and board. By this hasty letter I hope to arrest your attention and open a correspondence on the subject. Will you confer with Rev. M.H. Gardner of the Seminary.

Respectfully yours,

J.H. Smith

Continuing William Hudnut's memories of old Fish House:

At the time the Fonda, Johnstown and Gloversville Railroad ran an afternoon train to Northville which was the line's northern terminus. Passengers going to Northampton got off at Cranberry Creek and went from there by stage, a distance of about six miles. Joe Rider drove the stage. The team was slow, the road mostly heavy with sand and there were several stops for the delivery of parcels and mail bags. So we had plenty of time for talk and from Joe I got my first information about the countryside and its people.

Historically, the name of the town was Fish House. Here Sir William Johnson came from his manor house in Johnstown to fish

the Sacandaga River. Under grant from the King he owned this
entire region, serving as Commissioner of Indian Affairs.

Robert Chambers, who made his home in Broadalbin, wrote
several novels, located in this valley of the Sacandaga, stories of
Sir William and his friends, the great Indian Chief, Joseph Brant,
and the Butlers, who were the scourge of the early settlers. So I
was being carried into the land of pre-revolutionary history.

To the West I caught glimpses of the Mayfield range of wooded
hills and to the East, Maxon Mountain and the beginning of the
hills that extend past Conklinville to the Hudson. The river,
breaking out through the hills at Northville, and there forsaking
its flow over many rapids, meanders in a winding sweep through
the valley, turning at last northward to lose itself in the mighty
Hudson.

And now I caught my first glimpse of the village. There
through the trees was the white spire of the Church of my summer
ministry. We rattled across the covered bridge of the Vlaie Creek.

Fish House was a beautiful little village. It had lost its opportunity for growth and importance some years before, when it
refused a right-of-way to the railroad. At its center five roads con-
verged, each with its own special charm and destination. They
were dusty, muddy, curvy, up-hill-and-down-dale roads of the
horse and buggy age. You could go over Hans' Creek to "Hager-
dorn Holler" and on to a ridge from which you could look across
the great Hudson valley to the far ranges of the Green Mountains.
Another way led south through Broadalbin, whose ancient name
was Fonda's Bush, and so on through Vale's Mills to Gloversville
where mill owners were making fortunes in tanning and glove
manufacture. The road over the hill to Fayville led down the
south side of the Sacandaga to Batchellerville, over which I drove
every Sunday afternoon for my preaching appointment in that
village. The road across the Vlaie Creek bridge was the stage road
from Cranberry Creek. And the fifth was the road through the big
old Fish House Bridge over the Sacandaga River, which then
divided, one branch to Beecher Hollow, the other to Northville.

Driving over any of these roads you experienced the rural
simplicity and beauty of the countryside. They were shaded by
ancient elm and maple; behind the houses were the cultivated
acres and pastures of farm land. There were a number of archi-
tectural styles in the homes but they seemed to me uniformly
handsome. Notable amongst them were two Cape Cod houses as
old as the river bridge and one large finely proportioned brick
house that antedated the Civil War.

Covered bridge at Fish House

There were at the crossroads two hotels between which there was a bitter rivalry. Each ran a bar and a livery and each had its partisans and patrons. This feud later culminated in tragedy.

Two general stores also divided the community. Their proprietors belonged to different churches, and represented diverse political parties. The post office went from one to the other according to which political party was in power.

I think you would travel far today to find in so small a place stores owned and operated by men of equal caliber. Mr. Humphrey was the older man, spare, fine featured, with a lot of native dignity and refinement. He had two sons, Liph, the older, who ran the store, and Al, who was the village nit-wit, a jovial, harmless creature.

While Humphrey was a pillar in the Methodist Church, J.H. Smith, the owner of the other store, was the Clerk of Session of the Presbyterian Church and a strong Republican. He was a born merchant and trader, shrewd, genial, with a keen sense of humor, generally very popular. William Henry Harrison's election had awarded him the post office. His store was on the right as you entered the village, and inside were rows of numbered boxes built about the central post office window for delivery of mail and sale of stamps, all easily transportable to the other store when a Democratic president should be elected.

The Smiths had two children: Page, who was studying law, who put on airs, possibly because he was the only representative of the village in a school of higher learning; and Elsie, a pretty child with long black hair, just in her teens. The Smiths were related to the Fays, a fine old Fish House family whose older son, Ed, was a Presbyterian minister. They had wealthy relatives in Albany who were commonly referred to as "the summer girls."

Country towns still have their general stores, but I wonder whether they show on their counters as varied a line of merchandise. They were certainly the forerunners of the great department stores. In Henry Smith's store you could clothe yourself completely and get everything you needed for your housekeeping. Here during the day you could meet your neighbors and friends and hear much gossip and shrewd talk of crops and politics and religion. But the supreme hour of the day was when the mail was being distributed and you waited with the rest of the village, keeping an eye for the private box, into which at any moment a letter or paper might be slipped, and an ear for the village talk. It always seemed to take an unconscionable time to stamp and sort the mail. Even then, when the world seemed young and you were far from the crowded city, and speed was not your familiar demon, you fretted over those lingering moments.

Unlike many small villages, Fish House was not then over-churched. The Methodists worshipped in a wooden building of colonial type on the road to Fayville. They were on a circuit and received the part time ministry of their preacher. The Presbyterians had once had their own minister, but at the time I was there, and for several years before, they had only had student "supplies" for the summer and these young men held a service at Batchellerville every Sunday afternoon, in addition to the morning and evening services at Fish House. These three services, together with Sunday School and mid-week prayer meeting, made a rather heavy schedule.

The Presbyterian Church, which stood on the Saratoga Road, was a red brick building with a well proportioned spire and small wooden Sunday School room in the rear. It was a remarkably good looking structure embowered amidst great maple trees. In the rear were carriage sheds and on the south side a small graveyard. The sanctuary had a vestibule and two aisles and would seat about one hundred and fifty people. The roof beams were exposed in the nave and the walls were freshly decorated. Behind the pulpit, which stood on a raised platform, an artist had painted a religious scene in an oval recess, elaborately framed. Such decoration was usual in churches of that period and seemed to me more sightly than batteries of organ pipes.

Beside the Church was a parsonage, at that time rented to the Gibbs family. They had a daughter who was engaged to Mr. Lincoln, the Methodist minister, who lived with them and had a room upstairs. My study and bedroom were on the first floor and, like Lincoln, I boarded with the family. Gibbs was a small spare man and his portly wife was a Roosevelt, a distant connection of the President.

From my study windows I looked across the street to the Baker house where lived a fair and rather precise maiden by name, Cora. She later became the wife of George Fraser, a Presbyterian minister who for years was the pastor of the Northville Church. Next to the Bakers in the old brick house lived the Starks. He was a farmer, a thin, wiry man of middle age, a very glutton for work. Like many another farmer who got what he had by the sweat of his brow, he had the reputation of being "near." But he was a man of integrity, a respected Elder in the Church, always in his place at services, lifting his voice in prayer at the mid-week meetings and greatly esteemed as teacher of the Bible Class. He was a man of few words, independent and unafraid. His wife was a buxom, placid woman, immaculate in her person and her home. There were three children, Will, who was also a farmer, and two daughters, typical country girls, shy, silent, but capable.

Next to the Starks lived Miss Wood, a little maiden lady, whose house was as old fashioned as herself. Every summer her nieces from Watervliet, Fanny and Grace Waterman, came to spend their vacation with her. They were fine girls, full of fun. Fanny was the older and more dignified; Grace was athletic and bois-terous. Then came Bidker Jones, a drummer, who spent most of his time traveling. His waist measure must have equalled his height. Mrs. Jones was as thin as he was fat. She was dark skinned, wall-eyed and frail—a most peculiar looking person.

And now we have reached the corner upon which stood the Osborne Hotel. This became in a measure a house of tragedy. For besides the murder of old Sy (the proprietor), there was his eldest son, Will, a passionate, uncontrolled, brutal type, mostly feared and hated, who became the proprietor of a small hotel in Specu-lator, and was instantly killed by a baseball that hit him in the temple.* Another brother, John, a sour, cross-grained fellow, attained an unenviable reputation as the proprietor of one of the worst saloons in Fulton County. Withall, the mother of the family was a mild, hard-working, much afflicted woman and her daughter, who married Will Stark, was a refined and gentle person.

Across the broad intersection of the divergent roads was the Fish House Hotel; beyond it, on the road to the big bridge, stood the most elegant home in the village, then owned and occupied during the summer by Mr. and Mrs. Frank Sinclaire and their family, whose winter home was in Brooklyn on Amity Street. Mrs. Sinclaire was a daughter of Dr. Langdon Marvin, for many years the general practitioner of the valley, who had built this fine house hard by the Sacandaga. Attached to the house was a farm whose many acres of fields and pasture extended on both sides of the river. The farm was chiefly noted for its herd of registered Jersey cattle and every week shipments of the finest butter went to customers in Brooklyn.

The Sinclaires were a large family. Besides the two sons, Frank and Tom, and the daughter, Lu, there was an uncle, John Marvin, and an aunt, Lydia Hough, her son Jack, and several servants who had been with them for so long that they were as members of the family. Amongst these the most notable was Ash, who was the

---

* Will Osborne, Jr. continued ownership of the Osborne House at Speculator, well into the 1960s.

color of his name. Brought up in slavery, he was fortunate, during
the Civil War, to escape to the North where he found shelter in
the Sinclaire home. For some forty years he continued in their service, living, unmarried, in this home at Fish House, taking charge
of their dairy, making and shipping the butter, and in many other
ways rendering devoted service to his "white folks," who, upon
their part, treated him with equal faithfulness, humoring him,
bearing with him when in his age he assumed the role of "Emperor
Jones," until at the last, still in their bonds of mutual service and
loyalty, they laid away his wearied old body in the family burial
plot.

This home was large and beautifully furnished and it was always
a treat to be a guest at their table. Mr. Sinclaire had spent his
time largely in the fields or about the barns. He was an alert,
energetic little man, devoted to his family, rather self-important
and full of his own opinions—an imported English squire. His
wife, Lucy, was a woman of considerable culture, making up for
her husband's lack of elegance, an aristocrat, very gracious in
manner, always beautifully dressed, the complete mistress of her
domestic affairs. Her daughter, Lu, was much like her, but more
vivacious. She spoke and recited beautifully. I wondered why such
an attractive, capable woman never married. It may have been
that her home life was too assured and comfortable.

Just beside the Sinclaire home was a lovely little Cape Cod house
that dated back to Revolutionary days. Here lived James and
Elizabeth Beecher with their three daughters. The daughters did
not exactly live there: the oldest, Ella Katherine, was a teacher of
English in Miss Mittlebergar's School in Cleveland; the second,
Harriet Shew, was teaching several elementary branches in Miss
Lewis' School in Brookline, Massachusetts, and Hannah Emily, the
youngest, was tutoring in Des Moines, Iowa. Their son, Leman,
was a farmer like his father. He did not take kindly to an education and whereas Ella, who was the ambitious, intellectual leader
of the family, had inspired and financed her sisters, she had failed
to thus inspire her brother. He married early, and by dint of hard
work on a farm near Elmira, New York, which his wife inherited,
was comfortably well off.

James Beecher was a heavy-set man of powerful build. He had
great, toil-worn hands and a massive head, with rugged, handsome long gray beard—a patriarchal or prophetic type, if you
please. He was a Beecher in build and feature, strongly resembling
his cousins, Henry Ward and Thomas K. He had grown to man-
hood in Dutchess County, and here he had married Elizabeth

Anne Northrup. She must have been a lovely maiden for when I knew her she was very beautiful. Her black hair, but thinly streaked with gray, was parted in the middle and combed back smoothly on either side. Her features were fine and strong, but her charm was not so much in these as in her expression. Here was settled calm, quiet dignity, gentle sweetness, an impression of purity and goodness.

When James Fuller Beecher moved his family to Fish House his children were all grown; he and Elizabeth were middle aged. The Sinclaires, whose land and family have been described above, were cousins: Lucy Sinclaire's mother was a Beecher, before marrying Dr. Marvin. And both James Beecher and Lucy Sinclaire were grandchildren of Deacon Abraham Beecher, who had come to Fish House from Connecticut after the Revolution with his wife, Lydia Day Fuller Beecher. Their tombstones stood in the little graveyard next to the Presbyterian Church.

Besides Cousin Lucy, there was also Uncle Chauncey Beecher, living on his farm to the north of the village near Beecher Hollow, now Edinburgh. James Beecher was the grandson of Jacob Shew, described here earlier as the leading citizen of Fish House, and long-term member of the New York State Legislature. So, when the Beechers moved to Fish House, they were in no sense entering as newcomers. They settled with ease into the simple white cottage that had been Dr. Marvin's home (just in front of the site of Sir William Johnson's Fish House.) Mr. Beecher soon became a leader in the community, and a trustee of the Presbyterian Church, where his daughter, Harriet, would meet the new minister.

Continuing the memoirs of that young minister, Will Hudnut:

It was at my first service in the church that I met the Beechers. None of the daughters was at home, but they were expected in a week or so and my interest in them was aroused by the enthusiastic comments I heard. Harriet seemed to be the most favorably known and at once I found myself looking forward to her appearance. She was then teaching in Miss Lewis' School in Brookline, Mass. When I heard that she would be home the next Sunday, I prepared my sermon with special care. But even so, I was overcome with an excess of nervousness when I saw her in the pew with her father and mother. She was a strikingly handsome girl. She had raven black hair, beautiful, large, black eyes, finely chiseled features and an expression in which gentleness and strength were mingled.

I must say that she did not manifest the slightest interest in me. And I was much chagrined that during my *show* sermon she leaned over once or twice to speak to her mother, and seemed not the least bit interested.

The young minister's Sermon Diary for that summer Sunday of June 9th, 1889, simply notes:

> June 9th - morning sermon text: Hebrews 11.
> Cloudy and wet. 80 out.

The memoir continues:

> How it happened, I cannot tell, whether I was piqued by her indifference or fascinated by her beauty; from that moment I loved her and my mind was made up, without knowing it, that I would win her.
>
> Then commenced a period of intense emotional excitement. The Fish House valley and the encompassing hills were more beautiful; the village folk more interesting; a magic mantle had been thrown over my world and the commonplace was suffused with glory. Never before had I experienced anything like this. I was a new creature —so wrought upon, so profoundly moved that I imagined I had a fever and went to the doctor to have my temperature taken.

Having read this tumultuous outpouring, I was amused to find this note, carefully preserved by my grandmother, Harriet, written to her at the beginning of their courtship, demonstrating how politely a Victorian gentleman tried to camouflage his intentions:

> The Parsonage
>
> Dear Miss Hattie,
>
> When you said that you wouldn't be out to meeting this evening, I entirely forgot to ask you if you couldn't make it convenient to be present at choir practicing, just at close of service. I am *very* anxious that the singing on Sabbath should prove a success, and deeming your presence *most* essential to the attainment of that end, I take the liberty of addressng you in this brief and hastily written note.
>
> But, however much I would like to have you present, I beg of you not to let my importunity set aside any regulations which you deem essential to your health. I am,
>
> Sincerely yours,
>
> WM. H. HUDNUT

Continuing the memoir:

Now I had to be at the Beecher's every afternoon or evening. I became a pest, a nuisance. I was clever at contriving pretexts for calls. I took Harriet for long drives in what seemed then to be quite a stylish turn-out, hired from the Osborne Stables.

Mr. and Mrs. Beecher were immediately my friends. There was no match-making about their cordial, simple hospitality. Often Mother Beecher would tempt me with spring chicken and flaky soda biscuits to stay for dinner.

So was the stage set for our love idyll and there was not lacking one favoring circumstance. Often on those summer evenings we would walk through the long, shaded aisles of the old covered bridge, a mile or so, to Uncle Chauncey Beecher's. He and his wife were aged people who had through laborious years attained beauty and serenity of life. I have seldom seem a finer face than his, written over with the peace of God. He had learned to accept life whatever it brought. They tell how one morning early in the fall there came a killing frost. He was up early and out to view the blackened ruin of his buckwheat crop. Coming in, he met his son, Burr, who in those later days had taken over the work of the farm, and all he said was, "Burr, there's been a noble frost."

It was on one of these walks, only a week or so after I had first seen her, that I proposed to Harriet. I told her everything there was to tell about my life and poured out the amazing tale of my consuming passion. Naturally she was deeply moved and taken by surprise. She confessed a great liking for me, but did not feel that after such a brief acquaintance she could become engaged to me. She felt that we should know one another better. To my pleading she at last promised that later in the summer she would give me her answer. It seemed to me then that, while this waiting would be intolerable, I could wait for her forever.

I had only been at Fish House a few weeks when my brother Frank decided to come up with his family for a vacation. He had given up general practice and had become a specialist in the diseases of the throat and nose, eye and ear. The practice of medicine had not yet become highly specialized and the average physician looked after his own patients and only in the treatment of very stubborn or obscure cases did he seek or advise such assistance. So financially this change was not very successful. I of course vigorously promoted their coming and secured room and board for them at a farm house across the road from the Sinclaires.

Mr. and Mrs. James Fuller Beecher

Home of Lucy Marvin Sinclaire, first cousin of James Beecher.

"Cousin Lucy" serving tea; Lu, her daughter, at right.

Fish House, the Beecher house c. 1890

Fish House Presbyterian Church in 1889

When Frank learned that the Sacandaga River flowed through
Fish House and that it was navigable as far as Batchellerville, he
decided to purchase a Naphtha launch. He was always very extravagant and could not deprive himself of anything he set his heart
on. The boat was a handsome affair with a brass smoke stack,
though why *any* smoke stack I never knew, as there was no smoke.
It would accommodate eight people and could make ten or twelve
miles an hour. He decided to sail it up from New York and I went
down to make the journey with him. We reached the Hudson
River on the first day and there I left him. The boat went well
and I never enjoyed a trip up the Hudson so much. The next day
Frank continued the journey to Albany and from there by canal to
Amsterdam. At Amsterdam they loaded the boat on a hay rigging
and transported it to the Sacandaga. Frank was always popular,
making friends quickly, and the boat proved to be a great asset
with everyone at Fish House. Everyone was eager for a ride. It
required some care in navigation as the river was quite rapid in
places with many winding ways and shoals and snags.

In such a small community it did not take long for the Little
Minister* to know the village folk. But some of the members of the
Church were farmers living far out upon the roads that centered
in the village. To this farm group I was introduced largely
through the kindness of the village physician, Darius Orton, who
was one of the Elders and the best educated man in that whole
countryside. Almost daily he would be visiting some of these folk
and as often as possible I would ride with him. I had a very
enriching experience with this horse-and-buggy doctor. He knew
everyone for miles about and some of our talk would be of those
homes—family histories, financial circumstances, sicknesses and
sorrows. But there were other topics, and chiefest among those was
his theory of our universe, which he conceived to be a vast
dynamo generating electric light and power by the rotation of the
planets about the sun. His conversation was punctuated with certain brief and abrupt expressions such as, "Well, say, I want to
know! . . ."

He had several places in the village and a farm on the Vlaie
Creek road. A great octagonal barn which he had built, and his
house, burned shortly before I came. After the fire he bought a
very ancient house which stood upon the highest point in the
village. It was a Federal style with square porch pillars. Mrs.
Orton was a pleasant, cheerful woman, very hospitable and a hard

---

* Grandfather used this phrase often; *The Little Minister* was the title of a popular
novel of the time, written by Sir James Barrie.

worker. She had a large family and no help. No one but the Sinclaires kept help and any woman who had won the right to be called a good housekeeper must of necessity keep her nose to the grindstone.

Among the most interesting and substantial people to whom I ministered that summer were members of the Batchellerville Church. Not living amongst them and only being there Sunday afternoons, I did not come to know them intimately.

It was about an hour's drive to Batchellerville, depending somewhat upon the conditions of the road. Down the valley of the Sacandaga with now and then glimpses through the wood or across the fields at the winding, softly flowing river, the valley growing narrower and the hills higher until you came to the village straggling along its ancient shaded highway. Almost the first building was the old white church with its colonial portico and square bell tower. The soft note of the swinging bell is pealing across the valley its summons to worship, the family groups are moving along the road, some farm rigs are being hitched in the yard, the bell tolls and the Little Minister takes his place behind the pulpit. The church is well filled, for these people are faithful church attendants, kindly and appreciative, and the age of motors and "movies" and multiplying distractions is not yet. And the peace of God flows through the valley like the river and there is without the hush of quietness with which, through the open windows, mingles the music of the hymns and the spoken word of God.

After my second year in the Seminary I was perhaps better furnished to preach than I had been when I went to Port Daniel, but even so it was a very simple, unadorned, scriptural message which they received and which they welcomed so generously. And now, after fifty years, when I find those afternoon services standing out as more effective and satisfying in comparison with other more liturgical, ornate and sophisticated, I am convinced that beauty and truth and sincerity are most appealingly expressed through simplicity, and that in religion as in art simplicity is the supreme attainment. Maybe against the background of my experience it should be said that there are degrees of simplicity and that mine was the nth degree. I had with me the same five foot library I had taken to Canada and the notes of the sermons I had preached there—a very small backlog against which to kindle spiritual fires. I cannot now see how I got the time for necessary preparation. Each week there were three sermons to preach and a prayer meeting address. Then there were the pastoral visits covering a wide area of the countryside.

But in conjunction with these duties there were many distractions or attractions — the trout in Hans' Creek or Clouchy's meadow, the pickerel up the Vlaie, the tennis games on the parsonage lawn just outside my window, the excursions down the river in Frank's put-put, the swimming parties in the water hole across the Sinclaire meadows, the invitations to bountiful country suppers — but supreme amongst these was our courtship. Never did time, palpitating with pleasure, fly more swiftly. My eagerness for our engagement became an obsession, and daily I pressed my suit and besought her favorable decision. We had only known each other about ten weeks when we became engaged.

The Beechers accepted me as Harriet's fiancé and I was very desirous to have my mother come to Fish House to meet my sweetheart. It was one of those rare and amazing periods in life when everything turns out as you wish and to my great satisfaction those two, whom of all I loved most, fell in love with each other. Here began an affection which never waned, which time and experience only served to enrich, and which was beautiful in its admiration, loyalty and devotion.

In those days in New York on the corner of Courtland Street and Broadway, was the Benedict Jewelry Store. I knew one of the old clerks in that store and now, being in great need of an engagement ring, I wrote to him. Of course it must be a diamond ring, but it could not be a large stone because I had less than a hundred dollars to invest. That about represented my net income for my summer's work. After some correspondence the ring was ordered. The waiting for its arrival was a real ordeal.

Finally word came that it was at Cranberry Creek and Harriet drove over with me. To pay the express charges, to hold the precious package in my hand, to rush out to the waiting buggy, to break the seals and remove the various wrappings, to open the small pasteboard casket and disclose the small sparkling brilliance, and then to press it down on the finger of her lovely hand — what rapture it was! She was pledged and by this lovely token bound to me.

And now the wedding day was set for the following June and it was decided that she would go back to her teaching in Brookline whilst I would enter the Senoir Class at Union Seminary. Naturally I would not return to Princeton. Union was then a Presbyterian Seminary and my being in New York would make it possible for us to be together more often.

As Union Seminary opened about the middle of September, it

was decided to hold a Communion service before my departure. We invited the minister of the Johnstown Church to exchange with me for that Sunday. He was an eccentric about whom many stories were told. It was reported that he frequented livery stables where he might be seen sitting with his feet against the building and his chair tilted back, and what was worse, that he was known to take a piece of pie in his hand and bite off large mouthfuls—a man uncouth. I recall when I met him that he had a short, rough way of speaking and that in our conversation about pastoral experiences he told me that a minister must have the skin of a pachyderm. I think he prided himself upon being thus protected. But while his suggestion, reinforced and brought home by his personal experiences, seemed to have much in its favor, I was never able thus to arm myself against criticism and abuse even though on occasion I sought such defense.

I wished very much to be present at that Communion, principally because amongst those joining the Church there was a young man who wished to be immersed. They took him down and dipped him in the Sacandaga, and I missed the show!

Shortly after the Communion service came the day of leave-taking. I did not want to leave that charmed valley where I had found such perfect happiness, and yet, now, with marriage in view, I was more eager than ever to finish my theological training. We thought our parting would be easier if we travelled together as far as Albany. But when we got there I couldn't tear myself away and so went on to Springfield.

We would have a June wedding; that was settled. It seemed a very long time to wait, but no earlier date was possible. We found that we each wanted a very small home wedding with only the relatives present, and we decided to ask Thomas K. Beecher ["Uncle Tom" to Harriet] to come on from Elmira to perform the ceremony. So with these important matters settled, we entered upon our months of separation.

CHAPTER 8

OVERTURE
TO A
FISH HOUSE WEDDING

It was, for me, like finding hidden treasure to come across a small packet of letters, bound in ribbon, written by Harriet and William during that year before their wedding in June of 1890. This was not just for the light they shed on the way things *were* for an engaged couple back then, though to be sure, letters from another age hold a certain fascination, and it wasn't simply their record of events, though these enlighten us. The *treasure* was the way they brought my then-young grandparents alive to me. Here is not the tall slender gray-haired queen I remember from my little-girlhood, reaching down a long gloved hand to my tiny one. Here is not the distinguished elderly gentleman with his goatee and eye-shade, remembered with my own veneer of love and veneration. But here, in a handful of letters from over a century ago, real people in living dialogue, preparing for their June wedding.

William, writing from Union Seminary in New York:

> My own true darling Harriet, I have got the blues tonight in true earnest. I feel *dreadfully* lonely. I am wild to see you. . . . I am discouraged about my work, my own ability, and energy. In fact I am in one of my old time Saturday night moods and what I

do need *so* much is to have you here to comfort me up!

Harriet, from Miss Lewis' School in Boston:

My own sweet Will . . . we were going to hear Phillips Brooks this morning but it is pouring—

William:

The professor of Hebrew is a young man, very nervous and very expulsive and I am always afraid that in one of his talking paroxysms he will blow his tongue out by the roots.

Harriet:

Ten napkins embroidered and hemmed, thank goodness!! I beg to differ with you, Will dear, I do not think I under-rate myself or over-rate you. It will indeed be a sad day for me should I awake and realize that you have fallen below my standard, that you are not as smart as I *think* you—I am confident I shall *never* awake!

William:

I said to Mother yesterday, "Oh, would to God that I had my own home and Harriet there. I care not then *what* happens. The happiness of that time is unimagineable and I can but form faint conceptions of what it really will be . . .

Harriet:

You ask me, "Will you never long to be rich?" I do not think I shall *long*, though I may sometimes *wish* it. All my life I have wished for money as a means to so many ends, but I do not *long* for it. I have always had a faculty for taking things as they come, and have a happy disposition, so do not see why I should take to pining or longing. For you know, my love, that
>   "What appears in sight
>   Most heavy,
>   Love will make most light!"

William (writing of his father's home):

For with all its wealth and beauty, with all its luxurious devices to please the eye and amuse the fancy, yet has it failed and that, through no fault of its own, but through the fault of his whose it is and who conceives that he can purchase happiness regardless of the fact that true happiness is from within . . . to me, as you

know, the idea of a *home* is the sweetest of all . . . with Harriet to
make it bright and happy.

Harriet:

I have longed for you — inexpressible longings today — I think a
wife owes her husband such loyalty, a husband owes his wife such
loyalty, that the minute either confides in a third, or owns a
disappointment that then the charm of married life is broken, it
could never be quite the same. When I am disappointed in you, if
ever I should be, dear, I expect to fight it out with God and
myself. But that day will *never* come, my own.

The letters reveal a bit about their few visits together, when Will
would take the train to Boston for a day with Harriet. He would delight
to take her to the Parker House for a festive luncheon. Then they
would shop together for carpet ("I think a dark steel blue . . .") or for
china, which they chose at Briggs', a Haviland pattern with coppery-
rose decorations, butterflies and hummingbirds.

They were a stunning couple by any standards, both tall for their
day, and I can see them in fancy, moving with ease through the Saturday crowds on the Boston streets, oblivious and utterly absorbed in
each other and the furnishing of the home they could scarcely wait for.

Christmas came, and Will had an invitation to Fish House. For this
young man without a home, the prospect was sheer joy:

We were to spend Christmas together at Fish House. That in
itself would make this Christmas the best I had ever known. I went
about the city trying to determine what present I should give to
Harriet. All that I had was far too little to pay for such a gift. At
length I decided upon a mahogany writing desk and chair, which
I purchased at Horners'.

Pa Beecher and Hattie were there to meet me when at length
the train pulled in to Cranberry Creek. He was driving Cousin
Lucy Sinclaire's small black team of mares. They were skittish and
afraid of the train, so he waited up the road until the train had
pulled out for Northville. Then Harriet and I were together on the
back seat, bundled up in carriage robes!

It was a green Christmas, chilly and disagreeable, no snow on
the ground and no frost, the roads deep in mud. Through this we
tugged and splashed our way to the warmth and welcome of the
Beecher fireside.

It was a dear, old-fashioned country Christmas, with presents enough to make each one happy, an abundance of good things to eat, warmth and cheer and laughter, and in the midst of it all a pair of ardent lovers, dazzled as they wove the rainbow pattern of their future plans.

Soon after Christmas, in January 1890, the First Presbyterian Church of Port Jervis asked Will to be their new minister. In Presbyterian language, they "extended a call." This he accepted, in a most handsome letter, and so, at last, he was to begin his real career in the ministry. For the rest of the spring term at Union Seminary, he spent weekends at Port Jervis, and when there was time to spare from parish duties, he was a busy young man getting the manse ready for his bride. The church was a fine-looking structure, of Colonial design, and next to it, fronting on a square park was the handsome red brick manse. By present-day newlywed standards, it was enormous, with plenty of room for a family.

The next months' upheavals in the Hudnut family worked to the advantage of the bridegroom, in this respect. Will's father, Alexander, decided to sell his estate in East Orange and the town house on West 36th Street, and move to England. This he proceeded to do speedily; curiously, even in his hurry, he took the time to write to his banished son, offering him anything he might choose for his new home from the New York house on West 36th Street, anything that might be of use to his son and "Miss Beecher," of whom he had heard "the highest praise." This was a windfall, indeed, for the young dominie and "Miss Beecher." It accounts for the fact that the bride and groom came at last to live in a manse that was furnished with beauty, and a degree of Victorian elegance, quite beyond even *their* great expectations.

The news of early springtime at Fish House, 1890, was that Harriet's sisters, Ella and Nan, had together bought a new home for their mother and father. This came about largely because James Beecher had now reached an age when his work as superintendent of the Sinclaire farms and dairy barns was beyond his strength. The old Marvin House, the white cottage in which his family had lived, had been a part of his income and would be needed for the new farm manager. And so the Beechers moved, just up the road to the large old house across from the Presbyterian Church, owned until then by Miss Baker, but henceforth to be known as the Beecher House. This would be the setting of the wedding in June, and summer headquarters for the Hudnuts for years to come.

Its rambling, gabled style would perhaps be classified now as Farmhouse Gothic, and its whole aspect was inviting. Cream colored, trimmed with dark-green louvered shutters, it was shaded by a large elm, a bountifully-spread umbrella tree and a vine that made a regular bower of the long front porch. Looking out on a clear day from this cool vantage point, one's eye would be carried down the village and the valley to the Mayfield mountains just beyond, a sure reminder that the village of Fish House was in the foothills of the mighty Adirondacks. The back porch, within a colorful stockade of hollyhocks, looked out on green lawn, a small barn, attached to the house by a woodshed, and a large garden, which would supply the table.

The house had been built in the 1860s. For a house with no pretensions to elegance, it had some curiously handsome details: a spacious center hall, high and airy, with a fine staircase and turned banister of dark red cherry; a large living room with long windows and window seats beneath. It was the sort of house that we are apt to remember as being more distinguished than it was in fact, but its charm was found in its nooks and crannies, steps up here and down there, softness of Japanese straw mats under foot, and lovely windows that gave intimate views of pastoral village surroundings.

The end of May came, and with the last of the daffodils and the first of the lilacs, the Beecher girls arrived at Fish House, one by one, from the cities where they taught. The old house must have vibrated with all the excitement. Even though it was to be a simple home wedding, it was an important event of the summer in the Fish House village, and few of the inhabitants were not, in one way or another, caught up in the preparations. Several days after Harriet arrived, the stagecoach delivered the boxes containing her trousseau, which had arrived by the afternoon train at Cranberry Creek. Great pasteboard boxes they were, embellished with labels that declared in scrolls and flourishes: "J. F. SWEENEY, DRESSMAKER, Successor to M. E. Church, WASHINGTON STREET, BOSTON, Opposite the Globe Theatre." I imagine the confusion of tissue paper as Harriet modeled this modest but stylish wardrobe for her sisters. There were pitchers of icy lemonade, Ma Beecher's thin ginger cookies, and wedding presents arriving daily: not just the nice, useful things from J. H. Smith's store at Fish House, or the fine linens, embroidered with satin-stitched monograms by Harriet's friends, but also the glamorous gifts that came in shiny city boxes from remote and elegant Hudnut connections, lending an exotic aura to the whole festival of opening.

If Mrs. Beecher had made the new house her own before her gifted trio arrived from their respective schools, she left it to them to gild the lily—and this they did, between diversions, with real purpose. Ella unpacked the books—a regular library, mostly her own—and arranged them in long shelves along the living room walls. She hung pictures—watercolors by friends; several lady-like oil paintings of flowers by Mrs. J.H. Smith; a gem of a primitive landscape, painted by an itinerant artist of the first Beecher homestead in Fish House. Her final touch was the arrangement of her treasures from abroad: she put a tall brass oil lamp from the Holy Land on the little rosewood melodeon, and her collection of jugs, pitchers, copper trays and English silver on the mantlepiece, bookshelves and tables. A brocaded covering from Italy covered the daybed, and it was heaped with a bounty of pillows of different colors, one embroidered with peacock feathers.

Nan Beecher painted the outdoor rocking chairs to match the window shutters. And Harriet made livingroom draperies, of soft gray-green with a top border of copper velvet, with window seat cushions to match.

I am sure that much of this decorating whirl was performed to impress the extended family of Hudnuts who would come for the wedding. In which case they might have relaxed, for at the last moment not a one of them would be there. Each of Will's family would be abroad when the great day came—and even his brother, Frank, who was to have been the best man, would be prevented from coming at the last minute by his wife's serious illness.

During these days of preparation at Fish House, we catch a glimpse of William in his final days at Union Seminary. He was preaching at Port Jervis each Sunday, and he writes of one particular time in April:

> In the audience that day were my father, sister Nell, and Professor Perkins, who had been head-master at Exeter when I was there. This was the first and last time my father heard me preach. A sort of reconciliation had been effected . . . but still I was preaching to one who had exiled me from my home . . . and it was a trying ordeal.

To become a full-fledged minister, he had to undergo what was then called a Trial for Licensure. These were assigned by the Presbytery of New York, before which he would be examined on the basis of a written sermon, an exegetical exercise and a Latin thesis. The subject chosen by William for the latter was "On Spiritus Sanctus Deus Est."

William Herbert Hudnut, 1890

Harriet Shew Beecher, 1890

Fish House summer, c. 1894. Left to right, standing: Maria Hudnut, Nan Beecher, Elizabeth Beecher, maid. Seated: Will Hudnut, Maude, James Beecher holding Marnie, Harriet, Beatrice Gattie.

Lucy Sinclaire, with parasol; Nan Beecher, center.

Herbert Beecher Hudnut, age six, with Fish House belles.

Nan Beecher, c. 1890

He later confided to Harriet, "I believed the Holy Spirit to be the third person of the Trinity but how was I ever to put the reasons for this faith of mine into acceptable Latin?

His memoirs record his ordeal briefly:

> I was examined before the Presbytery. Besides the papers I had handed in, I was questioned upon Theology, Church History, my motives for entering the Ministry, Presbyterian Government, etc. I was also required to preach at least a part of my prepared sermon. Fortunately for me, the time had not yet come when candidates were put on the theological rack and tortured into confessions of error!
>
> So I passed, and on the 12th day of May was licensed to preach. Considering what I had to do, and the inevitable distraction of my love for Harriet, I do not see how I managed to get through.

Between Easter, when Harriet had come to spend a week with the Sinclaires at the big house on Amity Street, in Brooklyn, and his arrival at Fish House on the Monday before the wedding, Will had not seen his bride-to-be. It takes little imagination to picture the happiness when they finally came together that June week in Fish House.

Only one happening spoiled this wedding week. Uncle Tom Beecher, dearly loved and revered by his cousins at Fish House, sent word that he could not come. Mrs. Langdon (a leading parishioner of Mr. Beecher's Church and mother-in-law of Mark Twain) was desperately ill, close to death, and he must remain with her. This was a real blow, for much as the Beechers also loved Mrs. Langdon, they all agreed with Ella, who had written in her positive way (and, ironically, prophetically), "I wouldn't BE married by anyone else! I'd rather give up the man I was to marry than to have anyone but Mr. Beecher tie the knot!" However, the bridegroom persuaded Dr. John McClellan Holmes, of Albany, to journey to Fish House for the Friday ceremony.

Will stayed at the Fish House Hotel, and records the week as a regular whirlwind of parties and preparations and the joys of opening presents together. Among the gifts was a set of silver coffee spoons from Miss Dana, headmistress of the school in Morristown, N.J., from which each of the Beecher sisters had been graduated. It was not only the gift, but also the letter that came with it that delighted them:

> I do not by *any* means remember all my "old girls" when they marry. I recall, however, with real pleasure, your unceasing efforts to make the other girls bright and happy. It is perhaps late to

show my appreciation of all you did for me, but I felt it then and do still.

I hope you will have a happy and useful life and be as much of a comfort to the one you have chosen for your constant companion as you ever were to your friends here. . . .

Ever with love,

E. Elizabeth Dana

All that we know of the wedding day is what the bridegroom wrote, years later, in his memoirs:

At daybreak I was awakened by the singing of the robins. It seemed as if there were as many robins as leaves on the trees. And what a full-throated symphony of delight! Cheer-up, Cheery, Cheer-up, Cheery. A glorious matins for our wedding day. Never was a bridegroom more sweetly serenaded.

It was such a simple wedding. Harriet was clothed in her traveling dress. There was no bridesmaid or maid-of-honour. There was no best man. What form of service was used by Dr. Holmes I could not tell. I only know that out of a trance I made my responses. And we were blessed. And we were husband and wife.

The living room in which the wedding was held was a pleasant room, amply large for the small company of Fish House friends, and visiting relations, among whom were Uncle Chauncey and Aunt Kate Beecher, from across the river, with Burr and Kate; Uncle Leman Beecher from Wilmington, Delaware; and Harriet's brother Leman, and his wife, from Elmira. Of course, Ella and Nan were presiding geniuses. The service was at high noon, and immediately thereafter, a delicious luncheon was served.

Our brief honeymoon was to be passed in the Adirondacks. Harriet loved the mountains even as I did. I was anxious to visit Lake Placid and Ray Brook, the Elysian fields of my boyhood delight.

Accompanied by Dr. Holmes, we took the afternoon train, traveling with him as far as Schenectady, where we changed trains for Saratoga. There, at the Warden [sic] Hotel, we spent out first night together. Next morning we walked about the spa and drank of a malodorous, nauseous sulphur spring, as though it had been the fountain of Pirene!

We took the same stage-coach route to Lake Placid that Mother and I had taken many years before, a journey of five or six hours over a hilly dirt road, in the same uncomfortable stage, and with a team of horses equally slow. But the weather was fine and the scenery beautiful.

If the transportation had not changed, Lake Placid had. A village had sprung up. There were other hotels than the old Stephens House, where we had quarters. Everywhere were signs of growing popularity. I should have expected these changes, but I had not — and they ruined the place for me. Its isolation and wildness were gone. The red gods no longer called to something hidden behind the ranges. So as soon as possible we pushed on to Ray Brook, where the transforming hand of progress had not yet been laid, and where Harriet and I could be alone.

Like all the ecstacies of life, ours was too brief. We had made our journey in the land of pure delight, and now, refreshed and exalted, we must continue to the adjacent realm of duty and responsibility . . . so, full of hope and confidence, to a new life in Port Jervis.

CHAPTER 9

THE
GOLDEN AGE OF
FISH HOUSE

Fish House, at the turn of the century, and up until the time when the coming of the Sacandaga Reservoir changed it completely, was much like our romanticized version of a typical rural American village. Its five country roads radiated from the village green, and each was an elm-shaded bower, as Grandfather put it, "leading to a land of the heart's delight." The Sacandaga River, close by, flowed serenely through sunny pastures and rich marshes, as it had in the days when Sir William Johnson's Indian canoe would glide along its winding miles.

It had lost its chance to expand some years earlier by refusing a right-of-way to the railroad. But, also, as Frothingham's *History of Fulton County* puts it:

> Fish House has not grown as fast as other villages in the county, and this may be accounted for by the fact that its inhabitants have mostly been wealthy, conservative people with a love for their stately country seats, and no desire to see their beautiful farms and gardens laid out into building lots. It is a place distinctly noted for its pleasant and substantial homesteads.

It was a different world now from the marshy and untenanted

Garden of Eden beloved of Sir William and tamed by Godfrey Shew. It
was a Victorian world, with its own gentle way of life. Almost any summer afternoon a group of ladies would be having tea on the vine-
shaded veranda of Mrs. Sinclaire's house, only a stone's throw from the
spot where the real Fish House had once stood in its protective thicket.
The young people would be playing tennis on the parsonage lawn, or,
later, create an exhausted tableau on the Beecher's porch around the
magnet of ice-cold lemonade. The men, up from the city for varying
periods of holiday, would be casting for rainbow trout in the Vlaie
Creek or Cluchy's meadow. Only the small boys would ever think of the
glorious days when the valley was alive with honest-to-goodness
Mohawks. They would spin the family tales about Sir William as they
dug for arrowheads in any likely mound along the Sacandaga—many
of them descendants of the pioneer, Godfrey Shew, and some with the
last name of Hudnut.

For Harriet and Will those early years sped by, the only consistancy
being change. Then, as now, there was a shortage of young men who
possessed the peculiar balance of qualities the ministry demands: the
skill and intellect of a preacher, the humility and empathy of a
counselor, the compassion of a shepherd, the drive of a parish-builder,
the spiritual gifts of the priest in worship. Will Hudnut fortunately
possessed the requisite qualities and he advanced accordingly. This
meant a progression from Port Jervis to Brooklyn and, finally, to
Youngstown, Ohio, where he was called to the pioneer church of the
Western Reserve, the venerable Old First Presbyterian. There he
would remain for thirty-eight years, performing a ministry of real
distinction. During these early years as the family grew and moved,
there remained one constant—Fish House. Will wrote of it:

> It had become our summer Mecca. But for the Beecher home
> and its hospitality we could not have had our vacations. Even if we
> had had the means—which we did not—we would not have gone
> to a hotel, because of the children. But aside from all such con-
> siderations we went to Fish House because we loved the place. It
> was there that our family life took its rise.
> There we had so many friends. There we found the peace and
> beauty and refreshment which we needed. It was such a tiny,
> quiet village. Besides ourselves there were other 'summer people'
> whom we were glad to see. There were dinner parties, evening
> frolics, games in different homes, and picnics on the top of Maxon
> Mountain, with its lovely views across the Sacandaga valley to the

Mayfield hills.

The Hudnut children, in birth order, were Dorothy, Marjorie, Herbert (my father), Katherine, known as Kit, and William, Jr. Their love of this childhood summer home and their stories about it, together with Grandfather's memoirs, have created for me a clear and perhaps romanticized picture of Fish House as it was back then at the turn of the century.

In considering the people of the village, one mentions the Sinclaires first — only because they were so distinctly the leading family. Theirs was the manor house — pre-Civil War, soft yellow brick with many windows, shuttered and shaded — and theirs, the large land holdings. They lived in Brooklyn Heights during the winter. The only member of the household to remain for the cold Fish House winter was Ash, the freed slave, who cared for the big house.

Cousin Lucy Sinclaire invited the whole family — Beechers and Hudnuts — for a big dinner once a summer, but Harriet and Will could often be found there with Lu Sinclaire, Cousin Lucy's handsome spinster daughter, who was a member of their intimate circle. Indeed, there were more spinsters than couples in that inner circle: Harriet's sisters, Nan and Ella Beecher; Fanny and Grace Waterman, nieces of Miss Wood, who came regularly to spend the summers in Miss Wood's white salt-box cottage; Elsie Smith, the daughter of J.H. Smith, the proprietor of the store; and Maude Hudnut, Will's sister, who spent occasional summer weeks in Fish House before she married Robert Chapin, of New York. Maude was a brown-eyed young beauty, with a pronounced English accent and, some thought, rather affected airs resulting from her family's winters in London. She played the violin, wrote romantic poetry, painted in both oil and watercolors, and would often depart with her satchel and stool to spend hours painting the Fish House landscape. She could be whimsical and full of fun, and her presence created a certain rarified air in the small village — certainly, at least to Hattie and Will's circle.

The only bachelors in this group of couples and spinsters were John Lovell and Grant Persons, both of whom lived (suitably enough) in Batchellerville. They drove over often, to join the picnics and tennis festivities.

Next door to the Beechers lived William Stark and his family. Mr. Stark owned and operated the food store, next to his big, brick house. The store had a large scale in it, on which the young Hudnuts delighted to weigh themselves. They were a little afraid of Mr. Stark, however. A grim figure he was, indeed, and his daughter, Emily, known to everyone as "Miley," just a bit younger than Nan Beecher, was never a part of the gay summer group. They saw her hauling water from the well, feeding chickens, always working. She was a small, bent creature when I knew her, many years later, close to eighty, with large eyes like a baby bird's, and a curiously dazzling smile. And even then she was always working, cooking huge meals, fetching and carrying, canning everything in sight.

Then there were the Ortons. Dr. Darius Orton was the very image of the country doctor, driving about the countryside in his horse and buggy — always in a hurry, dispensing pills and remedies with brusque common sense. His family, of English origin, were pioneer settlers of Warren County, and he had graduated from the Albany Medical College in 1866. He and his wife lived in a fine white house of the Classic Revival period, set on a knoll in the center of the village with a splendid view of the whole valley. They had five children — the oldest of whom, Percy, was a contemporary of Harriet's and Will's, and the youngest, Zenus Vanderhoef (Zene), just a bit older than young Herbert Hudnut. Percy's daughter, Jane Orton, known as Jenny, was a boon companion to Kitty Hudnut. Jenny had a horse, and on the rare occasions when Mrs. Vanderhoef would lend her mare to Kitty, the two girls would be off down one of the winding roads.

Those summers at Fish House would cement the bond of a lifetime friendship between Herbert Hudnut and Zene Orton. Zene followed his father and became a doctor, practicing in Salem, N.Y., near the Vermont border. Full of energy, short and athletic looking, he had a sharp, staccato way of speaking and a sense of adventure that appealed strongly to me as a child. There was a wonderful jack-in-the-box air about him, up and off at a moment's notice — a way of starting a conversation in mid-stream that gave an air of continuity to each meeting. Each summer you took up the conversation with Uncle Zene right in the middle of where it left off eight months before.

Besides Jenny Orton and Zene Orton, there were the young Haseys from Brookline; Sumner and Dorothy Campbell; the Howgates from Schenectady; and a whole family of William Stark's grandchildren, who came for the summer to the place known as the Stark Farm. Art Vandenberg, whose prowess as a crack shot lent him a certain distinction, lived year round in Fish House, and Burr and Catherine Beecher, distant cousins of the young Hudnuts, lived across the river — too far to

Maude Louise Hudnut in England, c. 1883

Miss Nan Beecher and Harriet

Herbert, Marnie, Maude, Dorothy and Kit

*Fish House lawn tennis: Marjorie, Dorothy, Kit, Maude, Harriet and
Lene Orton.*

be regular playmates, but nonetheless a part of this circle who grew up together over many a happy summer.

I think of Fish House summers as one long golden afternoon, Years afterwards I experienced them in this way—but they must have been the more so for that earlier generation, when the village was in its heyday and the tempo of life was slower. Young people then, as now, loved to congregate. And the valley of the Sacandaga spread out its lush green acres for their congregational activity. One of the favorite pastimes was taking the walk up to Han's Creek, around a five-mile square, past the house of the ancient spinsters Brown, who would invariably be out working in their garden, and who, either because of their wicked-witch look or through sheer mischief, used to regularly frighten the walkers.

Picnics were the favorite punctuations of the week—hiking picnics up Edward's Hill or Old Bald Top Mountain, cook-outs or swimming picnics on hot afternoons at any one of a dozen wonderful coves and bends of the Sacandaga. One spot, with broad rock ledges and a tiny waterfall, was the favorite spot for the amateur photographers of the day, and many a Fish House belle was pictured there for posterity in her long jersey bloomers and bathing bonnet.

Fishing, woodcock hunting in the low marshes of the Vlaie, tennis tournaments, costume parties, and carriage rides to Beecher Hollow or Broadalbin—well, there was no end of things for an interesting group of youngsters to do. But I like to think, too, that the cool old houses of Fish House, with their bounty of space, attic corners, nooks and crannies, provided the privacy that the growing years delight in—the kind of inner summer joy described in a letter written from Fish House by Maude Hudnut:

> I have just been reading *Jane Eyre*. Have you read it? I cannot
> speak of it, I am so enthusiastic—particularly the end of that
> perfectly fascinating story. I have also finished Mrs. Gaskill's [sic]
> *Life of Charlotte Bronte*, and Mr. Twain's *A Connecticut Yankee
> at the Court of King Arthur*, most amusing. I am doing plenty of
> everything, it makes the days go by too fast. Music is my delight,
> and I enjoy writing letters.

The following theme, written by Marjorie Hudnut in 1903, aged 11 years, conveys in its schoolgirl way and schoolgirl spelling, the essence of many an Adirondack outing in that time and place:

THE VIEW FROM BALD TOP

As we reached the top of one of the Adiarondack [sic] Mountains, a cool breeze sprang up and was so refreshing after our hot
walk that I could do nothing but sit under a little bush for shade
and look at the wonderful expanse of country so plainly revealed
on that afternoon. To my right lay the beautiful valley surrounded
by magnificant mountains that grew dimmer and more dim as
they lead away to the distant lake region. Down below me lay our
little valley amidst meadows of soft velvety green through which
ran our little river sparkling like a silver thread. Then I looked
beyond this to the left where another high range rose and faded
away, till only dim outlines of the Katskills could be seen, with
smoke here and there probably from some forest fire. Suddenly it
occurred to me that *it* might be from a train and that soon I
would have to come back to school. With this thought I watched
the little white clouds appear and disappear. Then slowly the sun
began to sink filling the western sky with the glowing embers of
the dying day. Facing this we descended the mountain.

As soon as the children grew older, the family took trips from Fish
House to surrounding territory. For these excursions, Will would hire a
team at Osborne's Livery, and they would be off: to the Fuller's home
at Catskill Landing on the east side of Lake George, to Lake Pleasant,
and, after 1900, to that wilderness area north of Wells where William's
brother, Richard Hudnut, was systematically buying up the entire
hamlet of Oregon, to create the estate that would come to be known as
"Foxlair."

At the center of those Fish House summers, was the little red brick
Presbyterian Church. It could be seen from the crest of the hill on the
road from Hagadorn Mills, a tall white spire around which the village
seemed to cluster. The historian, Washington Frothingham, writing in
1890, says:

The Presbyterian Church at Fish House is the oldest one in the
place and was undoubtedly the first religious society organized within
the present limits of the township of Northampton, in which for
many years there was no other Presbyterian church. The present
church edifice is a handsome brick structure, occupying a sightly
position near the center of the village.

Kathryn Roosevelt Sleezer, for many years historian of the village,
gave me a more detailed story of this little church, which had such a

catalytic role in our family story. She wrote:

> As far as I can learn, a young evangelist, Rev. T. Osborn, visited this region in 1814, and a great revival ensued. It seems many walked five and six miles to hear this man speak.
>
> The meetings were held on the west side of the Sacandaga River, on the Fish House Road.
>
> As a result of this revival in 1815 a church edifice was erected on or near the present site and was organized Presbyterian in form. The first deacons were Abraham Beecher and Isaac Noyes. [Abraham Beecher was the great-grandfather of Harriet.]
>
> In 1869 this church was taken down by Hiram Osborn and William Collins. The next year, 1870, the present brick building was erected. Josiah Carr was the chief mason and the village men were his helpers.
>
> The bricks used in building this church were made by local residents at the brick pond or yard about one-quarter mile from this church.
>
> A Revolutionary soldier, David Marvin, is buried in the cemetery that adjoins the church on the south. [Also interred there are Deacon Abraham Beecher, as he is designated, and his wife, Lydia Day Fuller Beecher.]

During all the summer of which we speak, Mr. James H. Smith, leading citizen and proprietor of the Fish House General Store, was a ruling elder and superintendent of the Sunday School. He was chairman of the "Call Committee" that brought the young seminarian, Will Hudnut, to be the summer preacher. Dr. Orton, William Stark, and James Fuller Beecher were other leaders of the church, whose names constantly recur as elders or trustees.

John G. Lovell, an earnest and scholarly young man, tall and slim, and in his gentle way, immensely appealing, had become the year-round minister. He was a close friend of the Hudnuts, a frequent visitor at the Beecher house and constant escort of Miss Nan Beecher. I was told that the reason they never married was because he was the sole support of his delicate mother and sister. I rather imagine the truth also would include the fact that this gentle man was simply no match for the strong Beecher personality of my well-remembered Aunt Nan.

Sunday morning service was the social high spot of the week, but the Wednesday evening prayer meetings were special, too, in a time and a town that had few other distractions. I imagine it was a lovely thing to come into the cool and quiet of the little church after the heat and dust of the day had settled. The bottom panes of the long, patterned-glass windows were open to let in the twilight, and the lovely valley fragrance of river, and the fresh cut hay, and the sweet dialogue of crickets and tree frogs. The Order of Service for Wednesday nights was a little more relaxed than Sundays. The hymns were the old-fashioned and familiar ones, there were more of them, and the tempo was slower. The minister gave a short talk rather than a long sermon. But the undoubted highlight of the Wednesday night meeting was the period of public prayer, when various members of the congregation would rise and pray out loud. This held a never-ending fascination for the Hudnut children. Often there were long periods of silence, very much like a Quaker Meeting; other times there was a regular groundswell of oration, delivered by the laymen, particularly Dr. Orton and Mr. Stark, and these prayers would often last forever, or so it seemed to the children, who watched every expression from between tightly laced fingers.

But it was Sunday morning church that was the center of the week. Often Will Hudnut would preach for Mr. Lovell, and then the church would be very full, indeed, for not only was he popular in the village, but it was reported that he was making a reputation as a fine preacher. He took his preaching very seriously, studied and prepared with great care ("at least an hour of preparation for every minute of text"), wrote the sermon in long hand, then worked at it long enough so that when the time came to deliver it, he was sufficiently free of the written words to preach with great freedom and emotion. It is doubtless true that the summer sermons were "pulled out of the bin," ecclesiastical slang that refers to the recycled use of ones previously preached to a different parish. Even so, Will would re-work and polish it on Saturday night. On such Saturday nights the Beecher house became the Manse or Rectory, and the study lamp burned late, and the children whispered!

The moments just before the service began had a charm all their own. Most families had a special pew where they sat, and so it was a simple thing to find out who was there and who was not. Harriet and the children always went in early, for Harriet liked to have a time of quiet before the service began. The children, scrubbed and dressed in Sunday finery, plumped down on the comfortable cushions of the family pew and proceeded to watch the arriving worshippers as they moved down the aisles. They especially awaited the Sinclaires and the Haseys who were the fashion plates of that small society. The organist pumped away in the balcony: this, her best opportunity to perform in more impressive dimension than the hymnbook could afford. And then, a hush would descend and the choir would enter followed by William, books in arm, wearing his long black frock coat, called a "Prince Albert."

The minute the Order of Service was over, almost before the last amen of the benediction, the organist would burst forth into a rousing postlude, pumping the little organ to its limits, sending peal after peal of joyful music out of the open doors. If we could have glimpsed this after-church scene from across the road, perhaps from the Beecher's porch, it would have made a charming pantomime: gentlemen bowing; ladies wispering and bending in their graceful long skirts; little children darting between in their ruffled dresses and shirtwaists, long black stockings and high button shoes. The children, let loose from the pious restraints of the sanctuary, played tag among the gravestones. The men gradually would move around to the carriage shed, to find buggy or buckboard, and the women would disperse reluctantly, having given and gathered the news for miles around. Home, then, to Sunday dinner and siesta, feet up, on the shaded porch. This was the village way of remembering the Sabbath and keeping it holy.

CHAPTER 10
THE SACANDAGA RESERVOIR: CHANGING TIMES

The force that forever altered the village of Fish House was the coming of the great Reservoir, which was completed in 1930. C. A. Sleicher, writing in 1960, describes it:

> Its creation involved clearing a valley floor of 29,000 acres of forest and brush and relocating 44 miles of road. During the job - which required three years' labor - three small villages and parts of eleven hamlets were moved bodily beyond the prospective waterline, along with 22 cemeteries that were replaced in toto. As the waters backed up, the newly created lake formed an irregular Y, affecting parts of three counties, scores of tributaries of the original river, and a vast tract of marsh known as the Vlaie - now lying many feet below the reservoir suface. There was a creeping of water levels from Conklingville to Northville and a greater spread south as far as Broadalbin and Mayfield.
>
> In building this lake the state did an admirable job . . . at Sacandaga the land was totally cleared (that is, first, before flooding). Before, as at Cranberry Lake, trees were left standing, and the results were ugliness and chaos in navigation for years.

The village was reduced to a hamlet of twenty-four permanent homes, some of which had been moved from their original sites to higher land. One of these was Miss Wood's house, long since known as "The Watermans"; its owners, Miss Fanny and Miss Grace Waterman, who were nieces of Miss Woods and descendants of the Fays of Fish House history. This charming salt box was moved to a knoll on the Broadalbin road, just past the beach. Another that survived the move was the old Marvin House, where James and Elizabeth Beecher lived when they first came to Fish House, the scene of my grandparents' courtship. This belonged for many years to Mrs. Mignonette Riker and is perhaps still in her children's possession. Mrs. Riker was a Marvin, also descended from Abraham Beecher, and it was her interest in our family history with, also, her research in libraries of New York State and New England, that provides much of what we know about our Fish House ancestors. She had a precise taste for history; she tracked down genealogies meticulously, was wary of romantic myths, and labeled heresay as such. Having carried her research farther, into the regions of my own particular branches of the Beecher family, I have true respect for her work, and feel so grateful to her.

Another keeper of Fish House history was Kathryn Roosevelt Sleezer. She was for many years the self-volunteered Fish House Historian, and was a central figure in collecting and preserving the story of this village. She wrote articles for the *Schenectady Union-Star*, one of which described the bypassed character of Fish House today:

> The nearest doctor today is either at Broadalbin or Northville. There is no industry of any kind in the Fish House area. Some residents travel every day to Schenectady to the General Electric Company or Alco. for their work; others have found employment in nearby villages and cities, and some have only part-time employment.

But Mrs. Sleezer did something more than write articles. Virtually single-handedly she was the prime mover in the restoration of the historic name of Fish House. For as long as anyone could remember, the official name of the village had been Northampton. This made for confusion, since the name was shared with Northampton Township and a quasi-distant public beach as well; furthermore, it seemed like a deliberate rejection of the rustic and colorful history of the place. Not that it mattered, for "Northampton" never really caught on. In the 1890s, as in the 1930s, most people referred to "Fish House," particularly those who had roots in the valley. And none of the summer people would dream of going to *Northampton*. They spent their summers at

Fish House!

Who knows why the name was changed? My own guess is that the itinerant historian Jeptha Simms had something to do with it. There are those who have nothing but contempt for this folksy historian and his nineteenth-century books about the valleys of the Mohawk and the Sacandaga. His detractors disapprove, among other things, of the fact that he gathered his material from the people of the valleys, the patriots, trappers and frontiersmen — instead of from the Tory population that constituted the early aristocracy of the area who were, therefore, presumably more reliable witnesses to events. What they dislike particularly, is Simms' earthy picture of Sir William Johnson: the stories of his amorous proclivities and the free and easy life he enjoyed at Johnson Hall. It is conceivable that revisionists, custodians of a Tory legacy, could, in discounting everything that Simms reported, advocate the change of a village name, to one more historically genteel. Northampton? Well, it is conceivable.

In the the late 1960s, Kathryn Sleezer, a few years before her death, wrote to me about her efforts to restore the original name:

> As for the correspondence in regards to changing Northampton to Fish House officially: I spent months getting this done. Much was through the kindness of Representative Sam Stratton, who helped me to get the ball rolling. After weeks of trying one government office after another (partly due to the fact that we had no post office here) Mr. Stratton advised me to contact Dr. Corey, State Historical Director, which I did. He and the Commission on Geographic Names had to study the request as they weren't sure the name "Fish House" derived its name from the lodge Sir William had built here in 1762 or from a Major Fish, who bought confiscated lands. Well, this made me plenty disgusted as Major Fish was never even heard of until after the Revolution, while the lodge, the Shew family, and other early settlers, were here years before the Revolution even began — and some gave their lives in it.
>
> I spent hours and hours getting information from Frothingham and other history books, plus what I had been told by people who had long since passed away. I copied paragraph after paragraph, giving the page of the history taken from etc., and finally our genealogy. It was only a short time after that I received word that the New York State Commission on Geographic Names approved, by request of 95 percent of the inhabitants, the change of name of the unincorporated village of Northampton to Fish House! I must say I am glad there are no more battles as I just couldn't keep

fighting anymore.

It was a proud day for the little village when Mrs. Sleezer's article in the *Union-Star* could begin: "Although nearly all the things that made the old village of Fish House historical are gone, it now has its original name back." And all largely because of the dedicated and persistent work of one caring woman.

On a gray afternoon in October of 1990, I drove down Route 8, past Foxlair and beyond, to Wells, then along Route 30, through Northville and Edinburgh, across the Batchellerville Bridge and down the south shore of the reservoir, now the Great Sacandaga Lake, to Fish House. I hadn't been there for many years and it seemed important to me to report here the present condition of that forgotten village, once so much the center of our family life.

The modest summer homes along the lake road were cared for and groomed; the boat liveries full and well-kept. Two inns, of my girlhood memory — their names forgotten until I saw them, were thriving: the Tumble Inn and the Come On Inn.

I was prepared to see the Beecher Home no longer standing. Better that than derelict, as it had been on my last drive there with Father some ten years before. I remember being almost glad, then, for his partial blindness, which served to conceal the sight of this family icon in its misery, walls sagging, porch removed, set in a long-neglected mass of weeds. I fully expected it to be gone, razed, a vacant lot.

But there it was, soundly rebuilt, missing the porches and vines and trees that had given it such grace and old-fashioned upstate character. Painted dark red, with white trim — boxy, plain — but healthy and lived in, roof intact. Nothing at all to elicit nostalgia for *our* Fish House — the old homestead where my grandparents were married, and my own parents had spent their honeymoon.

So we crossed the road to the little old red brick church. This had been a shambles last time; it was used for boat storage, and the old gravestones all lying flat on the ground under a growth of weeds and poison ivy. A screen of lilacs and evergreens today shielded us from what I assumed was going to be even *more* advanced decay, but instead, behind the screen of greenery we found a simple churchyard, restored to order! A mowed lawn led up to the old brick building, and, off to the side, were the ancient tombstones, leaning now at crazy angles but nonetheless upright on a hilly cemetery lawn. I found the tall, simple, gray stone marker of "Deacon Abraham Beecher"; next, a more elaborate stone for "Lydia Day [Fuller], his wife."

We wandered a bit among the tombstones with their familiar Fish House names, knowing that none was matched with the buried bones beneath. How had the whole churchyard been so pleasantly restored?

"The Town of Broadalbin done it," said the blonde woman who had come out of Percy Orton's old house next door. "They come a couple times a summer to trim the graves."

"And *mow*, too?" I asked, nodding toward the little church lawn.

"No, I do that m'self," she said, covering her mouth as she smiled.

"Did you know that your home was the parsonage a long time ago?" I wondered aloud, and she answered, "Oh yes, but it's a wreck now. We're fixin' to improve it—nice old place."

It was as different as could be imagined from the genteel comeliness of the Victorian village, or even the rural harmony of my girlhood summers there. And yet I came away with the feeling that in its present incarnation there exists respect for a significant past, and a kind of new vitality in the survival of those old houses and that old cemetery. Fish House village is alive.

Four historic markers tell the story of its past: one for Godfrey Shew, its founder; a second, at the spare old Shew House, a handsome relic of Godfrey Shew's and his son's construction after they returned from the French and Indian War; another at the Marvin House; and, finally, a marker to tell that some thousands of yards north of "this spot" once had stood the famous wooden bridge across the Sacandaga River, built through the good offices of Assemblyman Jacob Shew, son of Godfrey, and the first member of the New York State Legislature to be elected from the village of Fish House.

CHAPTER 11
THE LAKE PLEASANT YEARS: PROLOGUE

Fish House was the summer home of the Hudnuts for many years. A high spot of these summers for William was his expedition into the wilderness to the north, where he followed the lure of the trout stream and the memory of his early camping trips. We don't have a record of these first family years, when he would leave Harriet with her parents and Nan to provide care and comfort and company with the small growing children. We do know that with all the pleasures of an idyllic village life at Fish House, his eye was often roving to the remote blue hills on the horizon, and it was up into the Adirondacks where he would journey once a summer with a few friends from Port Jervis or with his brother Frank. The first time in his *Memoirs* that he describes one of these trips from the home base of Fish House we hear about an area that became increasingly important in our family's Adirondack adventures:

> Another summer we hired a team and two-seated phaeton and drove in to Lake Pleasant. It was a 36 mile drive over a winding, hilly road, upgrade all the way, following the torturous course of the Sacandaga, a swift-flowing, rollicking little river — and there is nothing that enlivens and distinguishes a road like the companionship of a river. None of us had ever before driven beyond North-

ville and when we left behind us the outskirts of that village we
felt we were adventuring into the wilderness.

Beyond Wells we lunched, sitting on great boulders in the midst
of a turbulent mountain stream. Here began a great hill through
the pass, a mile long, where we got out and walked to lighten the
load. The rest of the way to Speculator was through thick forests.
We passed two small mountain lakes and late in the afternoon,
from a hill we had a first glimpse of Lake Pleasant, gleaming in
the light of the westering sun. There was a small town at either
end of the lake, one at the foot and another three miles farther on
at the head. Thither we drove, for we had been advised to put up
at the Morley's.

Those little Adirondack towns were very much alike: one or two
hotels, a general store and post office, a white church (usually
Methodist), a blacksmith shop, a school, and a few houses close by
the road. In the summer there was some farming in the valleys
and lake bottoms, mostly hay and potatoes and patch of corn.
The harvest was always uncertain because of the frosts, which
could and often did blacken the potatoes by mid-August and sear
the corn as if by fire.

Many of the men worked as guides, taking 'sports,' as they called
us, to the forest streams and lakes for trout or deer. There were
lumbering jobs in the winter and those men were expert woods-
men. The felling of a tree by a lumberjack is a thrilling exhibition
of skill. Each blow of the axe bites the same place, the great chips
fly, and sound echoes through the forest—then with a roar and
crash the tree falls exactly where the woodsman meant it to.

We put up at Morley's at the head of the lake. It was a small
rustic inn whose walls on the first floor were panelled with spruce
bark. There was an open fireplace in the lobby and from the walls
several antlered bucks stared at you with glassy eyes. From a rise
of land across the road was one of the finest Adirondack views. To
the north you looked across Sacandaga Lake to the distant Blue
Mountain range, while to the east you viewed the full length of
Lake Pleasant to the far distant mountains of the Kunjamuck.

Our host was a small man dressed all in leather, which added a
touch to the rustic character of the inn. The night of our arrival I
was taken violently ill with severe pains in my stomach. I had had
several similar attacks and had found relief then, as now, by the
application of hot stoops. This that we thought was an upset
stomach was appendicitis, and had it there developed to the
operable stage, I should probably have died, for we were at least
fifty miles over dirt roads to the nearest hospital. In a day or so I

was recovered and we drove home to Fish House.

The oportunity for another trip was not an exploration like the first, but rather a camping expedition with rods and reels, the sort Will loved. His companion on this outing was one of the great friends of his Brooklyn years, S. Edgar Briggs, manager of the Fleming H. Revell Publishing Company. Mr. Briggs brought his wife, a close friend of Harriet's and known to the Hudnut children as "Auntie Belle," to stay with the family at Fish House, while the two young men set out for the Speculator wilderness farther north. This was to be an important journey, for it began Will Hudnut's long friendship with the family of Camp Perkins.

When I had driven up to Lake Pleasant I had heard much talk of the forest land that lay to the north of the Jessup River where Isaiah Perkins kept a shanty. There beyond the Blue Ridge, fifteen to twenty miles from civilization, were many lakes and little rivers: the Cedars, Whitney, the Canadas, Pillsbury, Trout Lake— all well stocked with trout, to whose wooded shores the deer came to feed. No sooner had Ed arrived at Fish House than I proposed that we should ride our bicycles to Lake Pleasant, there engage a guide, buy sufficient provision and journey into one of the wildest regions of the great Adirondack preserve.

The thirty-five mile ride to Lake Pleasant took us the better part of one day. There were few, if any, bicycle paths and the road was sandy and uphill most of the way. Above Wells, where the grade was steepest, a kind-hearted butcher gave us a lift on his wagon for a couple of miles. When towards evening we reached the inn at Speculator we were about exhausted. I was really worried about Ed for he was not as rugged as I and was less accustomed to hardship. However, after supper we began to make plans for the great adventure.

George Perkins appeared to be the best available guide for the Cedar Lake country. He had a camp on the Big Cedar and all we would need to carry in was food and clothing. Because of the shortness of Ed's vacation we could be in camp only three or four days and George could carry all the necessary provisions. He was a small, dark-complexioned, wiry woodsman, with a slow way of winking at you with both eyes when he was "considerin'." It did not take us long to find out that we had engaged a fine, capable man. He knew everything about guiding and he knew his country. He was resourceful, he was tidy, he was quiet. I never saw him take a drink, and he never was profane. He was a rare exception in a country where there was a good deal of back-woods roistering.

Early the next morning we started out with his black team and buckboard for the Jessup River. All the way through a forest of great stands of oak and maple, birch, hemlock, spruce and pine, up and down sharp hills, through sections of deep mud we drove, until beyond the seven mile marker we crossed the Jessup and entered the clearing in which stood the large, two-story log camp where George's huge and hearty brother Isaiah, and his trim, capable wife "kept shanty" for sports and guides.

There we left the buckboard. George shouldered his pack basket full of our duffle (he called this basket his "Calamity") and we started out on the forest trail. It was a long walk over a steep and arduous way, with many stops for rest on moss covered banks and for refreshing draughts at tiny, flowing springs. A part of the way, George told us, we were walking along a footpath that dated from Revolutionary times.

Our camp by the shore of the lake was in a small log house built years before by some lumbering outfit. We were very successful in our bag of game. We caught nice messes of trout and by nightfall had two deer. Ed had never before seen anything like it and was completely carried away by the beauty of the forest and the novelty and success of our brief adventure. Arrived back at Speculator, we hired a two horse stage and, with the deer heads showing behind, drove triumphantly to Fish House.

For many years then, until 1917 when Will and Harriet bought land from Isaiah Perkins and commissioned him to build the house they called "WAMAKEDAH," the Fish House summers would always include at least one expedition to Camp Perkins. They were male adventures; the women and children stayed at Fish House. These trips were gilded in memory with the primeval magic: woodland and the lure of game, manly journeys into wilderness, the call of the wild!

In the following passages from the WHH *Memoirs*, Grandfather describes other trips that held such wonderful adventures for him. They happened in the family's Brooklyn years — the last part of the nineteenth century, when the children were small and Fish House was still summer headquarters.

When I returned to Fish House, Ed, Curtis, and George Justin were there with their wives, who would stay with Harriet till our return. All was in readiness for a camping trip to the Cedar Lakes. We were a congenial group and we loved the woods — and so for a number of years we made these camping trips together. George

Perkins, who had guided Ed and me on our first trip, met us at Speculator. As we needed a second guide, he engaged Abe Lawrence. Abe was a wiry, hard-bitten woodsman, very colorful of language, who had lost a finger in lumbering.

It was always an interesting experience buying the duffle for such an expedition at the country store, deciding upon how much flour and salt pork, eggs and butter, corn meal and maple syrup, beside much else not so fundamental, it would take to feed six hungry men for ten days or two weeks. At last it was all loaded on the big buckboard and, with the six men, made a full load for George's big team.

The road into Jessup's River is a dirt road, without sloughs and mudholes, but full of curves and wooded vistas, one steep hill after another, a regular roly-coaster of a road. For all of its seven or eight miles it winds through the great forest. It begins with a long, steep hill from the top of which there is a wide view of Lake Pleasant and its flanking ranges of hills. Then it plunges into the forest, not to emerge from flecking tree shadows until you cross Jessup's River on a wooden bridge and come out into an old meadow clearing in the midst of which, in those days, was the big log house, Camp Perkins.

Jessup's River! The very name of it for me is an Open Sesame of pure delight. It is little wonder that over and over again in memory I traverse that woodland road which led to still water and the upper reaches of singing rapids.

Isaiah Perkins loved to go fishing and I was always trying to get him to go with me to the Mossy Fly or up the Jessup's. I never wore waders and would fish all day wet to my middle. I recall a reach of still water in a narrow brook overhung with alders, where the cold water was at times up to my arm-pits, which I fished until my knees were so stiff that I could hardly crawl out.

Once, when Isaiah and I were fishing the river we came, in the late afternoon, to a deep pool in a bend of the river. Just above, the beaver had built a dam across a tributary stream. We were sure there were good fish in that pool but we could not get a bite. Then Isaiah went upstream and tripped the beaver dam with his axe, thus roiling the water with the increased flow of the river. When this ruse worked its magic on the pool we caught several beauties. The beaver would repair the damage in their dam over-night. Ah! the Jessup's has caught me in a mesh of memories and I have seen again in its waters the reflected images of good friends I have loved and lost.

From Jessup's River the road to the Cedars is passable for a

couple of miles to Sled Harbor. There at the foot of the Blue
Ridge the horses were unhitched from the buckboard and rehitched
to a wood sled upon which all of our impedimenta were piled high
and securely lashed. Then came the long trek through that ancient
forest.

I was always counted a hustler in camp, and perhaps I did take
undue command. Each day it must be decided where we would
fish and who would accompany each guide. Then there was the
night hunting for deer to be similarly scheduled. We always had
enough trout and venison, though a well stocked larder meant
hard tramps to Pillsbury Lake, or the West Canadas or Trout
Pond—and long night vigils.

I loved to hunt deer at night. I have hunted them with dogs,
waiting for hours on some favored run-way, perchance hearing
from far away the baying of the hounds, now louder, now fainter,
as the chase took it tortuous way through the river swamp and
over the shoulder of Bald Mountain to be lost in the echoing
distance. I have hunted them in razoos, when my guide would
place me on a good runway where for an hour or so I was to
become a part of the landscape, whilst he made a wide detour
through the woods, barking like a dog, so planning his course as
to drive the deer past my station.

I am standing on a gentle slope not far from the lake. The
leaves have fallen and I can see over a wide sweep of the forest.
George has been gone only a few minutes and I have not yet heard
his razoo, when as if by magic, where a moment before there were
only the trees, now there is a beautiful doe loping through the
woods. I make a lucky shot. She is down. The ball has passed
through her neck just behind the ears. She is large and fat, in
beautiful condition. Her skin is so fine that I sent it to be tanned.
It is cut off below the head so there is no bullet hole and the taxi-
dermist writes to ask me if I took her with a hook.

But I found night hunting much more interesting and exciting.
You must hunt in the dark of the moon and when there are no
wisps of fog rising from the water. The best hunting was on the
Beaver Pond which emptied into Cedar Lake through a shallow,
muddy inlet. The pond was small and, like the inlet, its shores
were deep with mud and covered with lily pads. In the center was
an area of clear water, and at the upper end, a cranberry bog.
Any hot night in July or August you would be certain to find deer
in that pond. They came to the lakes at night to escape from the
flies, and to drink and feed on the lily pads.

Night hunting was done under a jacklight which was rigged on a pole about three feet high and set securely in the bow of the boat. In its crudest form this light was a kerosene lantern set within a semi-circular cone of spruce bark. Thus a dim light was reflected ahead while the boat itself was in darkness. The light was much better when the lantern had its own circular reflector. Later searchlights were used, tied to the gun barrel, doing away with the jack.

The boats were pointed at both ends and the man with the gun sat under the light in the gun seat facing forward. The guide paddled, seated in the stern. Even on so-called hot nights the air on the lake grew very chilly so you wore two pairs of pants, hip rubber boots, sweater and top-coat, and even so protected, you would shiver with the cold.

The guide paddles noiselessly into the pond and stops. The night is "brimful of hush." You sit without moving until your legs go to sleep. You strain your ear to identify every sound. A frog croaks, a hedgehog scratches a rotten log, a muskrat swims across your ray of light, a frightened beaver dives with a great thwack of his tail on the water. A great horned owl calls from the mountain. Once I hear a bear in guttural argument with himself as he makes his clumsy way along the shore. The cry of a lynx tears the night apart. I long to stretch my legs, change position, shift the gun, but I dare not, for the slightest flick on the gunwhale of the boat would frighten any deer that was in.

I am dropping off to sleep when the boat shudders and moves forward. The guide has heard a deer. It has walked through the woods without snapping a twig and has stepped into the pond with no greater splashing than the fall of a water drop. It supports its weight in the mud by stepping from one lily pad root to another. But for all its silence, the guide has heard it, and turns the light in its direction. The deer is fascinated by the light and stands quiet. As we approach the shore I see the reflection in its eyes and its form dimly revealed. It's a difficult shot at best. The light so distorts the long water grasses and the height of the shore, I aim low and fire. Maybe he drops, or maybe he gains the shore and is gone. A deer that is wounded never whistles and never flags with his tail. Well, I have missed that one and the shot has frightened the others. Now it must be a long wait before another will come in.

As the hours pass I watch the Great Dipper descend the northern sky until it seems to rest upon the flat top of that mountain. I try to fight off the blanket of drowsiness. Again I am awakened by the moving of the boat. We are pointed toward the sand bar this time, and there, standing broadside, with great antlered head

looking at me, is a large buck. It is a superb chance. Pushing my
fore sight out under the light, I draw a careful bead on him, but
my rifle misses fire. The deer is frightened, makes one or two
jumps, but is still there. Another aim — another miss — with a few
long bounds, the buck is clear of the water and crashing through
the forest. Only now do I discover that after my shot earlier in the
night I had failed to reload my gun. The best chance I ever had
to shoot a buck was lost to me, thus, through sheer stupidity. I
was so humiliated that I remember the sting sharply, even yet.

Romantic memory notwithstanding, Grandfather was more fisher-
man than hunter. He had no love of venison, unless it was cooked by
Ma Perkins; the only souvenir of the hunt which he coveted was the
deer head which today decorates a wall at Windover. And he never
went hunting with his sons, nor did he inspire any love of the sport in
the younger generations of his family. Fishing was something else
again. He fished for salmon in Canada and Scotland and the far west.
And he would follow the lure of the Adirondack brook trout until he
was a very old man.

In 1899 the family moved to Youngstown, Ohio. Will Hudnut had
received a call to the Old First Presbyterian Church, the first parish of
any denomination on what had been called the Western Reserve. From
now on, the journey to the Adirondacks each summer would be a long
and complicated expedition involving stage, train, sometimes a canal
boat, and later, motor cars. Often they would stop overnight with the
Beecher cousins in Elmira. Once, too, my father remembers that they
planned the route home to include a visit to the Pan American Exposition in Buffalo, where they spent two days in the week just before President McKinley's assassination there.

By 1906, Herbert, at eleven, was old enough to begin accompanying
his father on the trips to Camp Perkins. And so it was that, as the
family grew, William supplanted the camaraderie of the earlier trips
with friends with family members, spending more and more time at
Camp Perkins with his young son, for whom it also promised to be the
land of heart's delight.

As a postscript, however, to those earlier years when Grandfather
and his friends left the women and children behind and answered the
call of the wild, I treasure a story told me by Aunt Kit, who was a very
small girl at the time she saw it happen.

She remembered an afternoon when the family left behind at Fish
House were awaiting the return of the fishermen from Camp Perkins.

The men had been gone for two weeks, and now they were expected in time for dinner. Grandmother Beecher and Aunt Nan sat in rockers on the verandah, but Harriet and Auntie Belle Briggs were seated on the broad stone steps, and Kitty, aged seven or eight, was nestled between them. Harriet Hudnut, beautiful and eager, held the baby, William, Jr., in her arms.

Suddenly the buckboard from Speculator rattled into view, and no sooner had it turned in from the Batchellerville Road than Harriet sprang to her feet, thrust the baby unceremoniously into Belle's arms, and set out running to meet the stage. For Kitty, it was sight enough to see her tall mother, ordinarily so calm and composed, now a picture of flying white skirts and long black locks, racing helter skelter. But even more amazing, as Harriet reached the stage, Will bent low and swooped her up into his arms: the mighty hunter returning to his mate!

Aunt Kit, relating the story, said that as she grew up she wondered if this vision had been a dream. Could her now aging and dignified parents ever have looked so young and playful?

But Belle Briggs, years later during a visit to Brooklyn, told Kit the memory was real. "I'm still shocked when I think of it," she said. "It's the only time I *ever* saw your mother lose her composure!"

CHAPTER 12

THE FAMILY OF CAMP PERKINS

My generation of the Hudnut family grew up with the folklore of the Camp at Perkins Clearing. Was Isaiah Perkins really a little larger than life? In my father's stories he was. Was "Ma Perkins" actually the best cook in the Adirondacks? According to our grandfather: "Absolutely." Could any one of the four gorgeous Perkins daughters shoot a chicken out of a tree with one bullet? Father would add, "With her gun in one arm."

Since this mythology was created for us around the family at Camp Perkins, it has been reassuring to discover from various reliable sources that our romantic narratives did not greatly exaggerate the truth about a woodland kingdom where this most unusual family held court. Susan and Isaiah were the regents there, and they presided over a rustic way of life that captured my family's imagination and affection for many years to come.

Ma was the quiet center of Camp Perkins. Long before she was given this homely backwoods nickname she was Susan Emily Lawrence, descended from one of the great land-owning families of the Adirondacks, the Lawrences, who in 1791 had purchased the 36,000 acres known as the Lawrence Tract in what is now Hamilton County. By the mid-nineteenth century her branch of the illustrious merchant family had moved far from its roots. Susan's father, Marinus Lawrence, was a farmer and trapper in Newton Corners (later known as Speculator), often called the First Citizen of Hamilton County, and remembered as the earliest friend and host to Louis Seymour, the famous guide known as "French Louie."

When Susan's mother died at an early age, this young daughter, being the oldest, was left with the care of the twelve younger children. Luckily she was capable and industrious, and mothering seemed to come naturally to her.

"Mees SuZAY," French Louie called her; she mothered him, too. She was a tall girl with particularly keen and expressive gray-blue eyes. Louie would say, "When Mees Suzay she geev you da look, you know she really *see* you!" And in the spring of 1888 her look fell upon young Isaiah Perkins, who had come to the Hamilton County logging camps to work, together with his brothers, George and Ashley. Their home was in Pottersville, up near Schroon Lake.

Isaiah was the dominant one of the Perkins brothers. He was unusually tall and powerfully built, yet he moved with grace. He was a handsome young man, with thick black hair, broad cheekbones, and blue-gray eyes. And there was a genuine warmth to him. Father remembered that Isaiah had a quiet side, "that kind of interior quiet that was common to the finest guides, men of the woods," yet he was essentially a gregarious man, possessed of the most infectious high spirits, with a keen sense of hilarious occasion. And Grandfather, who became his truly devoted friend, remembered that there was a wild streak to Isaiah, somewhat tamed by Susie, at home with nature and restive in captivity. All of these qualities combined to make a man of no small attraction, and it is little wonder that he and Susan Lawrence were immediately attracted to each other. Their romance was the event of the year in Newton Corners. They met in the snowbound spring and were married in the warmth of July. Thus began the family of the Big Shanty at Perkins Clearing.

Four daughters were born to Susan and Isaiah—Annis, Gertie, Rose, and Maybelle—and they were near enough in age that a close companionship existed among them. No one quite remembers when Miss Susie started to be called Ma, but by the time Grandfather first met her she was Ma Perkins—or just Ma—to everyone in Speculator; that is, to everyone but French Louie. He called her Mees Suzay till the day he died.

In 1890 Isaiah began work on Camp Perkins. It was a huge log cabin on the Indian Lake road near the Jessups River, just beyond a plank bridge in a secluded field, framed by giant firs; a piece of unclaimed wilderness that came in time to be known as Perkins Clearing.

The cabin was a simple two-storied rectangle, made of chinked logs, with an enormous fieldstone fireplace, deeply sloping roof, and a broad plank porch running its entire length. Downstairs was the big living room, which served as dining hall as well, a large homey kitchen, the Perkins family bedrooms, and a game room, centered with a massive pool table. Upstairs were the guest quarters in the form of a long bunkroom under deep eaves, divided into many cubicles by curtains on long tracks, which provided privacy of a limited sort. My father remembers that the beds were "big and deliciously comfortable" and that the atmosphere of the little corners under the eaves was comforting and cozy, which pleasure almost, but never quite, offset the snoring of the other guests.

Most of the Speculator guides would bring their hunting or fishing parties to Perkins Clearing, for this was as far as a wagon would go. Often they would stay for a meal, or the night, and then, with provisions lashed to sleds, would take off by foot into the deep forests, bound for the little lakes and the upper reaches of the Jessups River.

French Louie, too, would often meet his parties at Camp Perkins. Perhaps this was due in part to the fact that he had a small lean-to in the woods back of Camp where he often went to sober up after his notorious three-week sprees in Speculator. More than once an impatient hunting party took him into the woods with them before he had completely slept off his merrymaking. They would lash him to a sled, just like the provisions; and before the trail found the first night's campsite, their guide would be shaken to sobriety.

Rose Perkins Gallup, one of Susan's daughters, reminisced that French Louie would come to Ma Perkins before one of his customary sprees in Speculator and hand her a fistful of money from the sale of the furs he had trapped. Susie would put the money in a baking powder tin on a very high shelf. "Mees Suzay, you weel keep for Louie," he would say, as he'd take off for town, with enough still left in his pockets to finance the legendary binge. Rose knew there were other people who shared this role of confidential Savings and Loan, such as "Uncle David" Sturges, but Susie was called upon more than any of them. French Louie was devoted to her and allowed himself, along with so many others, to be mothered by her.

Louie gave Mees Suzay a picture of himself, one that he delighted in.

It shows him in a state of advanced bucolic dignity, with a bottle of booze protruding from his well-worn shirt.

Rose told me that her mother would often ride back into the woods, on horseback, to see Louie for a brief visit. He had camps on all the lakes back in the wilderness behind the clearing, and he would move from one to another, both hunting and trapping. Sometimes he would simply build a lean-to up against a log. One spring Louie didn't come out of the woods. The Perkins had a real family feeling about him, as had the Lawrences before them, and so, after a while, Isaiah went into the woods to search for him. He finally found him way back on Sampson Lake. Louie told Isaiah that he had decided, on the spur of the moment, to go back to Canada to see his mother once more. According to what he told Isaiah, he waited hidden in the orchard until his mother came out of the old farmhouse where she lived with her second husband and a whole new family. Louie took a long last look at her — never spoke out, never made his presence known to her — then silently returned. That enigmatic little excursion was responsible for his tardy appearance at Perkins Clearing.

Isaiah and Susie Perkins boarded fishermen during the spring and summer and hunting parties in the fall. Ma Perkins was the hardworking mother of the rustic guest house. Warmth and comfort and delicious food she provided in abundance. And Isaiah, by nature genial, with his gift for getting people to enjoy life, came into his own as the towering host of Camp Perkins. The little girls, in their black stockings and pinafores, perfectly at ease with the visitors, enhanced the homelike atmosphere of camp, and helped their mother with the endless chores and duties of a backwoods boardinghouse.

The stationery from Camp Perkins was decorated with a fine old-fashioned rebus: "IF YOUR 👁's R ALL RIGHT YOU CAN KILL DEER AT CAMP PERKINS." The same letterhead proclaims the Deer Season from October 1st to November 15th and the Trout Season from April 16th to September 1st and proclaims FISH AND GAME DINNERS IN SEASON. Another later one features a photograph in the upper left hand corner: a group of guides, hunters, and the whole Perkins family, lined up at one end of the big porch, under eleven deer hanging from the porch rafters. The title beneath the picture is "Trophies of the Annual Hunt of the Jessups River Gun Club."

Isaiah moved the family out to camp in early spring and they stayed right through November. Several years they spent the winter at the Clearing, too. These seasons were wonderfully happy times for the little

The Perkins Family: Susie, Isaiah, Annis, Maybelle, Rose and Gertie.

Isaiah and Susie Perkins

Isaiah Perkins' camp at Perkins' Clearing

Camp Perkins' letterhead

The billiard room at Camp Perkins; Rose at table.

Logs at Perkins' Clearing: Susie Perkins, top, second from right.

The picture French Louie gave to Ma Perkins.

Jessup River near Camp Perkins

Louie's lean-to back of Perkins' Clearing

girls, with all the sports of wintertime right at their front door. There was the problem of school, but Ma dealt with this in the efficient way that was not only her nature, but also the characteristic of simpler life in an earlier day: she got a permit from the school board and hired her own teacher. This was Miss Caroline Dockstader of Amsterdam who came to live at Camp Perkins. She conducted classes each morning in the big living room, around the open fire. Rose recalled that learning seemed easier in that wilderness school. Ma's brother, Abe Lawrence, had a camp at Mason Lake, about three miles from Camp Perkins. Each day the young Lawrences would ride over on horseback and join the classes with their Perkins cousins.

Caroline Dockstader was a popular addition to the family. The girls adored the pretty young teacher and paid her the high compliment of imitation; to them she was the epitome of urbanity and polish. Long after she left to marry a promising young teacher by the name of Fred Turnbull she remained a close friend of the whole family. Years later, her son, Theron Turnbull, married his mother's former pupil, Maybelle, the youngest of the four Perkins daughters.

Much of Isaiah's life, or livelihood, was guiding. Together with this went the work of innkeeping, or "keeping shanty," as he called it. He did a goodly amount of farming as well, but with these all being seasonal occupations, and none too lucrative in that rocky and secluded corner of the Adirondacks, he worked at many other jobs. At one time or another he occupied just about every position in the township, from Town Supervisor to Fire Department Chief to member of the School Board. For several years he served as Sheriff of Hamilton County, and the whole family moved to the jail at Lake Pleasant, a comfortable stone and frame building which featured the least formal barriers possible. Indeed, the prisoners — usually not hardened criminals — were separated from the Sheriff's family only by the most conventional partitions; they were allowed freedom outdoors and were served the same excellent meals that Ma set before her family. Small wonder that some of the poor men tried to arrange a prolonged stay in such amenable quarters.

High-spirited and handsome, the Perkins girls were widely known and admired around Speculator. They were raised in the closest and most affectionate kind of family, under the capable eye of a mother who knew how to keep house and cook, efficiently and creatively. But they were equally schooled by a father who knew the woods and loved sports and delighted in promoting good times for his girls and, indeed, for all the young people in that remote community.

This close and happy family circle had its first real blow with the death of Gertie, the second eldest, when she was in her early teens. Ma Perkins was hard to comfort; the loss of this lovely young one was an ache from which she couldn't seem to get free. Rose remembers that it was French Louie who was finally able to bring Ma to herself. When the word got to him, he made a special trip out of the woods to see her. Louie had a curious but absolutely certain conviction about the after-life: his botanical theory of heaven was that evil folk came back to earth as weeds and good folk as lovely flowers. "Do not feel so bad, Mees Suzay," he said, "Gertie she come up a beautiful flower." And Miss Susie was comforted.

CHAPTER 13

THE HUDNUT FAMILY AT SPECULATOR

THE EARLY YEARS AT CAMP PERKINS

Although William Hudnut first came to Camp Perkins with George Perkins, the younger brother of Isaiah, and in the years to come, employed a number of different guides—Selah Page, Mead Sturges and Cal Wilber among them—he was always, after that initial visit, eager to stay at Isaiah and Susie's big shanty and would always regard it as a homecoming.

It was a friendship of opposites, this deep bond between the Dominie, Will Hudnut, and Isaiah Perkins. These were years of intense work for Will—years of study, preaching, parish development, and travel.

Distinguished-looking, sensitive, immaculate, the picture of the city-bred gentleman with his goatee, spectacles and fine features—something deep within him responded to the huge man of the woods who, as he grew older, bore a striking resemblance to Albert Schweitzer. Will seemed to "let down" at camp. Nowhere did he have such a lot of fun.

> The Perkins family was always playing tricks on me. One night they put a big frog in my bed. When I put my foot against his cold, clammy body—and both he and I leaped out of bed—there

119

were roars of laughter from downstairs.

Will called Isaiah the "Pond Lily Guide,"* to which Isaiah, in return, called the Dominie "Wood Butcher."

Will was often accompanied on these visits by one or more of his children. He wrote in the *Memoirs*:

> Usually besides the family there were several fishermen and their guides at Ma's long, bountiful table. Marjorie and Kitty came to know the Perkins girls well and Herbert, who went there with me many times, fell in love with Rose, who was the most refined of the sisters, and a great beauty. The first time I took him there we walked all the way from Fish House, about 30 miles. He was just a lad, and towards evening, before we reached Wells, he was so dead beat that he wanted to lie down by the road side and sleep.

That same Herbert (my father) wrote to me of Will:

> Father would take me on long hikes up to Perkins as soon as he thought I could "take" the camp experience. I would be so dead tired I simply had to lie down by the side of the road and he would have to wait impatiently til my strength returned. Sometimes a mountain brook would refresh us. One night on the way up to Jessups River we put up in an unoccupied guide's cabin. We slept in a bed up in a loft. Bed bugs attacked me ferociously but your grandfather was immune. Finally I got up and climbed downstairs and slept the rest of the night on a table. Next day I had welts as big as saucers—Dad was untouched!
>
> My fishing pole was bamboo, one piece with a white string as line and a hook with no leader. Your grandfather had a beautiful rod of split bamboo and could cast flies expertly. I don't ever remember even noticing the discrepancy between our rods and had just as much fun as he had, I'm sure.

My father's memories of the cuisine at Camp Perkins were also shared with me:

> The table was covered with huge plates of pancakes and eggs and big pitchers of hot coffee and syrup at breakfast. Ma would tell Annis that she wanted a few hens for dinner. Annis would step out back with her shotgun and pick off three roosting hens up in a tree with three shots. And there was our chicken-and-dumplings

---

* Pants Lawrence, Isaiah's brother-in-law, and the best guide of the area, was also nick-named the Pond Lily Guide. Which came first? Who knows?

Some Speculator guides: Left to right: Jim Sturges, Brick Demarest, Isaiah Perkins, unknown, "Pants" Lawrence and Aaron Arnold.

Herbert in boat at Camp Perkins with Rose

for dinner. Just like that. We had venison pretty often at camp.
Ma knew so many ways to make it delicious. Once when I was first
there I complimented her on the venison. Isaiah placed a warning
finger to his lips and said that they never used that word around
there. "You just enjoyed your first mountain lamb, Herbert.
Remember, mountain *lamb*."

Isaiah would drive his team of mules into Speculator for supplies every now and then. He'd say, "Don't look for me til y'hear
the boards rattle"—meaning the boards in the old wooden bridge
over the Jessups River. When he returned, he'd hit the top of the
hill that wound down to camp, then he would stand up in the
wagon, crack his black-snake whip and let out a yell that you
could hear all over Hamilton County. The poor mules would come
down the hill in high gear, wagon careening from rut to boulder—
you couldn't miss knowing Isaiah was home!

Father, as a boy, hero-worshipped the Speculator guides. One of his
favorites was George Perkins. "Once at the Cedars," he told me, "a
member of George's party became seriously ill. George came out of the
woods to Perkins' Camp through the dead of night, miles over rough
trails, and got a doctor. He hadn't a lantern or flashlight. That took
real bravery."

Father wrote to Warder Cadbury:

> I remember meeting French Louie at Perkins Camp when I was
> a little boy. Those guides of the old days were strong characters,
> shy with strangers, but tellers of tall tales around the camp fire.
> They would carry a heavy pack all day without a murmur, glide
> through the woods like Indians and at the end of the day be as
> fresh as daisies. They always knew where the deer were—and the
> big trout—and it seemed to me that they could make the best
> flapjacks in America.

Another guide who became a friend of Father's was Cal Wilbur,
often affectionately referred to as Cal of Kunjamuk. The thing he
seems to remember best about Mr. Wilbur was his characteristic ritual
of hair cutting—it was enough of a specialty that he often did it for
members of his hunting parties. He would simply put a bowl snugly
over the man's head and trim off any hair that showed beneath. Years
later when my father returned from the First World War as a second
lieutenant in the Balloon Corps, he did a turn-about and cut the hair
of one of the small Wilbur boys. A delightful picture shows the little
boy thus being sheared—via the method made famous by his father.

Father said that Cal Wilbur always knew exactly where Grandfather could catch a mess of trout. Never once did Cal fail him. My father said,

> I remember a curve in the stream near the Clearing. There was an unusually deep pocket there—a very deep hole. I let my worm down into it. Right away I hooked a big trout, about a half pound. I was so young, so new at it that I was beside myself, so thrilled. Well, he jumped away. I can still remember the physical *ache* of that loss. I just sat there by the side of the river for the longest time, heart-broken.

This eldest son of Will Hudnut, young Herbert Beecher, was a charming young man and a handsome one. Warm-hearted, possessed of an impressionable and rather Byronic nature, it was a foregone conclusion, I am sure, that he would fall deeply, romantically in love with one of the Perkins girls. In the first place, he was enamoured of their setting and milieu. Like his father, he was a city boy with a heart to lose to the silent forest and the wandering stream.

In the era of the Gibson Girl, Rose Perkins was a rather different type of beauty. Everything about her was utterly natural, and she was skilled in all the sports and occupations of her country life. Tall, lithe, with a mane of dark hair, and deep set eyes, she seemed like a true rose of the wild wood. She and Herbert fell in love.

In a different age it might well have come to a different ending. But this was the post-Victorian era. Harriet and Will firmly vetoed an early engagement, and my father remembered that they were hardly ever even alone together; when they were, all the cautions and reticence of the day provided a restraint as effective as a third person. In any event, the end of that summer came, and their very different real worlds crowded in about them. Herbert was off to Princeton, and a series of summer jobs that kept him away from the Camp at Perkins Clearing. They did not meet again for many years; by this time, both were married. The happy ending to this brief story is that they remained friends for the rest of their lives, meeting hardly ever, but always with affection and the bond of the memory of Camp Perkins.

WAMAKEDAH

In the summer of 1916, a trip to Camp Perkins resulted in the pur-

chase of Hudnut land on Lake Pleasant. This letter from young Billy
Hudnut, about ten years old, written to his older sister Kitty, away at
school, tells the tale:

Dear Sis:

I have an awful lot of stuff to tell you but I may make the letter
very short seeing who I'm writing to.

Yesterday I had about the best time I've ever had because we
made the decision whether to buy or not and it was the former.
There are 7½ acres* in the lot and it has about 600 feet frontage
on the lake. We have one beautiful point and one fine sandy
beach. We own from the lake way back to the road. Isaiah Perkins
will, if we notify him this fall, build a log cabin and a wonderful
fireplace.

There will be two bedrooms, a kitchen, one living room and two
porches, one screened in. We may live in a tent next year but I
hardly think so. The house and lot combined will cost approxi-
mately $2,000.00 and we are going up there Sunday to talk it over
and make final arrangements.

There is plenty of room for another house on "our estate," but
as Dad said, "This other house can be no more elegant than mine,
or the squatter will get kicked out."

Dad and I will chink in the cabin with moss and make many
improvements.

We are going home Tuesday and we will go through Utica,
Syracuse, Auburn, Rochester and Buffalo. We will also see
Niagara Falls and I will be very glad for I have never seen it.

Your loving little brother,

Billy

This first summer camp of their own they called Wamakedah, an
acronym arranged by Will and Harriet using the initials of the children's names: its Indian sound has always fallen sweetly on my ear.
Names thus chosen are frequently disastrous; they were lucky. And
they were fortunate, too, in the location and the design of the house
Isaiah built for them. It was a real camp, set into the woods with a look
of belonging there. The roof with a gentle, tent-like slope, rested on
birch log pillars on two porches that looked out across the lake to the

---

* I will venture a guess that this land, bought from Isaiah, was a part of Susie Lawrence's dowry—a part of the original Lawrence Tract handed down from Marinus
Lawrence to his eldest daughter.

"Wamakedah" at Lake Pleasant

Beach at Camp-of-the-Woods, Osborne House at center, Wamakedah waterfront at far left.

The dock at Wamakedah and the view of Lake Pleasant.

Hamilton Mountain range beyond. The log walls were sturdy and the stone fireplace was well proprotioned, the focal point of a big rustic living room. The whole house, rough hewn as it was, was proof of Isaiah Perkins' innate skill as builder, stone mason, and backwoods architect. In the summer of 1917 when it was completed, the Hudnut family moved in and settled down to what would be more than a decade of Wamakedah summers.

Already the family was separated during much of the summer. In 1915, Marjorie had married Jasper Coghlan, a young doctor from Newark, New Jersey, who would soon be going overseas as a medical captain in the famous Rainbow Division. Herbert had graduated from Princeton in June of 1916 and within a year, on May 11, 1917, had enlisted at Camp Benjamin Harrison. The following January he was commissioned a second lieutenant with the 1st Tennessee Regiment, and was sent overseas in March of 1918.

The three who were left at home were Dorothy, the eldest, who having had infantile paralysis at the age of two, which left her deaf and partially paralyzed, had completed her education at a special school for the deaf; Kitty, who was at the Finch School in Boston, and would soon enter nurse's training there; and young Bill, not yet of high school age.

At Wamakedah the summer's diversions were more rustic than those of the Fish House village. Father and son found wilderness fishing close at hand. Will had two boats now, a canoe and one of the famous Adirondack guide boats, this one built by John F. Buyce of Speculator, who turned to boat building after the invention of the automobile had sent his blacksmith shop into a decline. And, though there were not the many friends of the Fish House days for Harriet and the girls, there were new friends at Speculator, and visitors from far away, who came to spend a few days at Wamakedah. Fish House was not too distant, and, in a northerly direction, was Foxlair, Richard Hudnut's Adirondack estate, where Will and Harriet occasionally spent an elegant weekend.

In the same year that Wamakedah was built, George F. Tibbitts, a well-known Y.M.C.A. executive, then posted in Washington, D.C., bought fifty acres of land across Lake Pleasant from the Hudnut property. This acreage included an unusually long white sand beach which extended along a cove beyond the Osborne House as far as the eye could see. Here "Pop" Tibbitts, as he was known to everyone, was to establish his Camp-of-the-Woods. This family type camp, with its distinct evangelical, religious emphasis, grew by leaps and bounds. Campers lived in tents, organized into twenty-three divisions known as tribes. One—the young men's tribe, for example—was called the Hurons. Study groups, religious programs of all sorts, and campfire entertainments, together with a number of outdoor recreational facilities, offered a good deal to the camp's vacationers. The eighty-five young counselors, all college students, were chosen with an eye to their musical ability, and many of them participated in the camp's orchestra and marching band. The central focus of each week was the big Sunday church service.

Pop Tibbitts became a friend of Will Hudnut's, and occasionally asked him to speak at these Sunday services. Tibbitts was the author of a book, *The Mystery of Kun-Ja-Muck Cave*, published in 1928. It is an adventure romance with a good deal of uplift, and its best part, in my opinion, is a description of the Speculator territory, and some of the people we have been writing about. French Louie, for example, is described with colorful accuracy. Other local figures enter the story, often with names changed so slightly one wonders why Mr. Tibbitts bothered to change them at all. Cal Wilbur, for example, becomes Cal Wilkins and here is a paragraph about Isaiah Pikes, who figures largely in the tale and is the very picture of an Isaiah we have been describing:

> Isaiah Pikes was there as usual, settled down in his accustomed corner. He had spent the day on the Jessup River, just south of Indian Lake, and, tired by the long trip back to Orendaga, said little. That region was common ground to Isaiah, as he had kept a hunting lodge for years on the main road, the lodge being used as headquarters by groups of city men who came up in the fall for the deer season. The buildings were made of rough logs with great stone fireplaces inside. Pikes and his wife knew how to cook, and many men preferred this hospitable hunting lodge to the larger hotels in the vicinity.

Camp-of-the-Woods put out a booklet each season, and in it are to be found lyrical descriptions of Hamilton County and particularly Lake Pleasant. It is also full of testimonials written by well-known people, most of them exuberant bursts of praise for the wholesome air or the abundant food or the inspiring meetings. As different from these outpourings as my grandfather was from Pop Tibbitts, this affidavit carries a reserved accolade:

> I have known George Tibbitts personally for many years and have had ample opportunity for an appraisal of the gracious work which

he carries on at CAMP-OF-THE-WOODS and throughout the world. Those cooperating with him render him a service of great value to any church or community. I count it a privilege to bear this testimony.

WILLIAM H. HUDNUT, D.D., First Presbyterian Church
Youngstown, Ohio

Several times during the Foxlair or Fish House summers of my childhood I went to Camp-of-the-Woods with father and grandfather. By this time a great outdoor chapel had been built facing out over Lake Pleasant. The camp service appealed to me mightily at that impressionable age. I remember the urgent rush of the white clad young counselors, each bearing a swirling flag of many colors as they marched in to the swinging hymn that was their theme song. Then they would dip each flag as its country's name was called. In the midst of it all, first playing the organ, then bobbing up to lead singing or prayers, was the round little figure of Pop Tibbitts. He was a great man in his own field; to me he was like a summer Santa Claus, deeply tanned and all in white, with round bald head and white brows above rimless glasses. I remember that he would greet Grandfather with real affection and put an arm around my tall father and call him "Herbert," and always ask us to stay to lunch as his guests. So, after the service, we would follow the hundreds of campers up the winding trail they called "Fifth Avenue," which led to the enormous dining hall. This seated 700 people at a time, and its barn-like aspect was warmed a bit by log rafters, a huge stone fireplace and wide windows to the forest. Afterwards my sisters and I would be taken in tow by one of the girl counselors and change clothes in her tent before a long swim in that most beautiful lake. It seemed to me that this was the loveliest of beaches, wide and white, with sand like soft sugar, that extended out farther than we ever were allowed to go.

Now Pop Tibbitts is long since dead, he and his wife buried in a handsome tomb at Camp-of-the-Woods. And I hear that the Camp goes on, under its new direction, as successfully as ever. But we have never been back.

The summer of 1921, often referred to as the "Africa summer" by Kitty Hudnut, was described by her as close to idyllic. Will had been asked by the Presbyterian Board of Foreign Missions, of which he was a member, to make a Tour of Inspection of their West African Missions, particularly those of The Cameroons. The First Church of Youngstown, which never missed an opportunity to be generous with their beloved minister, insisted upon sending Harriet along, too, and so it was arranged that they would be away for at least three months. Their daughter, Dorothy, with her need for special care, was sent to Nan Beecher at Fish House. The family's seamstress from Youngstown, "Aunt Betty" Rogers, was engaged as housekeeper and mother superior for the Wamakedah group, which included Kitty and her friend from the Children's Hospital in Boston, Paulie Jefferson, then the head night nurse; and Billy, with his great friend from Youngstown, Hugh Manchester. Kitty remembers this summer as an endless succession of happy days. Interestingly, her only specific memory, when pressed for some by a curious niece, is that she often went berrying with Ma Perkins. Across so many years, the pleasure of that memory tells me better than most things what a wonderful woman was "Mees Suzay."

WAMAKEDAH WEDDING

An entry in the *Hamilton County History* under "Hudnut," tells the reader that on July 16, 1924, Ella Katherine Hudnut was married to Henry Bischoff in the living room at Wamakedah. The ceremony, it informs us, was performed by the bride's father, Dr. William Herbert Hudnut.

Ella Katherine, known as Kitty, was the family spitfire, with large, brown Hudnut eyes and a thin, gamin face—the kind of face that gloom or boredom could turn quickly plain, and happiness light up to beauty.

In the nine years when she was the youngest in the family, before Billy's birth in 1905, she had learned to defend herself; she was a tomboy, unafraid of confrontation, the family defender. Once in the heyday of the Women's Christian Temperance Union, which had many supporters in Will's church, the wagon of a local brewer stopped in front of their home. Kit, aged seven, rushed down from the porch, arms and legs in furious action: "You can't stop here," she cried, "This is Dr. Hudnut's house!" My father, a year older, witnessed the startled driver lay a whip to his horses for a speedy departure.

Her wit was as quick as her temper and she had a flare for drama and mimicry; she was captivating, and so in spite of the fact that she was neither as beautiful nor as easily charming as Marjorie, she was the unquestioned leader of the sisters. For all their lives, Kit and Marnie

Kit Hudnut, c. 1916

Kit and Henry Bischoff at Windover, c. 1930

were as close as two sisters could be, and when in later years they were each widowed they chose to live together.

The story of the Wamakedah wedding really begins in Fish House for it would never have happened but for the long relationship between the Sinclaire family and the Beechers and Hudnuts. These cousinly bonds had brought the Beechers to live at Fish House, and friendships were made and maintained from one generation to another. One of these friendships pertinent to our tale was that of Kitty Hudnut and Elisabeth Bischoff.

The Bischoffs were a Brooklyn family with business ties to the Sinclaires. Cousin Lucy's son, Frank Sinclaire, and Mr. Bischoff were partners in the ownership and management of Schenley Distilleries. Some time after the death of his first wife, Frank married the eldest Bischoff daughter, a beautiful young woman thirty-three years his junior. It was an extremely happy marriage, and they soon were a part of the village life at Fish House where they spent their summers at Cousin Lucy's big home on the green. Elisabeth Bischoff, Marie's younger sister, came to Fish House for long visits, and she and Kitty, much the same age, met and became fast friends.

Cousin Lucy's death and the heralded coming of the Sacandaga Reservoir prompted Frank Sinclaire to build his own home on higher ground and comfortably far from the path of the proposed flooding. He designed a handsome Georgian structure of cream-colored stucco, approached by a high iron gate and an avenue of poplars. He called it Rosslyn House, honoring the Sinclaire's Scottish heritage. When he and Marie and their children took up residence there was a special room for Elisabeth, and Kitty Hudnut was a frequent visitor after her family moved to Lake Pleasant.

In the summer of 1923 Kitty had completed her nurses training at Children's Hospital in Boston. She was poised at the beginning of a career, delighted with the attentions of several faithful suitors, but not yet ready to think about settling down. In the meantime she was enjoying a holiday with the family at Wamakedah.

One Sunday afternoon she and her brother Bill drove Hugh Manchester down to catch his train at Fonda. On the way home to Lake Pleasant they decided, on the spur of the moment, to stop and see the family at Rosslyn House. What they did not know was that there was a visitor whom they had never met: Marie and Elisabeth's brother, Henry Bischoff. While Kitty and Bill were being urged to stay for tea, this visitor strolled out on the terrace and was introduced to Kitty.

Uncle Bill said he might as well not have been there, for between Kitty Hudnut and Henry Bischoff it was a clear case of love at first sight. Long afterwards my Aunt Kit said that everything else about the day was a blur save for the absolute certainty, as she met those grave brown eyes, that *"This is it."* Henry was struck with the same lightning, and during these last weeks of the summer he drove back and forth to Wamakedah almost every day.

Henry Bischoff was a thoughtful, rather quiet man with a dry and ironic sense of humor, characteristics that may have come of his having had a heart condition since childhood. The grave brown eyes that had so taken Kitty were the finest feature of his appealing face. It was a love affair of complementary opposites: he with his quiet inner strength; she, so vivacious and full of panache.

All too soon the summer houses were closed and the families went back to their city lives and Kitty and Henry had to part. It was doubly hard, for they knew that they belonged together even if the way wasn't yet clear. Kitty was needed in Youngstown: Harriet had been seriously ill and Will prevailed on Kit to nurse her through the winter. It was Easter before the lovers were to see each other again.

When the train from Youngstown pulled into the station at Brooklyn, Henry was waiting with Sidney, the family chauffeur, and the big black Bischoff limousine. No sooner were they in the car than Henry reached out to close the glass partition to the front seat, and in a moment or two he had slipped a diamond ring on Kitty's finger.

The Bischoff home was on Willoughby Street in Brooklyn Heights and there to greet them were Marie Sinclaire and her daughters — Lucy, Katherine, and the baby, Clothilde. Elisabeth and Mr. Bischoff, Sr., were in Germany, visiting Bischoff relatives in Bremen; Frank Sinclaire was also abroad on business.

We have no record of the reunion or their time together, nor do we know whether they had begun to think about the time of their wedding. All we do know is that after a week Kitty left for Manchester-by-the-Sea, near Boston, for a visit with the Wicks, great friends of the Hudnuts.

No sooner had she settled in than an urgent call from Henry begged her to return to Brooklyn, for his brother-in-law, Frank Sinclaire, had died on shipboard while returning home, and had been buried at sea. The news which had arrived by telegram had put everything in a turmoil. It was clear that she was needed, and Kitty returned as soon as a train could take her.

Into the distraught house on Willoughby Street she went, with the comfort of her nursing skills, her capable hands, and her gift of sensing a need and taking care of it. Her care of Marie and the little girls and the large household's management must have made it clear to Henry that he had found a rare gem indeed! Everyone in the gloomy old house depended on her and she kept things going until Elisabeth and Papa Bischoff returned from Germany.

Marie Sinclaire was beside herself, her anguish only intensified by news of the true circumstances of her husband's death. He had contracted "the black smallpox," as it was called, in India, where two others who had it had been removed from the ship. When Sinclaire became ill at sea it was evidently assumed that he had the same dread disease. The ship's doctor was terrified of catching it and had to be ordered into the sickroom at gunpoint by the captain. When Frank Sinclaire died he was buried at sea because the captain and the crew were afraid to keep the body on shipboard. Such a burial was patently illegal but the family decided not to go to court about it; they must have felt that winning the case would do nothing to restore the young widow's loss or ameliorate the terrible knowledge of its circumstances.

After the Bischoffs returned, Kitty left once again to visit Laura Wick and her mother at Manchester. She was exhausted with the emotional responsibilities of the past weeks, and the sea air and the care of old friends were immensely restorative. However, she always remembered this as a time of unsettled feelings. The wedding, now planned for July, seemed endlessly far away. And perhaps she missed her family, though in a vague way she sensed what seemed to her a lack of enthusiasm on the part of her parents for her coming marriage. She couldn't put her finger on it, but it seemed real and it hurt her. It wasn't something they could talk about, nor did they openly oppose it; they simply didn't act overjoyed as, for example, they *were* over Herbert's engagement. One would have thought that the match, bolstered with family ties and Fish House sentiment, would have been warmly welcomed. Surely they admired Henry and saw how he and Kitty loved each other. She wondered if a part of it might be the source of the Bischoff family fortune: the Schenley Distilleries. While Will Hudnut had not been exactly a temperance crusader, as many ministers of that day were, he had a distaste for the whole industry, a feeling shared, at least publicly by many of the so-called better people of the day in a conservative town like Youngstown. At Rosslyn House Will and Harriet sometimes had a glass of champagne; they enjoyed the hospitality of the family there. Could it be that some perverse, puritan feelings were almost subliminally questioning the support of Kitty's new allegiance?

The parental reserve which Kitty rightly or wrongly felt might also have been their concern for Henry's health. There was no secret about his heart condition. They knew, as Kitty did, that he would always have to live carefully, to avoid pressures or any strenuous work or activity. Kit loved the quiet manner that was perhaps partly an intelligent adaption to this handicap; she treasured his deep enjoyment of everything—of nature, of her own high spirits—knowing the source of his extra appreciation. She knew that their time together might not be long, but she knew it would be the more precious because of that.

As for her parents, she also knew that they were preoccupied with the June wedding of Herbert and his fiancee, a lovely Youngstown girl, Edith Schaaf, who was related by marriage to their closest friends and neighbors, the Manchesters. It was to be a small wedding at the home of Edith's sister, Josephine Manchester, but it had become the center of a great deal of social activity. Harriet and Will were probably wishing that Kitty would come home and be a part of it all. In any event there was distance between them during that spring and early summer that somehow did not lessen even with frequent letters. Kit's only happy memory of the time was the day when Laura Wick, close and understanding family friend that she was, took her on a shopping trip to Magnolia and helped her to choose eight pretty dresses for her trousseau.

Kitty arrived at Wamakedah just a week before her wedding. If this seemed casual, it was a note that characterized this smallest and simplest of weddings from start to finish. That was the way Kit wanted it, she said. Her beloved sister Marnie was in the hospital; Herbert was just returning from his honeymoon; and Bill, after his sophomore year at Princeton, was tied to a summer job, so the only sibling to be present was Kitty's sister, Dorothy.

On the wedding morning, Harriet and Nan Beecher decorated the living room with ferns and flowers, and welcomed the car from Rosslyn House when it arrived bearing the Bischoffs and Marie Sinclaire and her little girls. Henry arrived, and at 11:00 o'clock, they all gathered around the fireplace and the bridal couple went over to stand in front of the bride's father, who conducted the wedding service. Kitty wore a slim dress of pale pink silk and Henry was in white flannels and a navy jacket. They were a striking couple and they were together at last.

Afterwards the whole party drove down to the White Owl Tea Room on the road to Piseco where a lovely luncheon awaited them. "But our *real* wedding party," my Aunt Kitty told me, "was after we got back from our honeymoon in Maine. It was at Rosslyn House, with champagne, and ices shaped like swans and lilies, and a wedding cake from Moracey's in Brooklyn!"

CHAPTER 14

SPECULATOR FAREWELL

For as long as anyone could remember, and before, Adirondack guides had built simple camps for themselves on state land. These differed in kind all the way from lean-tos to good-sized cabins where they could store provisions for their hunting and fishing parties and make base camp for an extended time in the woods. French Louie, for example, was known to have camps hidden away in many choice locations, and in his West Canada camp where he lived for much of the year, he built everything needed for his rustic life.

Camp Perkins differed from this network of hideaways only in degree of size, in its established character as an inn, and in the fact that it had for years supported a thriving, industrious family life. The principle was the same: it was built on state forest land, which ultimately came down to state ownership. Mabel Stanyon put it clearly:

> When the State began to take an interest in its Forest Preserve and conservation measures were adopted, a regulation was made that no privately owned camps should be allowed on state land. For this reason, the Perkins Camp had to be discontinued.
>
> (*The Quiet Years*)

Bill Hudnut, a young man at the time, remembered Isaiah's bitter-

138

ness over the confiscation of Camp Perkins. He felt it violated the principle of Squatter's Rights which had surely been a fact of life in the settlements since before the Revolution. When the State instituted this new policy it hurt so many of the guides whose camps were tucked away on what they had come to think of as their own hunting grounds.

From Susie and Isaiah, perhaps, it took the most. Camp Perkins had become a regular institution, with special groups that came year after year. It had been eulogized in sporting journals; the young mayor of New York, John Purroy Mitchell, was a "regular," and had, in fact, chosen to bring his bride there for their honeymoon. This and many another accolade attested to the deep personal character of this backwoods resort, the love and work Susie and Isaiah had put into it, and the loyalty of its patrons. Its closing down seemed such a loss. Writing of this, and knowing the sadness my family felt for the Perkins family and the other guides they had known, it is particularly heartwarming to be able to report that the site of Camp Perkins is memorialized now, by act of the State Legislature, as Perkins Clearing on the Hamilton County map.

It was not in Isaiah to brood for long over what he saw as an injustice. It was his experience, as it had been for most of the men in those remote parts of the Adirondacks, to be flexible in the matter of earning a living.

> Mr. Perkins continued active in projects which would make of the village an attractive resort area. To him belongs the credit for building and operating the first and only movie-house within a wide radius.
>
> Mr. Perkins may also be considered a pioneer in the making of Speculator the popular winter sports resort which it is at the present time. On his land were built the first ski jump and ski lodge and, cutting a wide swathe down the side of Sturges Mountain, continuing through Mr. Perkins' property, and crossing the road to the lake, ran the first toboggan slide.
>
> (*The Quiet Years*)

Bringing the wonders of the silent movies to Speculator suited him to a "T," for he had always been a bit of a showman and an entrepreneur and had loved nothing better than promoting good times. The theater was a huge success; its screen brought the whole world right to the little mountain community. The piano was up in front by the stage, and its music provided the only continuity of sound for the motion picture.

The demands of this part of the entertainment were considerable, flexibility of mood and repertoire being of the essence. Isaiah's pianist for a season or two was young Bill Hudnut, my uncle, then a student at Princeton.

———————————————

For more than ten summers now the Hudnut family had lived at Wamakedah. It's possible that they might be there still but for Speculator's rising fame as a summer training ground for champion prize-fighters. It was an era when "society had selected prize-fighting as its foremost fad." Uncle Bill wrote of its effect on the family:

> In the summers of 1925 and 1926, the peace and quiet were threatened by the arrival of a champion heavy-weight boxer who established his training quarters at our end of Lake Pleasant, near the Osborne House, the leading hotel, and not far from the Camp of the Woods. The name of the boxer was Gene Tunney, and we all became instant partisans, pulling for him to whip Jack Dempsey.
>
> His sparring partners and camp attendants took violent exception to the bell that rang at Camp of the Woods every morning at seven o'clock. A delegation waited upon Pop Tibbits to complain that their morning slumbers were disturbed by the ringing of the bell.
>
> Pop replied, "So long as we are here that bell will ring. It's a call to prayer. If you don't like it, I suggest you move."
>
> Some fifty years later I met Tunney in Scottsdale, Arizona, and he remembered Pop Tibbits and the ringing of that bell.

Those summers of Gene Tunney's training camp put Speculator on the map of famous resorts.

> "Those were great days in the fight racket, those days with Tunney at Speculator," wrote Bill Corum in his syndicated column. Pugilism had just been taken up in a glittering way by what Tex Rickard delighted to describe as "the best people," and there were times when millionaires were so thick underfoot that you had to fight your way through them to buy a picture post card at the drug store.
>
> (*Hamilton County History*)

Ma Perkins' brother, the well-known Adirondack guide "Pants" Lawrence, became Tunney's daily companion and guide on long walks through the nearby woodlands; this friendship must have encompassed the whole Perkins family. "Neighbors like 'Pants' make my training camp in Speculator a delightful place to train," wrote Gene Tunney, and largely because of his love of the whole township of Lake Pleasant, it became known as "a goodluck place to train."

The crowds that boosted the prosperity of Speculator abolished much of the backwoods peace and quiet that had attracted Will and Harriet to Lake Pleasant, but they had not yet actively planned to leave Wamakedah when a realtor came to them with news of a prospective buyer for their property. Grandfather replied, perhaps over-quickly, that it was not for sale, to which the real estate man parried the suggestion that he name a price, "just for fun." So that is how our grandfather happened to name a price for Wamakedah — a price that he felt was beyond reason, something more than six times what he had put into the property. What he didn't know was that the prospective buyer wasn't in this "just for fun." He wanted Wamakedah, and agreed to pay the exorbitant price that had been named.

Now, then, Will Hudnut was in a dilemma of his own making. He and Harriet truly loved Lake Pleasant, yet on visits to Foxlair they had glimpsed the wilderness farther north, where larger properties could be had for very little. Perhaps it was the crowds. Perhaps it was the lure of the new and the unknown. Perhaps it was that the family was growing and would soon need more room if they were to gather in the summer. Whatever the reasons, all were weighed in the light of the handsome price that was being offered. Thus, in 1927 the sale of Wamakedah was completed.

The remainder of that summer, and all of the next, the family spent at the Foxlair guest house, known as North Cottage, where Will's brother, Richard Hudnut, invited them to stay until they found their new summer home and it was ready to occupy. Harry Armstrong, the superintendent at Foxlair, was instrumental in finding the new property for Will and Harriet and their family. The Speculator chapter was ended.

It was not, of course, the ending of the bonds between the Perkins and the Hudnut families. Their friendships had been too strong and had spanned too many years. But time was short for Susie and Isaiah. For several years, Ma Perkins had been in poor health, although people didn't really know how seriously, for she remained the kind of person who gave herself away to other folks' needs and kept her own troubles to herself. On February 20, 1930, just a week after coming home from the hospital in Amsterdam, she had two heart attacks and died. She was just 60 years old.

Her obituary, unusually detailed for a woman at that time, made it clear how highly Mrs. Susan Emily Lawrence Perkins was regarded in the whole area, and how greatly she would be mourned. One of the letters Isaiah would treasure the most came from his old friend, Will Hudnut:

My dear Isaiah:

Someone from Pittsburgh brought the sad tidings of Ma's departure. It seemed to us that there must be some mistake, that it could not be that she who had always seemed to us so vital, had gone. I suppose that her going will not seem real to us until we have come to Speculator and have sat down with you in the old home and have missed her from the familiar places. It is very difficult to realize what you will do without her.

The relationship was a very beautiful one and you have every reason to be proud of it and to thank God with all your heart that He gave you such a loyal and lovely wife and your children such a devoted and competent mother. She was very truly a child of the wilderness, loving the wild, and at home in the great open spaces. She had the vision and daring and romance of the pioneer, and wherever she was, in the settlement or in the deepest forest, there was an ordered home.

Her innate refinement and dignity were evident in all company. She wore the hallmark of a lady. To my thinking she was the Queen of Speculator and of all that region and her steady Christian influence will be sadly missed. She saw clearly what was right, and she had the courage of her convictions. She had capable hands and a kind heart. The sick and the poor will miss her.

Your daughters and their children have a great heritage. She set them a high mark. And so we, too, rise up this day with you to call her name blessed. We loved her dearly and honored her greatly and we shall miss her always.

Someone will write us of the circumstances of her passing from life unto death. God comfort and keep you and open the way before you.

Your loving friend,
William Herbert Hudnut

And so Ma Perkins was laid to rest in the little graveyard at Speculator, close by her parents, Phoebe and Marinus Lawrence, her young daughter, Gertie, and her old friend, French Louie, whose grave she had been bringing flowers to since 1915. If Louie's belief was true that the good will return as flowers, then that corner of the old cemetery should blossom like a garden.

Isaiah survived her by four years, dying at summer's end, 1934. Although the paper said that my father would conduct the service, he had, in fact, returned to the city and the funeral was conducted by Grandfather, quite rightly, one of Isaiah's dearest and oldest friends. Uncle Bill also took part in the service. It was one of the longest funerals anyone could remember in Speculator—over an hour and a half. Mrs. Robert Stuart wrote to Uncle Bill afterwards: "Your Dad's message at Isaiah's funeral was like a visit with God, Isaiah, and your Father. I shall never forget it."

Here is his obituary, in its entirety:

Isaiah Jefferson Perkins, prominent resident of Hamilton County for a half century, passed away Monday afternoon at 2:15 at his home in Speculator, after an illness extending over a period of three months.

Mr. Perkins, who was 71 years of age, was born February 2, 1863, in North Hudson, Warren County, the son of Isaiah and Annis LaVanway Perkins. He was united in marriage to Susan Lawrence, July 22, 1888.

Mr. Perkins was well known as a guide and woodsman and for many years was engaged in the lumber industry in that vicinity. He was the organizer of the Winter Sports Club of Hamilton County.

The late Mayor Mitchell of New York and Mr. Perkins were close friends, the former often visiting him at the hunting and fishing camp which he conducted at the Jessup River.

He was also prominent politically, having served two terms as Sheriff of Hamilton County and as Supervisor for several terms.

He was a member of the Speculator village trustees and was a hotel proprietor in the village for many years. Mr. Perkins was the owner of the Adirondack Theatre in Speculator and was connected with other amusement enterprises in that locality.

He was a trustee of the Methodist church of Speculator, of which he was an active member. During his long residence in Hamilton County, Mr. Perkins had surrounded himself with a host of friends, all of whom will sincerely mourn his passing.

I cannot close our story of this colorful Adirondack man with the formal phrases of an obituary; his spirit will not be so contained. Nor does any recounting of his various jobs and offices capture the essence of Isaiah. In his farewell, my father pictured him again at Perkins Clearing: "Look for me when you hear the timbers rattle," Isaiah always called out as he saddled the mules. Returning he would stand in the buckboard at the crest of the hill, push the giant sombrero back on his head, and roar. The wilderness spread out about him like his own green kingdom; smoke in the chimneys showed that Ma had dinner going; the girls would soon tumble out to meet him. Crack the long whip across the lazy mules! Streak down the hill, rattle across the bridge and into the clearing. Isaiah Perkins is home!

CHAPTER 15

OREGON

There is no record of Richard Hudnut's reason for coming to the remote territory known as Oregon. His brother Will knew about it from Cal Wilber, one of the Speculator guides who had his farthest camp there, and sometimes spoke with something like reverence of the beauty of its long valley, walled in by mountains, through which the east branch of the Sacandaga ran a winding course. The road up from Wells was rough and often impassable and it was thought of as a far wilderness, something like the Oregon Country out west for which it was named.

For a brief time, toward the end of the nineteenth century, it had been the scene of considerable lumbering. Much of the Oregon land had been acquired by Stephen Griffin, a lumberman from Warren County, and in 1877 he built a tannery there, to make profitable use of the bark of the trees that were cut down. In the late 1880s the lumbering was finished, and in 1890 the tannery at Oregon burned to the ground.

By 1900 only a few small, struggling farms remained in a valley that had supported a village and a sizeable work force. The ruins of the tannery were almost hidden by the undergrowth of a decade; the area that had even in its busiest years been isolated, was now almost deserted. As

I reread the memoir of the tiny farming community, written for me by Ouida Girard (and included in the Appendix here), it seemed even more a mystery that Richard Hudnut found his way there in the first place. Most of all I marvel that he had a vision of what it could become.

What we *do* know is that before 1900 he set about buying the whole valley; one little farm after another, the tannery lot, the school house lot, until at last the land was his. The State of New York must have bought many of the thousands of acres Stephen Griffin had bought in the 1870s because Richard's final holdings of twelve hundred acres were completely surrounded by state land. It took several years for the acquisition of the property to be completed. As families departed, Oregon became a ghost town.

Most of its buildings were destroyed — razed, burned, carted away, and as the sites of these structures were filled in, leveled and planted, the shape of one man's mountain kingdom emerged. This was to be known as Foxlair: in its days of glory one of the great estates of the Adirondacks, and yet even then, like Oregon, so remote and isolated that it was virtually unknown.

Before we continue with the story of the place, I will tell you what I know of Richard Hudnut, for the character of the man was so much a part of the rise and fall of Foxlair.

CHAPTER 16
RICHARD HUDNUT

It would be hard to find two brothers more different than William and his older brother, Richard, even though they shared the same father, Alexander Hudnut, and their mothers were sisters.

Will was warm and affectionate; Richard was cold and imperious. Will needed constant reassuring and was never an excellent student, whereas Richard was completely self-sufficient and brilliant in school. Will had a strong conscience and a deeply spiritual nature, whereas Richard was worldly and materialistic, his "religion" a sort of hedonism. Will was a life-long appreciator of natural beauty; Richard *created* beauty.

It could be said that Richard Hudnut was first of all an artist. He possessed an extraordinary sensitivity to fragrance and color; these were his mediums. But while he was an artist, he also excelled as a businessman. These opposite gifts combined to make his name something of a household word in the world of cosmetics and perfume for many years, one valued by elegant women all over the world. Vanity was a constant in his nature and catering to the vanity of women, he made his fortune.

He was educated at military academy and at Brooklyn Polytechnic Institute, for he planned to go into his father's pharmaceutical busi-

Richard Alexander Hudnut, c. 1881

ness. Indeed, Alexander Hudnut had encouraged his son's interest in chemistry as preparation for carrying on the work that he himself had founded with such auspicious success.

During the early years with his father, Richard developed his skill in creating and blending perfume. He was keenly aware of the new interest in cosmetics. Up until the period we speak of, the 1880s, any aids to beauty had been in the exclusive domain of the actress or the demimonde. Richard's creativity first of all perfected the finest cosmetics of the times for these eager professional women, and then he pioneered the creation of a market among "respectable women."

Will, as a very young boy in Llewellyn Park, remembered Richard coming home late from the city, dining in solitary splendor, and between courses, sniffing a variety of scented blotting papers, shifting and combining, lingering over each new combination. In this way he created the perfumes that were to make the House of Hudnut famous with women for years to come; names such as Gemey, Cardinal Lily, Three Flowers, and Violet Sec.

Will remembered little enough about Richard in those days, except for the following:

> He was aloof and we thought him incomparably handsome. He was slender and quite blonde, with the imperious beak of a young eagle, and ice blue eyes. Sometimes he would let Paul and me watch him fencing or wrestling. And sometimes he would join us singing around the piano, for he took a deal of pride in his fine tenor voice. But normally he lived at a far remove, for this was a period of intense work and self-development for him. We would scarcely see him for days at a time. Meals would be served him at any hour. We thought him very social. He loved parties and cared very much about his appearance. With his horses or his clothes or his attitude, his aim was always to be elegant.

In 1881, Richard was married to Evelyn Beals at St. Thomas' Church, New York. It was a small family wedding, for, although she had resumed her maiden name, Evelyn was a divorcée. She was the daughter of Horace Beals, the owner of a large quarry in Quincy, Massachusetts, and granddaughter of Hannibal Hamlin, Lincoln's vice-president. She had one son by her first marriage.

Evelyn was a highly intelligent, well-connected woman, and was unquestionably a driving spur in Richard's already rising career. He had always been ambitious to make his own fortune, not content merely to lead a comfortable life as the successor in his father's business. So it was that at the age of thirty, just a few years after his marriage, he left his father's stores and launched his own. He opened the Richard Hudnut Pharmacy at 925 Broadway. His brother, Will, later wrote: "It was small but elegantly furnished. He specialized in his own perfume and cosmetics and elegant toilet articles, all beautifully packaged to appeal to his fastidious clientele."

After an initially difficult first summer, during which critics may have murmured that "a drug store should be a drug store and not pretend to be a palace," the store caught on, and Richard's career was established. The pattern after that was simply rapid ascent. Soon he had established his own factory on East 29th Street and had opened a branch in Paris. It was not long before the pharmacy was a modest memory, replaced with a salon on Fifth Avenue, furnished with French antiques and bearing the name of HUDNUT in bas relief on its marble façade. Another salon was furnished on Bond Street in London, and the finest of all would be in Paris, on the Rue de la Paix. Like his father before him, Richard was a millionaire in his own right before the age of forty.

Unlike the sons of many rich men who seem to have been trained to anxious thrift, Richard seemed bent on surpassing the last of the big spenders. My grandfather always considered him wildly extravagant, and even used the patronizing term, nouveau riche, to describe him. But I think it fair to remember that my beloved grandfather spoke as a younger brother, strugging on the proverbially modest ministerial salary, with a growing family to support. Despite the judgmental prejudice of a younger brother, Richard and Evelyn, even in a gilded age, pushed the boundaries of luxury.

One of her maids from the Foxlair summers remembers Evelyn Hudnut as looking like "a mighty God." And it is true that her monumental size is remarked upon in any reminiscence of her. But it was her manner, too, that the little maid remembered: a hard, arrogant chill that could intimidate all but the most intrepid. This was exactly as she wished it. She made no secret of the fact that she had no time or use for people who were not amusing, attractive, or "ticky-ticky," in just about that order.

Yet people liked her, if they bothered to get past her manner, and they found her handsome despite her enormous size. She was strikingly blonde, by grace and favor of an excellent hairdresser, and her penetrating eyes were a blue-violet like hyacinths. She carried herself erect and dressed in her own distinctive style. Caring nothing for the caprice of high fashion, she wore long robes of heavy lace over silks or wools. These materials came from the lace mills of her mother's family in Ireland.

By all accounts, Richard adored her. He considered her brilliant, fascinating, and vastly witty. Like Richard, she was given to cruel innuendo; because she was sharply articulate, no one seemed to challenge her. Once, in the midst of a large gathering, my father heard her say of her son and daughter-in-law, "What he needed was a red-blooded woman. Look at him there with his little white rabbit!" My father could never forget it.

A common bond between the couple must have been a mutual bolstering of monumental egos. Clippings, articles, commentaries on their life at the turn of the century show a consciously developed plan of living: peripatetic, epicurean, carefully orchestrated, status-seeking. They would not just make cuisine an art in their lives; they must have one of the finest French chefs in captivity, the famous Grattard, Cordon Bleu, tempted away from the kitchen of the Baroness Adolph de Rothschild. Their lights would not be hidden under bushels. They entertained regularly, drawing their friends from many echelons: from the family years; from the emerging, yet still unlabled, "cafe Society"; from that company of minor royalty whose diminishing fortunes made them doubly receptive to the luxurious hospitality of the Hudnuts. How Richard and Evelyn loved titles! It was as if the glittering life they chose to lead was like a mirror, reflecting back to them an image of who they were and what they had attained.

During the years of his marriage to Evelyn, Richard seldom saw William, although he took more responsibility for maintaining the bond than did his younger brother. They had correspondence on family matters, and the letters from Richard often issued invitations to Greenwich or to the Biltmore, which Harriet and Will seemed never to accept.

Once, Will, in the years of his Brooklyn ministry, called on Richard in his New York office, and upon arriving there collapsed in a faint. Richard's doctor was summoned immediately, and Will was rushed to the hospital. Afterwards, Richard wrote to Harriet, and the letter shows a brotherly concern which is seldom credited to him:

> I was much disturbed about William's health after seeing him so
> ill the other day, but had no idea the attack would prove so
> serious. Dr. Slater, whose services came in so opportunely, said
> that it might be the forerunner of appendicitis. William has been

Evelyn Hudnut and friends at Oregon

Evelyn Hudnut, Richard's first wife

overworking himself, evidently, for some time past, and if you
have (as I do not doubt) the necessary influence on him, it will be
well to watch him closely and to compel him to let up and rest
for awhile when you see him running down. The Hudnuts are
ambitious without doubt, and full of nervous energy, but we all
lack the necessary stamina. William has the advantage of youth
and the best of attention. I feel sure he will come through it all
right. If you need me in any way, don't hesitate to say so. I will
be glad to do anything in my power. Please keep me informed of
William's progress.

Yours faithfully, Richard

As often happens in families, a new generation would bring the
brothers together again. In 1912, Herbert Beecher Hudnut, eldest son
of Will and Harriet, entered the freshman class at Princeton. (This is
the young Herbert of the Speculator chapters, who fell in love with
Rose Perkins at Perkins Clearing.) Now, far from home, he soon had
an invitation to dine at the home of his uncle in New York City.

At that time, the Richard Hudnuts owned a town house in the East
Forties. Herbert (my father) remembers that he felt like an intruder in
a small, but very chic, museum, and that while he was drawn immediately to his uncle, he recognized Aunt Evelyn to be the most curious
and formidable woman he had ever met. He had not moved in cosmo-
politan society: Youngstown was a provincial city and he had never
come upon a woman as unconventional or uninhibited as this new-
found aunt. However, growing up in a clergy family, he had been
prepared to meet a variety of people, and while this was surely a dazzling milieu, it did not put him totally off-balance. He was wide-eyed
and at ease, and this, plus the natural warmth of his nature, charmed
both Evelyn and Richard. They found it a novelty to have an innocent
and undoubtedly handsome nephew about. His manners were good;
his blush was amusing, and his youth was like a breath of fresh air. For
Richard, who never had children of his own, Herbert became, for a
period of time, like a son. Will, far off in Youngstown, noted in his
memoirs: "Richard loved Herbert, and contributed towards his education at Princeton."

For the next four years, they were close. Richard took Herbert with
him to parties and on trips, and enjoyed going to Princeton, especially
for football games in the autumn. He and Evelyn got Herbert invited
with them to parties in the castles on the Hudson, and the ballrooms of
New York. Before long he was receiving party invitations of his own,

the result of this family "sponsorship."

During this period, Foxlair was in its heyday, and Herbert came as often as he could. Once on the journey up to the mountains Richard's party put up at the United States Hotel in Saratoga, where he was always given the special place in the dining room known as the Abraham Lincoln table. My father remembers that on this occasion, as on so many, Richard criticized the food in an imperious manner. This never failed to embarrass his nephew, and Herbert never knew how to cope with it, or sympathize with the waiters who would flutter about and cringe. In spite of Richard's demanding and difficult nature, the bond established between them during Herbert's Princeton years lasted until his uncle's death.

CHAPTER 17

THE EARLY DAYS OF FOXLAIR:
WILLETT RANDALL'S TALE

It is hard to be exact about dates in the early years of Foxlair. I have always heard that Uncle Richard started to buy the properties of Oregon before 1900. However, I have copies of the recorded deeds that tell when the various parcels of land were legally conveyed, and according to these, the first 400 acres were bought in September 1904, and the last in 1911, being the Boarding House and Tannery lots.

The first purchase completed was a piece of land formerly owned by William Barker, a shirt manufacturer from Troy, New York, who had built a handsome camp at the far north end of the Oregon valley on a high bank above the Sacandaga. Richard called it North Cottage. This dwelling, and a big frame farmhouse with its barns, some distance away and across the road from North Cottage, were the only buildings of Oregon that were preserved. Here the Hudnuts and their staff lived before the building of the Big House. Since according to Grandfather, they occupied North Cottage as early as 1900, it must be that the title search took a long time; it is probable that in the interval Richard leased the camp from Mr. Barker.

Willett Randall was the third superintendent of Foxlair. He was an ardent conservationist, and long after he had finished with caretaking he ran "The Ark," an animal farm outside North Creek, where he bred

North Cottage

Bust of Richard Alexander Hudnut

Richard visiting Herbert at Princeton

Foxlair

the famous Patch beagles, and wrote nature columns for North Country newspapers, including the *North Creek News*. When he was ninety-four years old he agreed to write his memories of Foxlair for me. This he did around 1964, shortly before his death. They are a unique, and in some places, fairly unpleasant record. Dates were as problematic for him as they are for me: he believed that Foxlair was already a going concern some years before the early deed's dates would suggest. For example, Willett thought that the Big House was built in 1904, and Grandfather had always said that, too—but if that was so, it was built on land that hadn't legally been totally conveyed to Richard yet. The people and the papers that could provide us with more conclusive facts have long since departed this world. We may read Willett's memoir as beginning somewhere after the turn of the nineteenth century, and the lack of authentic dates doesn't seem to lessen its interest at all.

From the Foxlair memoir by Willett Randall:

> When Richard A. Hudnut acquired the extensive tract of land including the Village of Oregon, he unwittingly set the stage for according public recognition to a new and unprecedented focus of power that swiftly followed in his wake—namely the purchase and development of available wild acres which had been lying idle for centuries. This project was later to become known as "Foxlair."
>
> Mr. Hudnut was a man of sterling qualities, wisdom and forethought. He early recognized the value of these wild acres not only for recreational development, but for their aesthetic value as well, and particularly what they would mean in after years to the vanishing wild life whose home this was by right of birth.
>
> For years it had been his dream to find a haven among the high peaks of the Adirondacks, where he might shy away from the maddening crowds and relax in peace and quiet that awaited him, where his fertile mind could reach out and weld together both facts and fancies needed in the perpetuation of his business as a manufacturer of the finest perfumes in the world.
>
> When Mr. Hudnut first set eyes upon this property, it was called "Oregon"—the tannery part. It rested upon a level rise of ground on the banks of the historic Sacandaga River, hemmed in by high mountain peaks. Originally the town was built to house the workers who moved in to work at the huge tannery located upon the river bank where raw hides were tanned and made into leather. The Oregon tannery was one of many located in various parts of northern New York.
>
> During the first year of Mr. Hudnut's occupancy, my trail

crossed with that of Eugene Beals (a son of the first Mrs. Hudnut by a former marriage). Mr. Beals was very much interested in the development of Foxlair and actively participated in the multiple works that followed. Upon his first visit to me, he brought a message from Mr. Hudnut, which, as I recall it, read in part:

> It is my sincere wish that you will grant me an audience at your earliest convenience to consider your possible employment here at Foxlair. You have been highly recommended to me as a specialist in the field of wildlife, which is one of my first considerations and must receive immediate attention.

Signed: Richard A. Hudnut

I complied with this request and spent most of a day with Mr. Hudnut in his temporary office, located in one of the then existing buildings. My first (and last) impression of him was a man of few words dedicated to the immediate task he set himself. He did not elaborate upon the building of what would soon be known, not only as a wildlife haven, but as an "Institution" in itself. He outlined the program which he had jotted down on paper pending my arrival; these things, he said, we can work out together concerning the wildlife already existing on the property. And if he found me available, he would assign other tasks which he felt sure I could handle to his satisfaction. Other than this outline there were no details. He handed me a short contract which I read carefully, signed, and then handed back to him. I was to report the following Monday.

My work at Foxlair was one of the highlights of my career, and, I have no doubt, played an important part in the future shaping of my destiny. I was still young and ambitious. I was a naturalist, and I was born in this wilderness where I had every opportunity to study my chosen profession: the first hand study of our native Adirondack wildlife.

While Foxlair was my first major assignment, I had been employed by Collis P. Huntington on his estate, Pine Knot, at Raquette Lake in the year 1900. I had only been there a few weeks in July when Mr. Huntington died there at the estate and the place was suddenly closed.

If I had been somewhat reluctant to sign a contract, feeling I might not be equal to the occasion, my fears—if any—were soon dispelled, and the days that followed were never long enough.

One of my first assignments was the building of a real fox lair upon the hillside where a native red fox would make a permanent

home. To the Hudnuts that was of paramount importance and
took precedence over all other plans. Mr. Hudnut explained to me
that this estate in the future would be known as Foxlair, and as
such the lair and its occupants would play a significant role. Men
with picks and shovels excavated a cavity in the hillside where an
underground den afforded seclusion and comfort. The den itself
was a 6' by 6' palace built of brick and cement. The outside run
was 6' by 12', with one inch iron bars set upright.

Once finished my next task was to catch a fox—alive and
unhurt. This was easier than the building of the den. A family of
reds had made their home at the foot of the mountain above the
estate and we succeeded in digging them out. Five pups were subsequently brought in, together with their mother, but since a
single fox would complete the picture, only one pup was retained.
The mother and those remaining were replaced in their home
den. It might be interesting to state that during the first night the
old pair quickly moved the family to a new and secret place, and
we never saw them again.

During the months that followed both Mr. and Mrs. Hudnut
found great pleasure at the new fox den where they personally
cared for the captive. By late fall he was fully grown and sported
a glossy red coat. His feet and ear-tips were glossy black, and the
tip of his tail pure white. It is my understanding that many foxes
came and went during the lifetime of the den, but the original fox
was still there when I left the estate.

The Hudnut family were all nature lovers and while they had no
previous personal experience with wildlife, they pressed into service
every opportunity to learn. Like myself, they were most interested
in the species which were native to their land, and whatever the
species, they were made welcome. Soon they had acquired a
knowledge of practically all the wild inhabitants of the estate, and
kidded each other on how much they "really knew." There were
the coons and woodchucks, the ruffed grouse and the squirrels—to
say nothing of the hoards of chipmunks who had accepted their
hospitality to the extent that some of them had become a nuisance.
The height of the excitement came when the big, husky quilled
porcupines visited the cottage (North Cottage, where they stayed
until the Big House was finished) during the night and left their
calling cards in the shape of chewed holes in the canoe. They had
even gnawed a paddle in two, and made a good start on the sills
of the cottage. I explained to them that these animals crave salt or
anything that may savor of it. Once when Mr. Hudnut left his
camera on a log to look for wild flowers, an obliging porky came

along and stripped off the leather cover. When I protested that this was the limit, Mr. Hudnut reminded me with a bleak smile, "This is a wildlife Refuge."

Aside from the study of native wildlife, certain domestic animals were to be acquired for the same purpose. The sheep flock was the first. At the far end of the estate near the chauffeur's cottage, a large area was enclosed by a six foot woven wire fence, and the first half dozen animals were released therein, to be followed by others until the total approximated twenty. While the Hudnuts visited the enclosure often, the personal watch over the sheep fold fell to Mr. Beals.

From the start the flock multiplied and prospered and waxed fat on the luscious green foliage, along with the white clover that carpeted the rolling hillside, and the lamb and mutton was a welcome addition to the various species to be raised for the table. But the hand of fate was hidden among the foliage, and emerged to plague us when the sun went down. One rainy night a mother black bear with her cubs raided the sheep fold killing several of the animals, and left others maimed and dying; it was a ghastly picture, and there was but one answer. The sheep flock was dispersed.

During the first summer a pair of stately mute swans was brought to the estate and turned loose upon the river above the old dam that once furnished power to run the tannery. There had been no repairs since the Hudnuts came, although a new dam was to be built the following summer. When spring came and the mighty Sacandaga went on a rampage, the old dam let go, and the swans, which had been their pride and joy, were swept away on the crest of the flood. I never saw them again.

Another of the special animal attractions was a pure white heifer, first of the bovines to reach the estate. Mrs. Hudnut insisted that the animal be given full liberty, believing it would stay around the buildings where it could be seen and petted, but the heifer had other ideas, and promptly took a "French leave," ending up at her old home near Bakers Mills. This continued to happen until my patience was taxed to the utmost. Finally this thorn in my flesh was removed, the pretty white heifer found a new home.

Later a small herd of Mexican burros (or Syrian donkeys) were brought to the estate. These well might have been the final answer to the domestic animal collection—only for one thing, they persisted in telling the world about them that THIS wasn't Mexico, nor Bolivia, nor the Andes, or for that matter any other country where their remote ancestors held sway—they just didn't like it, and kept up their incessant braying into the wee small hours of the night, keeping the whole household awake and disrupting the repose of the workers who rebelled in no uncertain terms to the midnight serenade to which they were subjected. Soon the donkeys vanished.

Upon Mr. Beales first visit, he brought a pair of handsome beagle puppies; these were allowed the run of the property. Being young they did not stray, and soon were members of the Hudnut household, even though they often left their tiny footprints all over the furniture. When Mr. Beales went home in the fall, he took these pets along with him, and they never came back. Next spring in their place came a pair of big red setters, mature and huge for the breed. These dogs had been trained to the gun, and it was only natural that they pick up the trail of the first wild animals they came across. Since they found themselves within a veritable game paradise, they lost no time in reverting to the ways of their ancestors. Before their coming the deer about the estate had become so tame that they fed along the fringe of the meadows, often venturing upon the lawn near the residence. The Hudnuts enjoyed studying these animals through the field glasses; they fed them at the garden's edge, placed salt along the runways.

Of particular interest was a doe with twin fawns that came out to feed at sundown. She was early christened "Old Rhoda." Soon they had gained her confidence to the extent that she would feed from their hands, but the fawns kept in the background until they were well grown. About that time the red setters appeared, and the deer family vanished, never to return.

We were given to understand that any animal coming to live at Foxlair was to have absolute liberty (except the fox), so the red setters continued to cruise, even though we had long since come to realize that hunting dogs and deer were not compatible.

One weekend I had a day off. When I returned, the setters were gone, I never asked any questions.

During the early part of the first summer Mr. Hudnut summoned me to his office. "I have something important to say to you," he said. "I am making some changes in personnel about the estate, and beginning today *you* will become the superintendent of Foxlair. You will supersede Mr. Bowles who will be leaving in the morning. I believe you will be able to handle the affairs of the estate in a satisfactory manner, and together we will work out the problems as they present themselves. I wish you to please bear in mind that it is my policy to tell an employee *only once* what I expect him to do. I am sure you understand."

The once-thriving village of Oregon had long since reverted into a Ghost Town. The dilapidated old houses for the most part had already been razed during the past summer, yet there still remained much to be done. Since there were no bulldozers available, the task of cleaning up fell to the workers with pick and shovel.

This was a laborious undertaking: — old lumber was carted away and burned; foundations were removed; cellars were filled and leveled; and grass was planted everywhere. Soon the spacious green lawns stretched away to the edge of the forest, and there was no sign to indicate where once the thriving village stood.

Passing there last summer (1963) I paused to meditate "what changes." The fox den was gone. A new state road cut in half what was once the most beautiful estate in the section. The great windmill erected under the guidance of Mr. Hudnut was nowhere in evidence.

All that remained of the farm buildings was the Pigeon Loft upon the hill. It had long since gone to decay: — the windows were broken, the flag pole missing, and the dilapidated doors hung limp on rusty hinges.

I recall one instance that impressed me. The only building of Oregon left standing when I became Supeintendent was the old schoolhouse perched upon the hill where it had weathered the storms for more than a century. Mr. Hudnut pointed it out, standing silently before he spoke. He said, "It may be sentimental, but I'm going to leave the old land-mark here." That old building could add a chapter of interest here.* It held fast to its old foundations during the life of the Hudnut family.

I can't recall that any of the family ever left the estate during their summer stay. Otherwise I never knew when they would arrive or when they might be leaving, — usually not until the night before, when I would be instructed to have the horses ready so as to reach North Creek in time for the 10 a.m. train.

During the winter only a small maintenance staff were retained — about half a dozen. One of the oldest and most trusted of the servants was Josephine Hunt, a charming woman in her early seventies. She was well versed in the workings of the Hudnut family, having been with them for many years. We recognized her as head of the estate during the long winter. Few persons that I have met possessed her sterling qualities. She was deeply religious. I was instructed to see that her every wish was gratified, and it was my

* Miss Ouida Girard's Memoir is about this school. [*Appendix I*]

custom to drive her to church every Sunday morning. Often the
roads were blocked with drifts that came early and stayed late. In
those days there were no snow plows. We beat our own trails as
the horses wallowed belly deep much of the way; we made the best
of what was—and were a happy family.

Mr. Hudnut spent much time walking about the estate, gathering wild flowers which he would spread out on his office table and
arrange in systematic rows. Often he would sit for hours with
elbows on the desk poring over them. What, I thought, was his
purpose? But I never asked any questions. Was there a link
between those flowers and the secret formulas used in the
manufacture of his famous perfumes?

While some of the domestic animals were not all that could be
hoped for, the pigeon loft with its prizes was an exception. The
pigeons were housed in a palace all their own at the hill-top near
the Beales cottage and adjacent to the dormitory where Mr. Hudnut
spent much of his time with his physical instructor.

The loft was one of the first buildings to be built, and was occupied by some three hundred birds. I was thrilled at the number of
varieties; there were Jacobins, Pouters, Mondines, and Fantails in
a multitude of colours. There were the Flying Homers—perhaps
most numerous of all—and lastly, the giant White Kings which
supplied squabs for the table. [Aunt Winifred used to remark
dryly that each bird they ate cost about $200.00] Mr. Hudnut took
great pleasure at the loft and usually fed the birds himself—except
on rainy days.

There was a flag pole mounted atop the loft where a large flag
dominated the scene. When the flag was raised, the pigeons dashed
through the openings, mounted high on silken wings, circled a few
times, and then would take off, rising to dizzy heights where half a
hundred of them—or more—would be etched against the blue sky.
This was a thrilling event which their owners watched in awe and
wonder. Time without number the birds would circle the estate,
cutting wider and wider circles until they sometimes became lost
to view. When the flag came down, the birds came with it, and
lost no time in entering the loft to settle in the nave with their
numerous offspring whose voracious appetites seemed never to be
satisfied.

While the Flying Homers have been bred for countless generations for sustained flight, the little spotted Tumblers were another
show. These, too, had been bred for a special purpose:—to perform their acrobatic stunts in mid-air. They would rise slowly, toss
their heads backward, spin like tops in mid-air, and repeat a series

of somersaults as they plunged earthward, but halting abruptly before their little feet touched the earth. Without chart or compass their timing was perfect. When finally they had spent their fury in the air, they would skim along the ground, stop for seconds to preen their feathers, then resume their series of somersaults over and over again until I often became dizzy myself, watching them.

If some of our domestics had been a failure, the pigeons surely made up for it, and I believe Mr. Hudnut found his greatest pleasure among them.

At long last much of the heavy work about the estate had been completed; then came rumors of "The Big House," long in the offing. It stands today upon the hill, a silent sentinel of all it surveys—a living tribute to its designer—a monument that will long endure—and keep alive the dying memories of a happy past. [The future was to prove him wrong.] The Big House was not completed during my time.

As I mentioned in the beginning, Mr. Hudnut was a man of few words, yet always to the point; there was no surplus or sixty-four dollar words used when a simple one would answer. During my stay with him we never grew to be close friends; yet we saw eye to eye the work before us, and as he had told me in the beginning, we would work out each problem together—and we did.

Our closest ties were when we would pick up the threads that Mother Nature had strewn upon the forest floor, as we delved into the private lives of denizens of mountain and forest, as we walked among the land-marks where generation after generation of wild things had fought their battles for supremacy—had lived and died—and devoured each other, just as they had been doing since the dawn of Creation. Looking down from a towering peak one afternoon, thrilled at the panorama spread before us, we sat in silence for some time, and then he spoke, "It would be my wish that those who succeed me will keep this wild refuge inviolate." It was said in those few and simple words, but the sequel there was far greater than the mighty mountains that surrounded us.

Once you asked if I could give names of early workers of the estate, so I am jotting down those I recall who were retained as a staff after the estate got into working gear. These are probably not all, and they may not be of interest. So far as I know, there's but ONE of them still living.

I don't remember the name of the first physical instructor who brought along two children. These were forbidden, and because of them this man was speedily removed. The second one came shortly after and stayed through the summer.

The following are names of workers of the staff who performed various jobs such as those upon any estate of this type. Darius Waldron, North Creek, was a son of the first Superintendent. Joe Hackett, the stone mason, a very important person because of his skill. There was much for him to do. The Hudnuts liked him.

Dan Griffin, Wevertown, the farmer. He kept the lawns and used the horses for various work.

Thomas Thornlow, the architect, whom Mr. Hudnut brought up from the city. He was the principal designer, and builder, of the Big House. He was there when I came and still there when I left. He was an excellent man in his profession, but could talk more and say less than any person whom I have yet met.

John Davison and his son, John Jr., of Wevertown, did mostly extra work near the Hudnut cottage. Lemon Morehouse and Irving Armstrong, Johnsburg, did the pond work, shrubbery and gardens.

Jim Piper of Bakers Mills was road manager. There was much along this line to be done. Piper kept half a dozen men busy. The road was terrible when the family took over the property, but improved greatly thereafter. Piper was then a man well past seventy. He married one of the house servants brought in from New York. It was a swift courtship, created plenty of laughs but was a huge success. They lived at the old Piper place the first you arrive at leaving Foxlair. Mrs. Piper [later, Mrs. Bowman] lives at North Creek with her married daughter, their only child.

Will Hudson of Ticonderoga was the coachman. He was a quiet, unassuming man, nice looking and sported a black mustache which Mrs. Hudnut *ordered removed*! It *was* removed—but he removed himself along with it.

Max Gabeline, a young German fresh from the dock, was brought in from the city. He was a man of all work, especially about the laundry and the kitchen. His hands and feet were larger than needed. He was shy and bashful and would startle at the fall of a match! He was afraid of everyone and slunk away at his own shadow. Max was the scapegoat but was not justified. He was a good boy, needed pity, and seldom got it. I felt sorry for him and watched over him.

Nellie Malarchey, the fat Irish cook at the Men's Quarters, was imported along with some others from New York. She was "Ireland personified," carried a map on her face; a merry widow who kept all of us laughing. Nellie was most loved of all the workers—before or after my time. When cooks failed at the Cottage,

Nellie was often pressed into service, and liked it; if she had no keys to the kitchen, she'd remove the screws in the doors, then help herself.

Nellie LaPrairie and her husband "Coon" of Glens Falls were retained for the winter under the direction of Miss Hunt (Catholics, as was Josephine). We all got along as one big family through the winter.

Cats with the Hudnuts were taboo, but Nellie sneaked in a pet, and kept it all winter because Josephine said "yes." Her word was LAW; we all respected her. Once each week she wrote advising the family of conditions at the estate.

There were many other characters that came and went, but the above are best remembered.

That same evening Mr. Beales came to my room and announced that Mr. Hudnut wished me to be at his office promptly at nine the next moroning. When I entered, he was sitting beside his desk, clad in bathrobe and slippers. He did not appear to notice me when I came in, and I went to the chair that had been assigned me upon my first visit.

It seemed an Eternity before he turned abruptly in his chair, then looking straight at me, he said (in a gruff and unfamiliar voice), "YOUR SERVICES ARE NO LONGER REQUIRED" — period. I was not stunned nor shocked — for hadn't I seen dozens of others get the axe with far less fanfare?

When I got up to leave, I extended my hand in a farewell and friendly gesture, — he refused it! And then added — "I guess it isn't necessary."

This was not a happy ending, for I had loved the estate from the first, and gave them all I had to give. Perhaps I should not mention these happenings, but you asked me. I have told you only the truth.

CHAPTER 18

FOXLAIR: THE ESTATE

In the first decade of the 20th century, the remote valley that had been known as Oregon was transformed into one of the more lavish and least known of the great Adirondack estates. First the barns, staff dormitories and service buildings, then the Casino—or Teahouse— and finally the Big House: all were built, according to local memory, under the supervision of an "architect" from New York named Thomas Thornlow.

"Old Man Thornlow was, no doubt, the best in his day," Willett Randall wrote me, "else Mr. Hudnut wouldn't have considered using him. Italian landscaping and design were among his gifts, with sculpture work a runner-up. He was elderly then, 70 years or more, I'd guess, with a conspicuous faded goatee."

Well, Mr. Thornlow may have been good, but he is not listed anywhere in any New York annals of architects of the period. I have searched. And searched. My guess is that he was an artistic jack-of-all trades whom Richard met in the course of his business building, and that he was hired to carry out designs of Richard's own making.

Together they watched the buildings take shape. They were advocates of imported labor. Richard simply couldn't believe that the native carpenters or stone masons could build *his* kind of house. And he may well have been right. In any event, all the craftsmen were at first imported from New York City. Imagine the glee when it became apparent that the "experts" knew next to nothing about laying rough field stone. At that point John Robbins of Bakers Mills, then a young farm hand on the place, put Mr. Thornlow in touch with two fine native masons, Frank Robbins of Sodom and John Dutchwasher from down below Johnsburg Corners. John Robbins became a tending mason, and Will Ward, of Sodom, was engaged as one of the carpenters. As far as any who remember those days are concerned, this was the entire local contribution to the construction force. The rest came from New York, a few from Saratoga.

The Big House was built on a massive shoulder of solid rock, a knoll that rose at the westerly end of the long valley. The only Adirondack building I have seen that looks as if it belonged in the same design family is the Boathouse at the Antlers. The Big House at Foxlair was considerably larger and altogether more complex. Two hundred and seventy-five feet long, rising on high arched foundations of field stone, it was hip-roofed and many gabled. With balconies, sky lights, ornate pillars, sculpted eaves, carved pediments and protuberances, here a collection of old English chimney-pots, there a colonnade with a look vaguely Italianate—the effect was interesting and original. The glory of the house was its enormous verandah that encompassed the whole valley end, twelve feet above the ground, with a sweeping view of the valley and its mountain walls, as beautiful as any I have ever seen. The house, huge and inappropriate as it always seemed, nonetheless inhabited the crest of the hill as if it belonged there, settled comfortably into its site as surely as a great ship settles into the waves it rides. From the other end of the valley, rising into a frame of tall black pines, it looked like the Hall of the Mountain King.

It was painted, as all the buildings were, that soft, grayed, olive green that I always think of as an Adirondack color, having seen it from earliest childhood on so many little railroad stations and mountain camps. The tall stone ledges of the verandah were recessed for plants, and at one place a huge aviary was built into the wall, an elaborate screened affair, a full story high, in which you would see an ever-changing show of rare and beautiful birds.

Inside, the house was rambling and comfortable. The first floor was dominated by a lofty, lavishly furnished living room, some fifty feet square. Huge picture windows, far ahead of their time in design, made a mural of the mountains on three sides, and the south wall was cen-

Foxlair looking towards the Big House.

Another view of the main house at Foxlair.

Foxlair from Big House lawn shows tennis court, river and North Cottage.

Tea House at Foxlair

One end of the drawing room at Foxlair

tered with a cavernous Norman fireplace; its hood, tunneling straight up to the ceiling, was hand-painted with heraldic scenes of glory, and its massive andirons, forged in Spain, were over five feet tall. The chandeliers were of sculptured copper wire, and its carpets, like those all over the house, were flame-patterned and woven to order in Aubusson, France.

The entrance hall had painted murals on the walls, extending up along the staircase to the second floor. These murals depicted a regular Garden of Eden of flora and fauna, handsome in a florid way, but rather more Tahitian than Adirondack.

Almost all of the furniture was of French manufacture, much of it, particularly the bedroom chairs and settees, especially designed to incorporate the use of lace from Evelyn's family in Ireland. This lace, woven of thick, ivory-colored linen threads, was patterned like Toile de Jouy, with figures and landscapes and laid over colored silk as upholstery in all the bedrooms.

The master bedroom was almost as large as the drawing room beneath it, and its treasure was a porcelain stove, brought tile by tile from Limoges, and assembled at Foxlair. It was tall and narrow, with a crenelated top and it burned tiny birch logs. The tiles were white, decorated with wildflowers in shades of rose and pink.

The Big House was an amusement. Like the other great houses of the Adirondacks, it was called a "camp," but it made no attempt, as many another camp-castle of the mountains did, to graft luxury upon indigenous art. Here there were no Native American Indian rugs or birchbark commodes. Foxlair was an Adirondack stronghold furnished like a French chateau. Richard Hudnut loved the wilderness . . . outdoors.

And though he truly gloried in the magnificence of Foxlair's natural setting, he would mold even that to his imagination. The winding valley was sheared and pruned into a nine-hole golf course, with a sprinkler system to keep the greens like velvet. A stone-walled pool was stocked with trout; a sequestered curve of the Sacandaga was dammed to make a special showplace for Richard's rare and prized collection of fish, which glinted like many colored gems in the clear river water. The wilderness, so wild and beautiful, became a landscaped showplace.

The Casino, where afternoon tea was served and dances were sometimes held, was vaguely Japanese in style. Nearby was the tennis court; further along the river was a shingled pump house, built with twin turrets, a little folly from the Brothers Grimm. The Pigeon Barn was pure

Aubrey Beardsley, with half-timbered arches in art nouveau style. The chauffeur's house and carriage barns were solid Dutch Colonial, and North Cottage, used as a guest house after the Big House was completed, was a beautiful typical Adirondack "cottage," with deeply sloping shingled roof, gabled windows, and a criss-cross railing on the porch that ran around three sides. The caretaker, or superintendent's, house and barns at the northeast end of the estate, had the look of a New England farm. As we said earlier, it's hard to imagine any unity of style composed of so many disparate parts, but there *was* a Foxlair ambience. The grayed, mountain-green paint color drew everything together, but the force that united the very different buildings was the land itself. The high mountain walls, in some commanding natural manner, gathered the many parts, incongruous separately, into a harmony of sorts. Foxlair had its own character, more so than many another great estate where everything is designed alike. It was a monument to the eclectic taste and arrogant individuality of Evelyn and Richard Hudnut.

CHAPTER 19
FOXLAIR:
THE PEOPLE

Life in the early years—up until 1917, when Evelyn Hudnut died, had an anecdotal quality, for Evelyn was eccentric, or at least "a character," and everything she said or did seemed colorful. In the flamboyant society of New York and Paris she was just one of many, but to the people of Johnsburg and Bakers Mills, Sodom and North Creek, who made up the working forces and "neighborhood" of Foxlair, she was a rare bird, indeed, and as such her activity was frequently reported, in wonder or derision.

Just her *size* was the stuff of folklore. Occasionally she would be driven to North Creek by Mr. Waddell, her coachman, in a brilliantly decorated carriage with fringe, tassels, and lamps, and I have heard how people would stop on the street just to stare at this enormous woman, who never left the carriage, but sat there in state like a huge blonde Buddha, indifferent to her audience or to the attention she attracted.

Many articles of household convenience had to be specially built to accommodate her outsize proportions, causing no end of amusement. Time and again I have heard old-timers allude to stories about Aunt Evelyn that "we *could* tell you but we *wouldn't*," as if the tale would shock our later, less exotic, generation of the family. That she had a sharp bite and a raunchy sense of humor, was well known. But there were darker tales too, which neighbors have felt they were doing me a kindness in forgetting. However, I pried the following story from Willett Randall and have always wished that I had not.

In his written memoir, Willett mentioned the fact that a twilight diversion for Richard and Evelyn was to go to the fox's lair, and watch it being fed. What he did not write, but later told me, was that the sport for Evelyn was to feed the hungry fox a *live* chicken and watch, fascinated, as he tore it apart, and devoured it.

She used to sit on the balcony outside her bedroom with a spyglass trained on the farm hands and gardeners at work around the golf course or tennis court. John Robbins told me that several men left because they were unable to bear the discomfort of this distant scrutiny. She loved to drive about the place in her Sicilian donkey cart and often supervised or criticized, sotto voce, the farming procedures.

Evelyn's personal maid for many years was Elisabeth Ahoe, who was brought straight to Foxlair after she debarked from the boat which had brought her from Denmark. She had been hired through an agency in New York.* She had kinder memories of her colorful mistress. She remembered that Evelyn loved nothing better than arranging flowers in huge bouquets which were placed all about the house each day. And she would paint, for hours at a time in the studio alcove of her enormous bedroom, beneath the skylight installed for this purpose. She remembered, too, that Richard would often spend his mornings in the Casino, where he had a vast array of chemical equipment for experiments with new fragrances and emulsions.

She described parties in the Casino for the weekend guests, and dances, with orchestras imported from New York for special occasions. She remembered, too, a well-stocked wine cellar, and added rather primly, "Not that the Hudnuts drank at all. They only kept it for their guests."

Finally, Elisabeth said that although they had many, many guests during her employment at Foxlair, the "nicest ones that ever did come were Mr. Hudnut's brother, Dr. William, and his wife. They used to come from down Speculator way. They were *real* people." She said this, not realizing in the least that these were my grandparents.

A fact of life at Foxlair, which undermined each working day and robbed it of pleasure, was that the lord and lady of the manor treated

---

* Elisabeth married Jim Piper, once superintendent at Foxlair. After his death, she married Mr. Bowman: she is now deceased.

most of their servants and helpers with little-disguised distrust. This did not go down well with the local people, who are a proud and independent mountain folk, not used to being patronized or suspected. The estate provided dozens of jobs in its heyday: "Most everyone worked there, one time or another," but that is not to say that the people were happy there. Much of the time there was an undercurrent of contempt for the city folk who acted so almighty. It is true, as we said earlier, that Richard Hudnut was cold and impersonal, and you have read of the curt and unpleasant way in which he dismissed Willett Randall from his employ. It should be said (not in defense but in an effort to understand) that he was brought up in a world where there was still a clearly defined servant class and some servants cultivated an obsequious demeanor that put their employers on their guard. Many of this type came to Foxlair; almost all the house staff fit into this category. They were a breed apart from the proud natives, who eyed their subservience with disgust. Petty thievery doubtless began with the imported staff at first, but the local people saw it happening and some were bound to follow suit. Whether the Hudnuts' lack of trust was the cause or the result of the steady pilfering that went on is a matter for conjecture. But I am certain it created an unhealthy atmosphere, and accounted for such daily indignities as, for example, unlocking the stores each morning to measure out what the cook would need, then locking them up again.

The chefs were French or Danish; the seamstresses, French; the masseur, Swedish. There were seldom less than three butlers and footmen, usually Italian, lording it over a retinue of Irish maids. It would have been a wonder had there *not* been plenty of backstairs politiking and shenanigans with such an international assortment in this isolated, lonely situation. Add to this the natural rivalry of house and hamlet, and it is understandable that beneath the ordered surface of life at Foxlair there seethed a daily cauldron of intrigue.

The essence of the tension was clear when my father showed me the great leather mail pouch that carried the mail to and from Foxlair to North Creek. Each morning its clasp was padlocked by Uncle Richard, and unlocked by the postmaster, who alone had the matching key. He would take out the mail for New York, put in the mail that had arrived, lock it up again, and send it back with the coachman.

The kindest way I ever heard it summed up was by old Mr. John Robbins, who remarked in his dry way, "Guess you might say that Mr. Hudnut put too much confidence in some of the help, not enough in the others."

This memory of arrogance and distrust on the one side and feelings of offended pride on the other made a tension between the family and the valley that remained to haunt us for many years afterwards. When my grandfather came to settle at Windover, ten miles distant from Foxlair, it was a long time before he was accepted by anyone as the neighbor he wished to be. To this day you can hear an old one marvel that "two brothers would be so different."

Evelyn Hudnut died in 1917. I have been told that for Richard, she seemed almost an alter ego, an emotional twin as well as a wife. Surely Foxlair was their joint creation.

Grandmother remembers Uncle Richard calling at the time of Evelyn's death to say, "Please tell William that the dear little woman has passed away." She said that he sounded sepulchral, a heartbroken and wounded man.

CHAPTER 20
THE VALENTINO SUMMER

Three years later, in the summer of 1920, Richard Hudnut brought a new wife to Foxlair. The general concensus of the resident staff was that she was a great improvement over her predecessor. She was the former Winifred deWolfe, three times divorced, a successful interior decorator, and a person of great charm and style. One of her forebears was a great Mormon patriarch, Heber C. Kimball, Brigham Young's first lieutenant and pioneer of the Utah territory. She brought high spirits and warmth to this marriage, and new life to Foxlair and its master.

She also brought a grown daughter, a fascinating young woman whose professional name, chosen in an earlier career as a ballerina in the Kosloff Ballet, was Natacha Rambova. She was an artist in Hollywood, a designer of costumes and sets, and she was evidently so compatible a part of the new marriage that Richard adopted her; her legal name became Winifred Hudnut, second to her mother, but she was never called anything but Natacha. It was her marriage to Rudolph Valentino that put Foxlair in the news for a season, and provided that remote valley of the Adirondacks with its own drama festival. The story, as I have pieced it together from Valentino biographies and particularly from the relatively new Rambova biography, *Madame*

Richard Alexander Hudnut

Winifred Hudnut, second wife of Richard

Herbert, Winifred and Richard Hudnut

Richard Alexander Hudnut at Foxlair

Valentino, by Michael Morris, began in Hollywood.

Alla Nazimova, one of the greatest stars of her day in early Hollywood history, was a mentor to Natacha. She had met her through Alexandre Kosloff of the Kosloff Ballet, liked her immediately, knew her work, admired her ability, and persuaded Cecil B. DeMille to employ her as designer in charge of casting and production for all of Nazimova's pictures. "Nazimova never argued with Natacha Rambova, who was cold in her fury and usually correct in her judgments."

> Natacha Rambova was a recognized genius in Hollywood. Perhaps she was accorded the title of genius because many didn't understand her work. She was years ahead of her time in set and costume designs. She was daring and original, tireless and independent. She was good and she knew it. She did not need others to praise her to recognize her own talents.
>
> (Oberfirst)

At the time that Natacha and Valentino met, Nazimova was to star in Metro Goldwyn Mayer's forthcoming production of *Camille*. They were having a hard time casting the role of Armand. The actor must be sensitive, but not too much so, boyish but not too much so; above all he must have a romantic quality. Nazimova had seen the new Italian, Rudolph Valentino, who had had his first role in *The Four Horsemen of the Apocalypse*, and now he was at work in a secondary role in *Uncharted Seas*, a movie about Eskimos, in the process of being filmed on the MGM lot. She was convinced that he was perfect for the part of Armand, but she would do nothing without the consent of her art director, Natacha. Oberfirst describes the meeting:

> When Valentino met Natacha Rambova, he wasn't "just right" for the part—he was bundled in a fur-lined coat and was wearing thick-soled, high laced boots. Flakes of mica (imitation snow) still lay upon his lashes. He had just finished shooting a scene in "Uncharted Seas" and had rushed across the lot for the meeting with Nazimova and her art director. He was perspiring freely and the make-up streaked his face. Natacha walked around him slowly, raised an eyebrow in Nazimova's direction, nodded and disappeared.
>
> "You've got the job," Nazimova said.
>
> Valentino was happy. He didn't know why he had gotten the job, but he was glad to get it. . . . From the first moment he saw Natacha, he was entranced. Her dark flowing hair encircled a delicate face. Her blue eyes were like rare jewels set off by her soft white skin. As Nazimova expressed it to a Hollywood columnist, "You should have

seen him! He stood there staring at her as though he had never seen a beautiful woman before in his life."

He had been married earlier to a rising young star named Jean Acker. Now, deeply in love with Natacha, he set about getting a divorce. The new courtship was long, and a less optimistic or romantic soul simply never would have put up with the obstacles. Natacha told him from the first that her career meant more to her than anything, and she meant it! He was beautiful to behold, it was true, but he was too worshipful and slightly gauche in the eyes of this cool and highly polished young woman. Still, he made himself a fixture in her life. When he could have been the center of parties in the boom town of Hollywood, he chose instead to sit in his car and wait for Natacha, who worked at the studio late most nights. He planted her garden for her, painted her furniture, brought her animals — a pair of Great Danes, a Pekingese, a golden lion cub. He cooked wonderful Italian meals for her, nursed her when she was ill — in short, cherished her. And he brought fun into her organized and ascetic life. First he just made her laugh, and then he wore her down, and at last she loved him, and they became engaged. The Hudnuts went to Hollywood to meet Rudy. Winifred was dazzled by him. Richard was delighted by the genuine warmth and ingenuousness of the young Italian, but most impressed, I suspect, with his worldly success.

In March of 1922, Valentino's interlocutory decree of divorce was granted, but it was not final until a year from that date, and in the meantime he and Natacha could not legally marry. However, in the face of all legal advice — and it is hard to understand how Natacha Rambova could have joined in such a spontaneous bit of folly — they decided to elope to Mexico. It was all the fashion, and others among their friends had done it and gotten away with it. But Rudy was already too famous for such anonymity and they would pay for their escapade most dearly. Natacha wrote this account of the wedding, which took place in Mexicali on May 13th:

> The ceremony was performed at the Mayor's house, with a stringed orchestra on the porch and the Civil Band in the yard to lend a musical background. The whole town turned out for the festival.
> The wedding breakfast, composed entirely of real Mexican dishes, was also held at the Mayor's house. This lasted until seven in the evening, when we finally took our leave with much shouting and band playing, the Mayor and the Chief of Police accompanying us to

Natacha Rambova and Rudolph Valentino

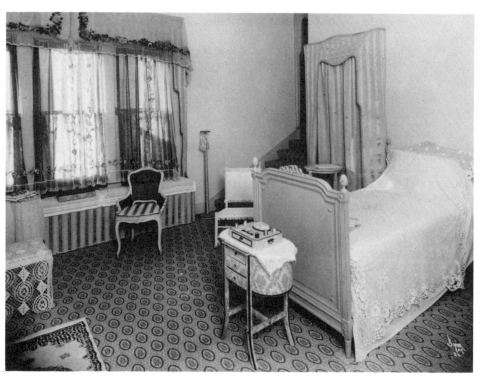

Natacha's pale blue room

Valentino's room adjoined Natacha's.

the border in their car.

The tragic and immediate ending to all our dreams came the next day. From the studio, by long distance telephone, we were frantically summoned back to Los Angeles. We left without even a coat or suitcase, motoring continuously until we arrived that evening at nine o'clock.

The trumped-up charge of bigamy, Rudy's arrest, and my hurried departure for New York on the advice of Mr. Gilbert, are too well known to be gone over again.

(Rudy)

It is precisely because we do *not* know these details today that I include them. The whole thing seems archaic to us now, but in those days divorce and quick remarriage, even in Hollywood, were neither common nor sanctioned; the studios, immensely powerful, feared public disapproval, which could seriously jeopardize a star's career. All this was responsible for the year of hide-and-seek played by this illegally married pair. And I have always suspected that Valentino's agent played the agony of their separation to its hilt. Seldom has any movie romance received more day-by-day coverage in the press. Tabloids, movie magazines—even the respectable *New York Times*—kept the movie-going public informed of Valentino's every move. Natacha, who hated any intrusion of her privacy, went into seclusion. Winifred wrote:

> After Rudy's and Natacha's marriage in Mexico, Natacha immediately came to us at the Biltmore. We were here for a few days, intending to sail for Europe. When we saw how wretchedly unhappy Natacha was, we cancelled our passage and decided to open Foxlair.
>
> After being settled in the quiet of all that mountain loveliness, we found Natacha's grief inconsolable. She worried constantly for fear that the newspaper notoriety might ruin Rudy's career. The children [i.e., Rudy and Natacha] wrote and telegraphed back and forth daily and Natacha rode for miles two or three times a week [to North Creek] to put in long distance calls to Hollywood. Rudy was at this time doing "The Young Rajah" which was expected to be finished in a few weeks.

(Rudy)

My father, Herbert Hudnut, was at Foxlair during part of those weeks. He found it hard to warm to this icy step-cousin; even Natacha's beauty failed to move him. He said that she always wore long skirts to hide her legs, which were heavy, and that she also wore turbans to match the skirts — all in exotic, glorious patterns of silk. He remembered that Natacha's gloom was impenetrable, that the atmosphere was funereal, and that he was delighted to get away.

He also told me that the telegrams back and forth from Hollywood were the gossip of North Creek. They would arrive each day, often five hundred words or more; classics of Jazz Age baby-talk. Valentino always addressed Natacha as "Babykins." To the telegraph operator, who had grim occasion to meet her every day or so when she came to wire or telephone, the pet name seemed hilarious. But then, Valentino referred to Winifred as "Muzzie," to cold Richard as "Uncle Dickie"; his language was flowery and laced with Italian like a secret code. Small wonder that these messages, clicking in and out over the wireless each day, were circulated through these valleys of the Adirondacks. They were the very stuff of class humor — the inanities of haughty and pretentious people.

But that summer the laughter gave way to a kind of grudging anticipation, for it was on the grapevine that Valentino was coming to Foxlair. For some reason not at once apparent to modern view, there was great need for secrecy. At any rate, Valentino traveled incognito, disguised in a black beard, which only identified him more readily for the throngs of reporters and gossip columnists who met each train as he progressed across the country. With him was Douglas Gerrard, an English actor, film director, and old friend, whose exaggerated attempts to shield him inevitably attracted all the more attention. But his public seemed to adore the whole farce. They idolized the man, and they had an image of the romantic hero, tracking down his cool princess in the remote mountain lair where she was hidden by her rich family. People in North Creek knew he was coming and pretended not to. Either they cared little — or did him the honor of believing that he really wanted secrecy. Mountain people tend to take celebrity lightly.

Fletcher Dunkley and his family lived a few miles from Foxlair on the country road that wound its way from North Creek, passing through Sodom and Bakers Mills. He was a farmer, and he supplied eggs to the Big House larder. One of his daughters, a dark-eyed youngster named Sophronia, was limp with excitement. Valentino was going to drive within a stone's throw of her own front porch. Phrony, now gray-haired, remembers that they took very seriously the fact that he was incognito, that she and her sister were told that they might watch from the bedroom window, but on no account was anybody to be out on the porch as if they were *expecting* anybody, God forbid. She said that they waited and waited — it seemed like hours — and then in a cloud of dust a long touring car roared by, scattering pebbles in all directions. Phrony thinks she caught a glimpse of a man with beard and dark glasses and a beret, but she's willing to admit that it was more a feeling than a bona fide sighting. After so many years, with an apologetic laugh, she admits that it was a thrill, even just to see his passing car, and to know that he was *living* so close by.

Natacha's mother, Winifred Hudnut, continues her first-hand tale:

> It was the first good laugh Natacha had had for weeks when Rudy arrived at Foxlair. His own mother would hardly have recognized him. His face was covered with a heavy beard, and his eyes hidden by big dark goggles. He wore a tweed golf suit, with a golf bag slung over his shoulders and soft grey cap pulled well over his face. He also wore a smile that reached from ear to ear.
>
> Douglas Gerrard [Gerry] came with him. Our small party was now complete. Foxlair was an ideal place for a happy vacation. Its twelve hundred and more acres of mountain land with its lake and fishing pond and golf links and deer hunting, gave the children plenty of opportunity for good sport.
>
> They practically lived in their bathing suits, swimming, boating and golfing the whole day long, never thinking of dressing until time for dinner. I used to sit up in my boudoir and hear those three screaming and laughing as if no cloud had ever come to shadow their happiness. This exhilarating country life with good food, alternate exercise and rest, soon brought the ruddy glow of health to their cheeks. They were no longer the fretful, anxious children of a few weeks before.

Winifred's retelling of events for Natacha's book was written in the style of the fan magazine, but then, she herself must have been overcome with the romance of the situation. Even so, the visit was not all as lyrical as she described it. The Hudnuts were formal and fastidious. While Winifred reports nothing but sweetness and light, the memories of some of the others who lived through those days at Foxlair are rather different. Katherine Armstrong, whose father, Harry, was the Superintendent, remembers distinctly that, according to the servant's reports, Rudy's somewhat primitive table manners annoyed Uncle Richard immensely, that each meal was a tense affair with everyone making an effort not to notice his incredible sound effects.

Katherine remembers the marked difference between Natacha and

Valentino as she saw them walking each day. Far from being in bathing suits all day, as Aunt Winifred remembered, Katherine reports that Natacha was always a perfect picture in lovely linen or silk dresses and picturesque leghorn hats, and that Valentino slouched along beside her, uncouth looking, often in riding breeches that looked as if he had slept in them. "But Katherine," I remember saying, "Mrs. Bowman said he was *beautiful*." "She's right," Katherine freely admitted, "He was a beautiful man."

And here is an adventure of those days, written by Winifred Hudnut, for Natacha's book, *Rudy*:

> At Foxlair we never troubled to close or lock the doors and windows at night. But at about six o'clock one evening, one of the maids saw a man drive up in a Ford car, which he parked in the heavy shrubbery below the kitchen. This appeared rather suspicious to her, but as Mr. Hudnut had gone to New York that morning on business, and I was in bed with a sick headache, not wishing to worry me, she did not mention the incident but locked up the entire back of the house.
>
> After dinner the night grew intensely dark and heavy showers came on. It was the blackest night we had had.
>
> Natacha, Rudy, and Gerry were playing poker in the big front living room which had a screen door leading onto the verandah. This verandah stood twelve feet from the ground and surrounded the house. From where Natacha was sitting she could look out to the verandah, but because of the darkness could but dimly see through the screen door.
>
> Suddenly this door began to slightly and cautiously open. This startled Natacha and she said in a low voice, "Don't appear to notice but I think someone is on the verandah—I saw the screen door pulled open a little."
>
> "Nonsense," said Rudy, "It's only the wind."
>
> "There's no wind blowing," answered Natacha, "the night is too sultry."
>
> Just then she saw the door again carefully opened and back of it the slight outline of a man. In a still lower voice she said, "I see a man looking in—Uncle Dickie's revolver is upstairs in his top bureau drawer. You go up and get it, Gerry, and Rudy and I will keep playing as if we noticed nothing."
>
> Saying in a natural voice, "It's my turn to get the drinks tonight," Gerry arose and left the room.
>
> There sat Natacha and Rudy, waiting for Gerry, never dreaming that he had taken the revolver and gone down the back stairs, out the kitchen door, and tiptoed stealthily along the verandah to the front of the house.
>
> Suddenly they heard Gerry's voice ring out, "Damn you, hold up

your hands or I'll shoot!" Gerry had taken the eavesdropper by surprise. The man now rushed to the edge of the verandah, and as Gerry thought he was about to jump over, he clutched him by the coat.

Catlike, the man turned on him and, seizing him with both hands by the back of the neck, pitched Gerry over the wall to the ground twelve feet below. Gerry fell flat on his back, but as the rain luckily had softened the earth, no damage was done. Strangely enough, in all this scuffling the revolver was not discharged. The fall quite knocked the wind out of Gerry, and it took a few seconds for him to collect himself. Springing to his feet and turning toward the sound of the man's departing footsteps, he fired in rapid succession three shots. Out of the darkness there sounded an agonizing scream. Then dead silence.

The children, who had been standing spellbound listening to this, rushed to the window and loudly called for Gerry. No answer. Then Rudy, knowing there was a shotgun upstairs in my room, rushed up to get it, Natacha at his heels.

At Foxlair we had no electric lights, depending upon oil lamps and candles. As I had one of my bad headaches I was lying in the dark, terrified at all this excitement.

Rudy rushed in saying, "The shotgun, the shotgun — Gerry's been killed!"

"The gun's in the bay window," I answered. In a second Rudy had it in his hands.

"Don't you do it," screamed Natacha, "You may be killed or disfigured for life! Remember you belong to the screen — the public!"

Then another tussle began in the dark. Natacha was trying to get the gun away from Rudy. Chairs and tables crashed to the floor. I could hear my photograph frames and bowls of flowers smashing. I jumped from the bed and tried to find the matches to light a candle, but trembled so from intense fright that it was a minute or two before I succeeded.

By this time the children, like magic, had rushed down the stairs, Natacha hanging on to Rudy's coat tails. I followed, holding the candle, only to see them madly dashing out the front door and down the side path. As I entered the living room, there stood Gerry. And this was my greatest fright of all. I mistook him for the burglar — the spy — or whatever he might have been.

It was impossible to recognize Gerry as he was soaked to the skin and so covered with mud that only the whites of his eyes and his white teeth showed through. At sight of him I threw up both arms and let out a shriek for help.

In a mud-muffled voice he piped up, "It's Gerry. Don't you know me? I hit him alright, but I can't find him!"

Then we both called from the verandah for Natacha and Rudy to
come back. But there was no answer. In a short time the rain-
bedraggled children returned. They had found nothing. Gerry was
still convinced he had killed or seriously wounded the man. So, taking lanterns, the three of them went out again in search of the victim.

I remained, huddled in my dressing gown, and in my bare feet,
chilled through and through, but too frightened to return to my
room. After a vain search they all returned. The man had evidently
escaped. It was useless in the pitch darkness to search further.

After all had quieted down and the children were fast asleep, I
heard in the early dawn the chug-chug of a motor. Stepping out to
the upper verandah leading from my bedroom, I saw the little Ford
disappearing rapidly down the drive and out the big front gates.

That morning we found the man's footprints and the imprint of
his body where he had fallen over a low wall. Several broken cigars
had tumbled from his pockets and lay in the mud.

After breakfast the three young people motored to North Creek
station and inquired of the station master if anyone had left by the
early train. There were so few homes around North Creek that this
man knew everybody. He told them that a stranger had driven up in
a Ford with another man. The man, he said, was well dressed, tall,
slender, and good-looking. He seemed to be in pain, as he walked
with two canes, holding one foot from the ground. This man, having
bought a ticket for New York, boarded the train, while the other
drove quickly away.

Who and what this man's mission was—whether a burglar or a
detective—I am sure he hopes never again to meet Gerry.

Soon after this excitement the whole party left for New York,
Natacha and Valentino going through the farce of traveling separately.
I imagine that at Foxlair they enjoyed the greatest measure of privacy
they would ever know. Adirondack people of the old school are by
nature respecters of privacy, not apt to be thrown off balance by a
famous face; they may have snickered at their baby talk, so ludicrous
over Western Union, but once in their midst they were treated with the
elaborate indifference that often marks the proud mountain person's
communication with outsiders.

One of the few people to see them was Elisabeth Ahoe Piper [Betty
Bowman], who had come as personal maid to Evelyn Hudnut and remained as former workman, Jim Piper's, wife. By now she was mistress
of a farmhouse on the road to North Creek, mother of several children.

Every other day the Valentinos would drive up in their long low sports car to bring their personal laundry to her. They could not tolerate the heavy hand of the Big House laundress with their monogrammed silk underwear, and implored Mrs. Piper, who had a true European respect for fine fabrics, to do their work.

She later described them to me in her shy way: "He was a *beautiful* man, so kind. And she was beautiful, though not so kind. Oh, they were a *beautiful* couple."

They never came to Foxlair again. After their second — and legal — marriage they led an increasingly frenetic life, traveling back and forth from Hollywood to Europe. They made their European headquarters the Hudnut Chateau at Juan Les Pins on the Riviera, where Winifred had decorated an entire apartment for them in the then modern Beaux Arts style. The furniture was of satin-black lacquer, and their enormous bed was completely round, covered with one of the magnificent Spanish shawls that the Valentinos collected. Rudy installed elaborate motion picture equipment so that his movies could be shown at the chateau, and this quickly became a feature of any visit at the big house.

Rudolph and Natacha also became deeply involved with the world of psychic phenomena, spiritualist manifestations, and automatic writing. They believed passionately, and were accompanied on many of their travels by a trusted medium. He was always installed at the chateau when they were in residence.

Natacha divorced Valentino in 1929, a short while before his death. After his studio had removed her control over his pictures, she seemed to lose interest in his career. She hated life in Hollywood, called it a "gilded hell," and took no trouble to disguise her disdain. Off to France she went, and was at the chateau the summer my grandparents were visiting. Valentino followed her and arrived to find that she had left the day before. He died on the following August 23rd, tragically young, mourned by millions of fans. "On his deathbed and into his permanent tomb he wore the slave bracelet Natacha had given him. It was the emblem of the only true love of his life."

Most biographers of Valentino blame Natacha for the fact of their marriage's failure. They blame her artistic ambition and classic taste, as well as her coldness of temperment. But Natacha's own book gives a very different impression: Hollywood itself came between them, and she was strong enough to leave a life that became unbearable to her. The book also describes a kind of spiritual reunion with Valentino, and gives messages that came to her after his death through the medium who was constantly with her.

Natacha remains an enigma. After Valentino's death, she pursued several careers and married a second time to a Spanish nobleman. She wrote prodigiously—columns for syndicated newspapers, a standard text on judo used in the training camps of the U.S. Army during World War II, and she edited three volumes on Egyptian religions and artifacts for the Bollingen Foundation. She studied the work of Carl Jung, and was close to several members of the Eranos circle. When she died in 1966, the *New York Times* obituary describes a woman whose life was widely varied and fascinating, limited only by her own preference for seclusion and anonymity.

The only members of my branch of the Hudnut family who spent any significant amount of time with Natacha—my father, at Foxlair and my grandparents, at Juan les Pins—had very little to say of her that was flattering or endearing. They found her totally self-involved, they were unsympathetic with her spiritualist leanings, and they attributed Richard's abandonment of Foxlair to her lack of interest in returning after the Valentino summer.

Many years of enquiry and the sharper insight of Women's Studies have helped me to see Natacha in a very different light. She was in so many ways a remarkable woman, decades ahead of her time in her pursuit of excellence and integrity in her art. She has at last had an appreciative biographer in Michael Morris, author of *Madam Valentino*. Her varied achievements in later years give credence to Morris's belief that it was Natacha's real genius that created and empowered the myth of Rudolph Valentino. When they met, Valentino was an "impoverished Italian-born actor with but one hit on his resume." Morris continues:

> Together, their creative energies left an indelible mark on Hollywood history, and they became one of the most attractive and talked-about couples in the western world. Their story was Pygmalion and Galatea in reverse, the only time in Hollywood history that a woman fashioned a male star to an image of her imagination and shared that image with millions.
>
> (Morris)

He explains the shrewd and intuitive ways in which first the image and then the romantic character of the Valentino myth was created. He believes that the slave bracelet, worn to the grave, was Valentino's tribute to Natacha's role in his life and far more. Morris uses it to posit a most unusual perspective on their relationship:

> The slave bracelet was a symbol not only of Rambova's dominating artistic spirit, but of Valentino's unquestioning love. This image of the "Latin lover" was not a shrewdly calculated concept invented by Hollywood studios, nor was it even an artistic idea that sprang from Rambova's fertile mind. Rather it was the reflection of a very passionate physical and emotional relationship that existed between them in the mere six years together.

The honeymoon at Foxlair was perhaps the happiest part.

CHAPTER 21
THE LAST DAYS OF FOXLAIR

Uncle Richard died on October 30th, 1928 at the Chateau Juan Les Pins. Increasingly in his last years this beautiful place had become his chosen home. He came to America only when business called him, and even though he made elaborate plans to visit various members of the family while he was in this country, he invariably cancelled them and booked early passage back home to France. He wrote Father from the St. Regis during his last trip to New York, April 14, 1928: "Here I am once more in this modern Babylon. There are mobs of people everywhere, all in haste to reach somewhere. I feel among them, but not of them."

His last letter, undated, from the Chateau, urged my parents to visit him, and delicately but firmly offered the opinion that their three babies in three years could "put too much strain on Edith without having at least two servants. Do not think I am interfering," he continued, "but young husbands are sometimes thoughtless in such matters!" He told this nephew, whom he had always loved, that he was carrying his 73 years "with as much pleasure as one could ask," adding a note sure to please: "Herbert, I feel also that I am growing spiritually." Richard spared the young minister the fact that the direction of his growth was towards spiritualism, with two mediums installed at the chateau, and seances being held each night.

Foxlair had been discreetly up for sale since 1926*, but had attracted no buyers. Richard and Winifred had spent no time there since 1923. Each summer there was a small staff in residence, and the Big House was always groomed and ready for its owners. But they had abandoned their jewel in the Adirondacks. They never returned.

People have always wondered why. In the preceeding chapter I noted that my family has attributed this to Natacha's reluctance to return to the scene of her greatest happiness with Valentino. I am more inclined to think that Winifred found Foxlair the least bit haunted by her predecessor, Evelyn Hudnut. Winifred preferred the glamour and society of the Riviera life, and so in those later years did Richard — though to the end he maintained Foxlair as his legal address.

But there may have been another reason that even in business trips to the States, Richard Hudnut never returned to Oregon country, from 1923 until his death in 1928. Ernest Noxon, the respected proprietor of Braley and Noxon Hardware Store in North Creek, once told me — with the air of one divulging a dreadful secret — that on a night in the summer of 1923 a bunch of young fellows had been having a merry drinking party at Farrell's Hotel, and got the idea of riding out to Foxlair to do a little mischief. Their target was the pond where Richard Hudnut's prize fish were kept. These were rare and gloriously colored fish, some irridescent, some with fins like chiffon, that flowed and rippled in the moonlit water. According to Mr. Noxon, these young men, more in drunken prank than in malice, killed the fish. The story ended, "Mr. Hudnut had a lot of aggravation on the place that summer, and seems this was the last straw." He left next day and never came back, so goes the tale.

From Uncle Richard's death until the summer of 1938 when Aunt Winifred gave Foxlair to the Police Athletic League of New York City, she returned only once, after which she wrote my father, "The memories were too sad, and so I remained for only one short day." She was extremely generous in inviting our family to use the place. My grandparents spent summers there during the move from Wamakedah and the renovations of Windover, and they were also given as much Foxlair furniture as they wanted to use for their own Big House. Later,

---

* Katherine Armstrong told me only last summer (1992) that two interested prospective buyers were the Wright brothers, Orville and Wilbur, thinking to build a flying school. The golf course was to be the runway — but would need expensive lengthening. She said her father imagined that the Depression probably "killed the idea."

This gives at idea of the length of the Big House. It shows the skylight in the master bedroom.

Richard's chateau at Juan les Pins; Valentino and Natacha at the steps.

when I was very young, my father and mother had the use of North Cottage at Foxlair for three summers. Those summers shaped my earliest and indelible impressions of the Adirondacks.

During my childhood vacations at Foxlair I came to know and love the Armstrongs. Harry Armstrong came to be Superintendent of the estate in 1918 and remained in that post for the next twenty years. He and his wife, Nellie, were related to a host of families in that part of the mountains, from Johnsburg to Irishtown. They came with their daughter, Katherine, to live in the farmhouse at the north end of the property, a roomy old house that had originally been a part of the Oregon community. And it must be said that they came with a certain fear and trembling, for although Richard Hudnut hadn't specifically stated it to Harry, it was a well-known fact that his employees were not allowed to have children living with them at Foxlair. For the first few months their child, Katie, was kept well out of sight. Initially, things were nip and tuck anyway, for Richard had reneged on his promise to furnish the farmhouse for the Armstrongs. This had been his method of dealing with his staff in many instances, and had scarcely endeared him to previous employees. However, Harry Armstrong loved Foxlair and was determined to make a go of it, and so he exercised all of his patience and understanding of his eccentric employer, as well as the firm insistence that "Mr. Hudnut would surely want to keep his end of their agreement, and the plain fact was that he had promised to furnish the farmhouse for us." In the end Richard sent the furniture to them but with little graciousness and a great show of having been pressured. It was precisely this kind of behavior that caused people like Grandfather to judge him harshly. He could have afforded to be *so* generous, but seldom chose to.

Nellie Armstrong was tiny as a bird and bird-like in her sparrow quickness and bright, chirpy quality. She seemed to be related at least distantly to everyone in the Town of Johnsburg and this, plus the fact that Harry was just simply one of the most charming men in that valley or anywhere else, made them a well-acquainted and well-loved pair.

My grandmother and grandfather got to know them on one of their visits to Foxlair; it was a fast-formed friendship that lasted all their lives. When Will sold Wamakedah, he asked Harry to find a new property for him. They agreed that Harry Armstrong would act as agent for him and buy the property in his own name, for it is sad but true that any price in the valley would have been trebled if it were known that a Hudnut was buying it.

After the Ross property had been bought and was in the process of being transformed into "Windover," the Armstrongs spent several summers as close neighbors of the William Hudnuts; it was during these Foxlair summers that our families became fast friends. Harry and my grandfather hunted and fished together, and Harry acted as guide through these new areas of Adirondack wilderness. He also took on the job of laying out the vegetable gardens at Windover and supervising the planting of trees and landscaping. He became the first caretaker of the Windover property.

My summers at Foxlair were when I was aged six, seven and eight. They have the quality of a remembered dream — hazy, disconnected pictures, perversely distinct. Our home there was North Cottage.

North Cottage was a romantic house and I responded to it whole-heartedly. It smelled of cedar logs and kerosene lamps, and a less definable fragrance that I always thought of as French. It was a child-like notion and was probably the smell of mustiness or mildew. The large living and dining room had a handsome cobbled fireplace with bookcases on either side. Casement windows with leaded panes and a divided staircase to the second floor gave a story book character to the cottage, as did the windows in the eaves of the four upper bedrooms. There was a study, an extra bedroom and bath on the first floor, and beyond the big archaic kitchen was a servant's room as well. Everything downstairs was furnished nicely, with an incongruous mixture of fine rustic pieces and French furniture. The china was so beautiful, all one solid color, a deep pink which my later acquisition of worldly knowledge knows to have been French Rose Pompadour. How amusing to think of our using it for "every-day" in that cottage — a family with four tiny children. How much of it was broken by Elizabeth, my mother's cook, I shudder to think!

The days began, I remember, with the wild cawing of crows and the crowing of the Armstrongs' rooster in the barns far across the way. After breakfast Uncle Harry would come with the big milk cans full of warm milk, and perhaps invite us over to the barns that afternoon to see the new calf. Sometime during the morning we'd toddle across the fields and dirt road to knock on Aunt Nellie's kitchen door, to receive a fresh-baked sugar cookie and watch the cat drinking milk from its saucer.

Sometimes Aunt Nellie would be going up to the Big House to check on something or air the place or put out the mouse poison and I, being the eldest, might be allowed to go along. The distance was far, and we would be driven along the little road, over its three criss-crossed iron bridges, past the grave of the little Revolutionary girl,* past the silent barns and the mysterious closed-up Casino, up the great solid rock hill to the stone steps that twisted up, up, past massive iron lamps to the porch. The verandah, as everyone called it, seemed to a child like the deck of some vast ocean liner. As if drawn by a magnet, you would be pulled to the front of the mighty deck, from which you looked down the sweep of the valley, framed in the foreground by the giant pines, and in the distance by the narrowing mountains like enclosing walls. Around the porch I would trudge close on Aunt Nellie's heels, past the deserted aviary to the pantry door. Here Aunt Nellie would take out the chain of keys and unlock it, and we would slip into the cool gloom of that particular entry with its Chinese red walls, picked out in gold leaf.

I would inch up the wide stairway that was carpeted in pale green, each landing memorable and sinister for having to pass huge stuffed birds, poised on each turn of the balustrade with upswept wings, look- ing ready to strike. I would shrink against the wall, panicked yet fascinated by the confrontation with their beady eyes, too ferocious I thought to be just glass. A hawk at one landing, an owl at another, and then a golden eagle—they were the spectres guarding the place I loved the most, else I should never have braved that staircase time and time again. The place was Aunt Winifred's bedroom which seemed to me like the vast, deserted bower of the Sleeping Beauty. Here were two large brass beds from France, and many, many chairs and settees and dressing tables—Louis XV country pieces painted white, cushioned in sheer lace over pale pink watered silk. The great armoire had hand- painted scenes of bucolic shepherds—imitation Fragonard—and the silk draperies at the far end swept back to disclose a secret place with window seat and high skylight. Within this nook was a small silk cabinet with row after row of shallow drawers containing Winifred's collection of laces and embroidered ribbons. I never tired of sorting through this colorful treasure.

There was a gold room, too, and a room with densely flowered French paper, and the room where almost everything was pale blue silk covered with gossamer lace and tiny satin flowers. This had been Natacha's room, I was told, and I can remember wondering whether she had ever really used the dainty little sewing cabinet all upholstered

---

* Marked with a wooden cross; no one seems to know the origin of this story.

in blue silk moire. The bathrooms were faintly perfumed even after all these years of disuse, each one still with its treasury of Hudnut bottles, some covered with wicker baskets molded to their graceful contours, some made of French blue china with globe stoppers and inlaid labels of blue and white. Katie Armstrong was along with us one day, and she told me that once when the Shah of Persia had been visiting Uncle Richard, he had emptied an entire blue quart bottle of cologne into his bath water, which fact had been reported by an incredulous footman to all below.

It may have been the luxury of the furnishings that impressed my youthful mind, but I think it was far more the deserted quality of that Big House. I would strike notes on the piano in the great living room, and the sound would echo through the stillness and chill my young heart. Aunt Nellie would pull a silken cord, and a vast wall of draperies would whoosh back, flooding sunlight into the heretofore shadowy canyons of the room. The fireplace, twice as tall as I was, would be laid and ready; the huge brocaded pillows, smooth and plump; each table would disclose its jeweled boxes or carved ivories—all for *no one*. When we left, the house would be sealed up again, waiting for someone who would never come. The poignance of all deserted fairy castles was made real to me at Foxlair.

We all loved to fish at Foxlair. We would make poles of shaved-off branches with a string and a pin and sit by the creek that wound in and out along the road, a tiny offshoot of Kibby Creek that tumbled down to join the Sacandaga. Father took us fishing on the river now and again, probably in the hope of instilling a lifelong interest in us. It accomplished quite the opposite end in at least two of us. One time my sister, Doff, who must have been about six, leaned over the side of the boat, and her tiny, silver-rimmed glasses fell into the river. These could not easily be replaced, and I can vividly remember both the tense atmosphere as Father quietly eased himself out of the boat, over the side and into the water up to his chest, and the restrained ministerial swearing as well that emerged each time he surfaced without the glasses. He had to hold the boat steady with one arm and bend over and search with the other. Remarkably enough, he found them undamaged, nestled among the smooth and slippery stones of the river bed. He never took us fishing again. I wonder only that he ever did in the first place.

I remember the forest fires one summer. Father was recruited to fight them, along with all the other able-bodied men in the valley. A big truck would come to pick him up. Men would be standing in the back, packed in as tightly as possible. Mother and our cook, Elizabeth, would have filled a big Adirondack packbasket with sandwiches and this would be loaded in, too, along with other food from the neighboring farms. Many hours later the truck would return with its load of exhausted firefighters, their faces blackened with soot.

I remember going to the salt lick one night with Uncle Harry Armstrong. We drove in the car across the fields to a spot that must have been close to the rise of Harrington Mountain. It was eerie with no headlights on the car, and the motor so quiet as we merely edged along, not as loud as the covering song of the crickets. Then we stopped —quietly—and Harry turned on the lights. There in the sudden beam of the headlights was a mother deer with two fawns, one of the loveliest sights to be seen. They were utterly mesmerized by the lights, but did not seem even slightly frightened.

I was tutored in arithmetic by Katherine Armstrong, who was the teacher of the one-room schoolhouse at Bakers Mills. I loved going over to the broad porch of the farmhouse and sitting there at the table, watching her neat fingers fly as they added and subtracted neat columns for my kindergarten edification.

I remember visits to Windover, and visits from the family at Windover to us at Foxlair, and the winding dirt road between the two family places that took an hour to drive in those days.

But most of all I remember a piece of heartbreak in my last Foxlair summer. Mr. Pierce, Aunt Winifred's lawyer, was using the Big House for a week or so, and with him was a party of his New York friends. The women seemed dazzling to me in their elegant clothes, and with their long cigarette holders and sophisticated make-up. They seemed always to be laughing, although I cannot imagine why their memory is so vivid to me, having seen them at most only once or twice. Mr. Pierce met me at the Armstrongs several times and each time seemed to me extremely friendly. He talked to me as if I were an adult, and this delights any child. Then came the day when my father and I met him together. Mr. Pierce told Father that he was having a big party at the Big House that night, for people up from New York. And then he invited me to come. Not mother and father. Me. I can still remember the frost that was in my kind father's voice when he said no, I *certainly* could not go, that I was accustomed to being in bed before the party would even *begin*, and thank you very much indeed, but *no*.

I crept out of bed that night to the tiny gabled window of my room and looked out into the blackness of the long valley to the lights that blazed all over the Big House, so far away. There would be the great fireplaces glowing with real fire, I knew, and the house that I knew as dead would have come alive that night. I knew myself to be another Cinderella, but more tragic by far. Even after that, when I overheard the innuendo in Aunt Nellie's description of "that party" I still felt deeply, irrevocably deprived, as if my eight-year-old presence might have lifted it to a loftier level.

Other than this, my memories of Foxlair are pastoral and lovely; it was a golden summer world complete with deserted castle. Its wilderness setting, so secluded and remote, was my earliest vision of the Adirondacks, nor have I yet seen any lovelier.

Then in 1938 Winifred Hudnut deeded over the entire estate to the Police Athletic League of New York City "for the purpose of establishing a non-profit organization as a camp for the recreation and training of boys of inadequate means or opportunity, a training school for camp and boys' club executives, and for such other charitable and educational purposes as may be determined by the members, directors, or other proper representatives, from time to time."

Winifred, who was fond of the Armstrongs and once visited them during the P.A.L. years for a luncheon at their home in North Creek, ended their Foxlair employment with a settlement and a gift of most of the furniture for their new house.

Soon after they moved into the new house on Circle Avenue, Harry Armstrong died. Grandfather wrote the following appreciation of Harry and I include it because it seems to speak of many a mountain man we've known:

> You could not have had a better or more loyal friend. There was no limit to what he would do for you, and you will find many who took their troubles to him. Many and many is the man who got into difficulties on the old Wells Road and on the more dangerous ways of life for whose assistance he traveled miles and under whose stresses he put his wisdom and strength and resources.
>
> Harry loved folks, enjoyed visiting and meeting with people, knew most everybody who lived on the highways and byways of his own and adjacent townships, and wherever he went he acted the part of a neighbor. He loved to talk and was most interesting in conversation. He was happy-hearted, quick to laugh—with a very keen sense of humor. In all my favored years of companionship with him I never heard him swear or tell an indecent story. Had

he been a politician, I believe he could have been elected to almost any office, township or county, that he desired. Men liked and trusted him.

He was a most valuable man to those who employed him — honest, dependable, loyal, intelligent — thinking far more about the quality of service he rendered than of the amount of money he received.

He was educated in the school of hard knocks and proved himself an apt pupil. He was what you call a handy man, and while not a trained mechanic he was accomplished in many crafts. On occasion he could be a machinist, a plumber, a carpenter, a painter, a woodsman; and he was proficient in farming and animal husbandry.

All of his days were passed amongst the hills and valleys of the Adirondacks. I am sure he would not have been happy living in towns. He needed something of the primitive — the wide spaces, the silences, the horizons that hills make, and the sweet breath of the forest. He was much interested in the wild life about him, but he would not shoot a deer and did not care to fish. He was deeply sensitive to the sense of beauty amongst which he spent his days. Familiarity never robbed him of the splendor of sunsets, the glory of the hills and the song of the woodthrush. He was a native. He died where he loved to be, amidst the hills of his home.

He was a gentleman. Here was a big heart! Here was a loyal friend — and here a sincere Christian. We greet Harry Armstrong with a cheer.

From 1938 until 1964 the Police Athletic League owned Foxlair and for about twenty years operated it as a camp for boys from the slums of New York City. About six hundred boys would have two weeks there each summer, 130 at a time. Lieutenant Campbell was director for a number of years, but there was a full staff as well — counselors, a doctor, and special instructors in athletics, nature, and crafts. My brother, Herbert, during two of his undergraduate years at Princeton, was Nature Counselor there, and during those years, particularly, we had many opportunities to observe the good use being made of Foxlair.

We also had a clear idea of the changes that had taken place. The pink and white bedroom of the Sleeping Beauty fairly jumped with life those days, for twenty bunk beds slept forty boys there without any feeling of crowding. The walls were institution green now, and the Limoges tile stove had been boarded up to protect it from the boys' tendency to chip off souvenirs. The stuffed birds that had glared at me from each landing of the staircase were now put to use, along with the stuffed fox from the Great Hall mantle, in the Nature House, converted from the old boathouse where Natacha and Valentino had sunbathed. The camp newspaper was put out from what had been Uncle Richard's study and billiard room; the chauffer's house had become the counselor's house, now furnished with an odd mixture of Army-Navy store and fine French cast-offs.

Roy Dunkley was the superintendent of Foxlair during the P.A.L. years. He was one of a well-known family of the Bakers Mills and Sodom area, and was much respected for his work at Foxlair. He retired with a Police Department pension when the state bought the property.

Almost from the first the P.A.L. was plagued with money troubles. The buildings were not in the best of repair and required renovation to convert them to use as a camp. New buildings were needed as well, and the cost of everything seemed to skyrocket. However, when a fire inspection found the camp lacking in proper equipment, the inspectors threatened to close the camp unless this equipment was installed. The cost of the equipment was $45,000—which the P.A.L. simply didn't have. So camp never opened the following year, nor any year thereafter. Roy Dunkley remained there as caretaker, but it was impossible for any one man, no matter how capable, to keep a great place like that from disintegrating. Nature—and occasional vandals—began to take over.

About this time it became known to us that the P.A.L. was offering Foxlair for sale. The terms of the original gift had still to be legally met: only a school or camp or similar non-profit organization could buy the place. This prohibited land speculators from buying it, and not only speculators but later generations of the Hudnut family as well. Only a legal machine as stong as the State of New York's could have managed to break the terms of the gift.

It was the thought of the Limoges stove, boarded up in its forgotten corner of the master bedroom, that caused me to write to the Police Athletic League. I addressed it To Whom It Might Concern and explained my interest in what was going to happen to Foxlair. I asked that my husband and I be allowed to buy the tile stove, and perhaps any furniture that remained in the barns or houses that had belonged to the Hudnut family. I was able to describe this, and the deteriorating condition of everything that was left there, because Roy Dunkley had kindly taken me all through the buildings a month or so earlier. In fact, Roy always showed our family every kindness; during the years when he was a zealous guardian of the place, we were always free to come and go, to fish the river there, and wander around as we wished. He had known my grandfather and father and had helped to build Uncle Bill's house at Windover.

In response to my petition to the P.A.L., a letter from a Lieutenant MacManus came, saying that Foxlair was within his realm of supervision, but a decision of the Board of Directors would be necessary to deal with my request; he had no power to give away or sell anything. Soon after, on a trip to New York, I stopped in to see him at P.A.L. Headquarters. He turned out to be a most approachable man, and he, for his part, was delighted to meet a "genuine Hudnut"—the first he had ever met. In fact, he showed me all around, introducing me to all the police personnel. Many of the men I met had spent some time at Foxlair, and without exception they spoke of it in a way that made me feel a common bond—we shared a deep feeling for that beautiful long valley, its mountain wilderness.

A few weeks later a letter came from the Board of Directors of the P.A.L., giving outright to "Mrs. Clarkson, anything that had belonged to the Hudnut family." I promptly wrote a letter of thanks, sent a contribution to the P.A.L. which seemed commensurate with the gift, and then set about making all the arrangements for removing the last of the Foxlair furnishings. It took Dan and Vincent Nevins of Sodom, about six trips with their small truck to bring out the contents of barns and attics. Maurice Richards of North Creek, and Orbin Harrington of Bakers Mills, worked for two days to dismantle and move the Limoges stove. It is stored in the stone cave of our log house now, and it is a moot question whether or not it will ever be assembled again, but at least we rescued some Hudnut family relics—(most of them derelicts after years in fitful storage)—just before Foxlair was sold to the State of New York.

In an indenture signed and sealed on the 17th of November, 1964, New York State completed the purchase of Foxlair for what seemed to me the pittance of $40,000.

For a year or so nothing happened to the land. Rumors had it that the State might use it for a Forestry School or a public campsite. The last times I went to the Big House were to show it to house guests at Windover. A trip to Foxlair was an outing, like an excursion to a ghost town, and people never ceased to be fascinated with this giant spectre of an extravagant past. Roy Dunkley had moved out, and it was a scene of proverbial "wrack and ruin." The great verandah showed gaping holes to the caverns below, and to get to the house itself you had to straddle the rotten planks, hoping that you would not step on a weak one and crash through. Doors hung on their hinges and swallows swooped down the long halls. The Moyenage fireplace had been defaced. There was an ache in my throat for the indignity of this survival. Our visitors saw a lesson in the whole scene: Ozymandias in the Adirondacks. I finally vowed to myself never to return. It was just too sad.

My father, who had loved Foxlair, decided to take action and I quote his letter of February 2, 1966, to the Conservation Department:

> This note is in regard to the property known as "Foxlair" which was bought and maintained, starting before 1904, by my Uncle, the late Richard Alexander Hudnut. Upon his death the Estate was turned over to the Police Athletic League of New York, who operated the land and buildings for several years but found that they did not have sufficient funds to transport the boys back and forth from New York City. The Estate was then not used for a number of years and finally in 1964-65, was purchased by the State of New York and we understand that the 1,200 acres has become a part of the Adirondack Park and that the land will be forever wild.
>
> On January 1, this year, I made a visit to the main house on the property and discovered that vandals have been destroying everything in that great house. I think it is now a menace to public safety and call this to your attention because I think it should be burned or torn down before someone is seriously hurt on that property.
>
> The destruction of that house and the other buildings is unbelievable. We cannot understand how people could possibly engage in such vandalism. Every window is smashed, glass is scattered all over the place, door frames have been ripped out, plumbing has been taken, things too large to move have been wilfully smashed and the result is a scene of total desolation.
>
> A law suit against the State of New York could well be averted by the complete removal of the building.
>
> Yours Sincerely,
>
> Herbert Beecher Hudnut

On April 10th following, he received the following reply:

Photograph by Charles Severance

The front of the Big House burns.

Photograph by Charles Severance

The pigeon barn burning at Foxlair.

The remains of the Big House after the fire.

Dear Doctor Hudnut:

This is to inform you that last week our department forces burned down all the buildings on the Hudnut estate that we were unable to sell to the public. This was as per your request to our Albany office. This also included the mansion.

Signed,

S. M. Parmer,
Dist. Director of Lands and Forest
District -11.

Now there is nothing left to tell the tale of the town that was Oregon or the great estate that was Foxlair. Nothing except an ornately carved garden bench, which was too ugly to covet and too heavy to move. Even that is buried now in vines and creepers.

There is no one to regret the passing of Foxlair and that is the saddest thing of all. For my part, I am fast forgetting this sentinel of my childhood in the Adirondacks, or at least the buildings—and watching, fascinated, to see the wilderness erase its contours. The long valley was beautiful with the farms and lilac blooms of Oregon. And it was beautiful when it bore Foxlair on its clearings like an alien jewel. Now it is just another lovely stretch of the Adirondack Forest, forever wild.

CHAPTER 22
WINDOVER

Will and Harriet Hudnut bought Windover in 1928. Uncle Bill
(William H. Hudnut, Jr.) had graduated from Princeton and completed his first year at Union Seminary. He spent that summer with the
family, and he was very much a part of the acquisition and rehabilita-
tion of what was then a bedraggled farm property. As he wrote:

> The second summer we were at Foxlair, 1928, Uncle Richard's
> overseer, Harry Armstrong, found a place some five miles from
> North Creek, which he thought might interest us. Dad did not
> want to appear in the matter as he knew this would boost the
> price, since the name of Hudnut meant a wealth which Father, a
> clergyman, didn't have. So he sent Aunt Nan Beecher and me to
> inspect the property. We saw a mill, a barn, an old dam, an ice-
> house, and an old farm-house, run down, but essentially sound.
>
> The owner, Mrs. Balch, was eager to sell. She had been
> deserted by her husband, and had been trying to make ends meet
> running a sort of fishing and hunting lodge. She had let most of
> the water out of the small lake, through the sluice, in an effort to
> farm the lake bottom. This had not been successful. She wanted
> to sell the property and return to her family in New Jersey. Dad
> was able to purchase the one hundred and sixty acre property with
> a part of the money from the sale of Wamakedah.

The road into Windover.

"Windover" c. 1940 showing Uncle Jack's "Versailles."

Harriet Beecher Hudnut, c. 1930

William Herbert Hudnut, c. 1946

We saw real possibilities in an enlarged lake and a remodeled house. In order to accomplish this, Dad sold his Republic Steel stock in the summer of 1929 for eighty dollars a share. After the crash of October, '29, it was down to six dollars. This fortunate move enabled us to renovate the farmhouse, with the help of a Youngstown architect named Canfield, and to make a beautiful summer home.

Horace Hack of Johnsburg was the chief carpenter, and he had as his assistants his father-in-law, Mr. Straight, as well as Harry Hitchcock. Uncle Bill worked along with the others, and so, sometimes, did Grandfather. Will was sixty-five that summer, in good health and still vigorous.

The barn and the mill were torn down, and a three-foot concrete cap was added to the dam. This raised the level of the lake, which now more than covered the hundred-acre meadow, bounded by Eleventh Mountain to the southwest and Gore Mountain to the northwest. Smaller, wooded Edwards Hill seemed to rise straight out of the water at its farthest end.

And so Windover became the center of the family summers. Because our patriarchs were ministers, we had long summer vacations, and in due time a whole community grew up around that lovely little lake. First was the Big House, as we called our grandparents' home, the handsome white remodeled farmhouse with its dark green shutters and spacious porches, and its comfortable interior enhanced with Foxlair rugs and furniture. Harriet's touch was everywhere; the ambience of the house was her creation. But she had so few years left; the last filled with the pain of her fatal illness.

I have an image of her with Grandfather, leading us on picnics up a little hill beyond the tennis court to a shadowy pine grove, where a linen cloth was laid out on the pine needles and the big wicker picnic basket unpacked. Surrounded by her children and small grandchildren, like a tall country queen in her long summer dress and wide leghorn hat, I see her smiling the serene smile of a truly happy woman.

And there's another image in my mind as well—of a grandmother on the chaise longue on the back porch, wrapped in a dark plaid steamer rug, trying to smile for a young granddaughter, who adored her, and not being quite able to. We whispered that summer, and went away on tiptoe.

Harriet Hudnut died in 1935. Will and her children, who had never seen the Adirondacks in any season but summer, came in cold November to bury her near the pine grove she had loved, in the shadow of a huge rock. Here, the following summer, with a heart still full of winter, our grandfather created a lovely little cemetery around her grave. Bordering a large clearing, he had a hedge of cedars planted, and a master stonecutter came from New York to carve the outline of a large cross on the face of the rock. Underneath in simple block letters was spelled:

To the Glory of God

Harriet Beecher Hudnut, 1866 -1935

Harriet's son-in-law, Henry Bischoff, Kitty's husband for just twelve years, was buried there the following year. Now that quiet graveyard has many of the graves of our family. It is a place that feels holy to us — "a place where prayer has been valid," in the words of the poet T.S. Eliot.

Bill Hudnut married Elizabeth Kilborne in New York in November of 1931, and in the following summer they built the second house at Windover. Its design echoed the simple lines of the Big House and it, too, was white with dark shutters. Roy Dunkley was head carpenter with, this time, Horace Hack as helper. Others who worked on it were Howard Hodgkins, Vern Hitchcock, Harry Hitchcock, and Harry's sons, Jim and Burke.

This house was known as "Windover, Junior," or, in recent years, the Little House. Uncle Bill and Aunt Betsy lived there in all those early years with their family of six children. And Aunt Betsy lives there now, our matriarch and treasured elder.

In 1937 the ownership of Windover was assumed by Uncle Bill. It was in so many ways a helpful thing for his brothers and sisters, and it removed the running expenses of the property from Grandfather's shoulders. With part of the funds from this purchase of his Windover inheritance, my father (Herbert) was able to build his house on the other side of the lake. Its architect was Uncle Bill, and its chief carpenter was Horace Hack. Various young people brought to Windover that summer from the two brothers' parishes worked on it, as well as Uncle Bill and my father. It was built in six weeks of nine-hour work days, and was the first Adirondack-style camp at Windover. We called it "Windover Cottage."

The other building put up in those early years was Uncle Bill's one-room log cabin in the woods. It is a gem of rustic simplicity, and here the two brothers went each morning to study together and plan their sermons for the year ahead.

These houses, together with a few out-buildings, gardens, a playing field and tennis court, made up the planned spaces of our family place. The rest of Windover was seemingly endless: hills and forests and islands in the lake. We were free to roam and explore and create our own playground and domains, among which the Inlet, "Bunny Hollow," and the Old Stone Quarry were our special haunts.

I suppose that life at Windover was lived day by long summer day much as vacationing families spent them in many of the grander and lesser camps of the Adirondacks: morning chores or activities for the children (for the good of our character!), lots of swimming, mountain climbing, competitive sports, and excursions to such landmarks as Fort Ticonderoga or Ausable Chasms. We made up a lot of our own plays and adventures. We also did a fair amount of "grown-ups watching": the afternoon hours of the tennis court were reserved for them, and we were their loyal gallery; evening usually had bridge games at the Big House, and while we children often played our own hands at the big old kitchen table, it was thrilling to me to watch the skills and strategies and warfare (usually polite) at the grownups' tables.

I'm sure that other family camps had stunt nights like ours, when children learned to overcome youthful stage-fright with frequent and sometimes elaborately rehearsed evenings of performing arts. Others, too, must have reveled as we did, in Scrabble, and "*the* game" and square-dancing, which we at Windover were invited to take part in up at the Tibbit's Log House at Thirteenth Lake. And the hymn sings each Sunday night were by no means unique to Windover. The Lake Placid Club and the Lake George Club had them, as did some other family camps but in these they seemed to be more a popular old-fashioned remnant of nineteenth-century "high w.a.s.p." culture than a religious thing. What *was* different at Windover was that the spiritual element of a hymn sing was articulated from the first, when they were led by Uncle Bill at the piano, and later, by my father. It was also a part of our intentional shaping: we children learned to lead the responsive reading on demand, or to sing a solo or duet, and to behave in as civilized a manner as we did at dancing school; woe be to those who giggled when a cousin mispronounced a word, or hit a false note, or when Grandpa prayed too long!

It is hard to communicate the powerful beauty of the hymn sings in those high seasons at Windover. Our family has been blessed with ones who love to sing, many who have sung in their school glee clubs or

Photograph by Patricia Layman Bazelon

The Big House at Windover today.

Windover Lake, Eleventh Mountain in background

The log cabin Bill built as a study.

Trail from lake to Log House at Windover.

The Windover family matriarch, Mrs. William H. Hudnut, Jr. (Aunt Betsy).

Another William, (Wm. H. Hudnut IV), great-grandson and another Harriet, (Harriet Hudnut Holliday), granddaughter.

The "Windover Olympics," a long tradition for young cousins.

Tidbit Island, a most convivial picnic spot in Windover Lake (beaver house at left).

Trail to the graves at Windover.

The big rock at the family graveyard at Windover.

HARRIET BEECHER
1865 — 1935
WILLIAM HUDNUT
1864 — 1963

choirs and harmonize with ease. Those of us who have grown up through Windover summers know all the family favorites by heart, but guests seem to join the music with equal enthusiasm. And since these guests have represented widely varied religious persuasions—from Orthodox Judaism to High Anglican, from Buddhist to free-form, or none-at-all, I tend to think of our hymn sing as a kind of family art form, practiced and refined over many summers, rather than as a spiritual exercise. Though it is that, too.

All the years of my childhood at Windover, the last hymn sing of the summer featured, at its close, a little message to the family, given by Grandpa, our founder, the William of all these Adirondack chapters. He sat in his big old rose silk armchair, all of us children clustered around him at his feet in the lamplight; the grown-ups ranged around the periphery in the Foxlair chairs, benevolent. They knew what was coming, almost to the exact words.

But Grandfather spoke always to us grandchildren directly—to the third Windover generation. And whether it was that we adored and venerated him, or that the marvelous timbre of his old voice held us in thrall, or that we felt the gaze of our parents' expectations, we hung on his every word. It was always the same message.

It began with the story of the man who showed his children what family unity was meant to be by demonstrating how easily one stick could be broken, but how, if all their several sticks were bundled together, you couldn't break them. And he would go on to speak about his own boyhood broken home and his exile from it. He always ended with the words from the twelfth chapter of Luke's Gospel, "Every one to whom much is given, of him will much be required."

In the summer of 1951 when I was still a bride, I must have felt a new consciousness of the passing of time, for I decided to take down the words as Grandfather spoke—for posterity. Well, as it happened, there was no rush, for he was with us for twelve more summer seasons, increasingly frail, of course, but quite able to give the final homily for eleven of them. It was like this:

> When your Grandmother and I created Windover, we had the family's health and happiness in mind, but our main purpose was to establish a beautiful place where we could all gather together each summer, strengthening our family ties and welding a unity of our several generations.

Then would come the story of the sticks, and following that, his own experience as a boy—a family that seemed to have everything, but in reality, had so little of what mattered most.

> Out of such tragic memories, I resolved that if God gave me a family, I would use every means to bind its members together with ties of love stronger than death. We were so richly bless'd with children. They, in turn, have their own families—and there are twelve of you now in the third generation. Each of our several homes has its own structure and loyalty; each is making its own traditions, which is each child's birthright. It is quite possible for these homes to become independent of all the others, to become fragmented. Against such a possibility, we built Windover.

So Windover was to be our bundle of sticks. But there was more. For underlying the ideal of a family unity was a conscious intention, almost unimaginable in an era of a more laissez-faire psychology: a passion to shape the character of a whole family to high traditions of achievement in the service of humanity. As he spoke he would lean forward and his voice trembled with emotion. We children listened, wide-eyed, to these words of our grandfather:

> We aim to build a family tradition here—to raise young people who will distinguish themselves in the manner of their lives, in the service they will render.
>
> So many people today seem incapable of doing *anything* to help. We will try to make the most of ourselves so that we may make a real contribution to our world.
>
> And lest we work at cross purposes, and some tear down what others painfully build, I hope that our family will always strive first to build the Kingdom of God, through our various professions and vocations. I am persuaded that any lesser objective will not preserve our unity—will not be worthy to enthrall our descendants.

That was Grandfather's vision for his family. It was the essence of noblesse oblige. It was Puritan and Presbyerian and Princetonian. It was pure Grandfather. And we lived into it.

It was that vision, faithfully carried on in the second generation, and persevering in relaxed but respectful ways "unto the third and fourth," that has left its mark on the Windover family. The fifth generation is coming on strong, and in spite of the secular society we live in, which has so vastly lost the language and practice of things spiritual, I believe that many of William and Harriet's descendants will be gathering to sing hymns and enjoy the family camaraderie on summer Sundays for some years to come. Those gatherings may be the outward and visible sign of an inner family tradition that can be strong as a bundle of sticks in a scattered clan.

Now, other generations occupy the first family homes, and some of us have added new houses and adjoining lands to Windover's boundaries, and therefore go with frequency; many are able to go only occasionally. We come back to reunions; we come to bury our dead in the family cemetery on the little hill; we come to see the relatives, and to take a deep breath of belonging. And whether we are there or not, we all carry Windover in our souls, for distance is a matter of miles, not of the heart.

Will and Harriet Hudnut could have asked for nothing more.

APPENDIX A

More About the A.P.A. — the Early Days of the North Woods Club

Mr. Wessels' book, *Adirondack Profiles*, tells us that in 1890 Mr. Bibby built a sawmill and produced lumber, and that he subsequently built a new barn, the farm house, and many new cottages. From that day to this, however, the North Woods Club has preserved its essentially private nature and small membership — its beautiful and secluded lands known only through the paintings of Winslow Homer, one of its early members, and the writings of Hugh Fosburgh.

Mr. Fosburgh's uncle, the late H. Leroy Whitney of New York, kindly gave me permission to quote here from an article that he wrote for the Anglers' Club Bulletin; it adds to the brief picture given in my grandfather's memoirs:

> Eliphlet Terry certainly was the moving spirit in the formation of the Adirondack Preserve Association. He was a Civil War correspondent, and a sketcher, as was Winslow Homer. They, with the brothers Kitching — Frank and Amon — both Union veterans, were among the Founders. And as Terry was the only one who had ever heard of the place, he must have been responsible for bringing all of them here. Terry and Homer both let me carry their painting equipment. Terry's usually included a bottle, but Mr. Homer was nicer. He taught me to see things and sent me off exploring while he painted. I remember rowing him to different spots on Mink, to Thumb Landing, and to a place on Thumb Pond where he painted "Boy Fishing."
>
> The Kitchings and Terry were there every summer; Mr. Homer, not too regularly, but it was during those years he painted most of his Adirondack oils and watercolors. My memory is much clearer of later years, our camp on the Hudson near Fish Rock, and of the appearance of small-mouthed bass in Split Rock. It must have been some cyclone that dropped them there.

APPENDIX B

The Will of Godfrey Shew

"In the name of God, amen, I, Godfrey Shew, of the Town of North-ampton, county of Montgomery [Fulton County], State of New York, being of sound mind and memory, blessed by God for the same, do make and publish this, my last will and testament in manner and form as following, - that is to say imprimus, I commend my soul into the hands of the Almighty God who gave me and my body to the earth from whence it came in hope of a joyful resurrection through the merits of my saviour Jesus Christ and as for worldly estate that God hath blessed me with, I dispose of as follows: First, I give to my youngest son, Godfrey Shew, all my premises of the real property of Lot No. 2, out of No. 26 of Northampton patton which I exchanged with my son Jacob Shew, the whole containing 100 ackers and further-more I give to my oldest son, Heanery Shew, 12 dollars and 50 cense, and also to my son, Stephen Shew, 12 dollars and 50 cense, and also to my son Jacob Shew 12 dollars and 50 cense, and also to my daughters, Mary Jackson and Sarey Jackson (each) 12 dollars and 50 cense, also to my son Jacob Shew's oldest son, Godfrey Shew, being my grandson, the sum of 12 dollars and 50 cense, for barying my Christian name, for him to remember me thereby and make good use of the same; and fur-thermore, it is my will that my son, Godfrey Shew, shall raise this money to pay the above menshuned Legatees out of the stock of cattel, horses, or other creatures, or otherwise agree themselves, and if not, by appraisal by good men; furthermore, I give to my daughter-in-law, Catherine Shew (wife of Godfrey) two beeds and all the furniture for them that is in my room now and all the rest of the household furni-ture, excepting one chest, that I give to my son Godfrey's daughter, Susanner Shew and the contents therein I do further mak and apint Jacob Shew and Godfrey Shew to be executors of this my last will and testament, in witness thereof, I have hereunto set my hand and seal this 20th day of Feb. in the year of Our Lord, one thousand 8 hundred and 5, in the presence of Caleb Watson, Prudence Park and Sam'l Scribner - Godfrey Shew."

Source: *Descendants and Ancestors of Jacob Dunahm and Stephen Shew with*

Historical Accounts of the Shews, Etc. Complied by Sophie Dunham Moore, Kalamazoo, MI.

I used a mimeographed copy of 1933, and a bound volume, copyrighted and privately printed by the compiler in 1963, lithographed by Edwards Brothers at Ann Arbor - both loaned to me by Mrs. Bovee at the Johnstown Public Library.

Page 48 of the mimeographed copy reads:

> Godfrey Shew, supposed to have been the son of a German nobleman, came to America to visit the country in 1730, but after a perilous journey, refused to cross the ocean again, and so remained here. He fought in the French war under Sir Wm. Johnson and was wounded at Fort Ticonderoga. He also fought in the Revolution and was for several months a prisoner of the British.

APPENDIX C
The Putman Family

The following excerpt is taken from *The History of Montgomery Classis*:

> Sir John Johnson, the eldest son and heir of Sir William Johnson and Catherine Weisenburg. When Sir William left Mount Johnson in 1763 to found Johnstown, named after the heir, Sir John took up his residence at what is now called Fort Johnson. The mistress of this baronial mansion for a decade was the beautiful Clara Putman of the Mohawk Valley, by whom Sir John had several children. . . . Forgetting his promise of marriage to Clara Putman, he married Mary Watts, the daughter of a wealthy New York loyalist June 30, 1773. On his return to the mansion, Sir John had Clara Putman and her children removed, first to the town of Florida, then to Schenectady, where it is said he bought a home for her where she lived until 1840.
>
> (*Dailey*, p. 194)

Simms adds the tale of Clarissa Putman's visit to Canada to see Sir John (at his request) in the year 1810. He also mentions that the children of this liaison grew up to be most respected citizens, as was Miss Putman, as Simms puts it, "notwithstanding this liaison."

Vrooman speculates that the reason why Sir John never married Clarissa was because his father insisted that he marry someone of wealth and aristocratic lineage to help assure the title continuation. Sir John was never known for his "marrying ways," in any event.

Vrooman also gives a stirring account of the murder of our ancestor, Lodowyck Putman by Sir John's Indians during the Revolution, who returned with Sir John from Canada to raid the Mohawk Valley. Lodowyck was Clarissa's uncle, and she evidently tried to save him — too late. His daughter, Hannah, married Jacob Shew.

Sources: *The History of Montgomery Classis* by W. N. P. Dailey.
Frontiersmen of New York by Jeptha R. Simms.
Clarissa Putman of Tribes Hill by John J. Vrooman.

APPENDIX D

The Massacre of Lodowyck Putman

On Sunday, May 21st, 1780, [Sir John] Johnson, with about five hundred troops, British, Indians and Tories, entered Johnstown by the expected northern route. The object of the invasion was to secure certain treasure which had been buried and certain property which had been concealed at Johnson Hall by Sir John, just prior to his hasty flight to Canada; also to murder certain Whig partisans. The day before the raid several Tories residing in Johnstown mysteriously disappeared. These Tories joined Johnson and guided him to Johnstown so that he and his raiders might murder their former neighbors.

At about midnight the raiders appeared, and proceeded directly to the home of Lodowyck Putman, a patriotic Hollander, who resided on his farm about two miles north of the courthouse. Putman had three sons and two daughters living at home, but fortunately two of the sons were away; they had gone "sparking"; they were at a house located in what is now Sammonsville. Lodowyck Putman and his son who was at home were dragged from their beds and cruelly murdered and scalped. Mrs. Putman and her daughter* escaped and fled to the Johnstown Fort. (At this time the jail was palisaded, and, with several block houses built within the enclosure, constituted the Johnstown Fort.) Putman had another daughter, married to Amasa Stevens, who, like his father-in-law, was also an enthusiastic Whig, and had incurred the displeasure of Sir John Johnson. Proceeding directly to the home of Stevens but a short distance away, he too, was murdered and scalped, and his body impaled on the garden fence. In neither case were the women molested, and what was less common, the torch of the incendiary was not applied. These atrocities were committed at night, and fires were not set because the invaders did not care to warn the settlers and the garrison at the fort, but a short distance away.

* Hannah Putman, who married Jacob Shew in 1787. Note that the raid on the Putman farm and the massacre there must have occurred only days after the attack on the Shew home at Fish House.

Source: *The Morning Herald* (Fulton Co., NY), Sept. 8, 1922; article by John T. Morrison.

APPENDIX E

An Autobiographical Account of the Early Life of Harriet (Shew) Beecher Hudnut

In 1865 James Fuller Beecher and Elizabeth Northrup, his wife, lived on the high hills above Elmira, N.Y. On Jan. 14th of the year, early in the morning, a doctor was needed. The horses were hitched to a sleigh and away they went down the hill and through the fields and over the fences, as the snow was so deep and the crust so thick that it would hold up the horses. Mrs. Doctor Gleason of the Water Cure Sanitarium was brought back to the farmland. Before many hours, a homely little girl, with lots of black hair, arrived and was named Harriet Shew Beecher.

Father soon thereafter, bought a farm about half a mile further up the hill, where a cross road led to "Quarry Farm," Mrs. Crane's home, Mark Twain's sister-in-law.

I remember our white house, and especially the yard, in one corner of which was a grove of tall pines, a lovely place to play house with my younger sister, Hannah Emily, whom we always called Nan. Between the trees and the house there was a long grape arbor under which flowed a small brook, and on the bank beyond were beautiful flowers. Our older sister, Ella Katherine, was devoted to flowers and had many varieties planted. In another part of the yard was a large cherry tree. I can see it now full of white Oxharts, with their pink cheeks. What fun to climb the tree and pick them for Mother, at the same time eating our fill.

Beyond the yard was the barn where I spent a great deal of time jumping in the haymow. Climbing to the highest beam I would stand and sing with all my voice, making believe that I was on the opera stage. Then I would climb up on the backs of the horses and talk to them. Father had a team of pretty blacks, Fannie and Charlie. When I was about eight I used to ride Fannie bareback, taking as many children behind me as could hang on—often they slipped off over her tail.

A very humble family lived a short distance from us. One of the children, Mary, was my devoted playmate. Her father, Giles Harris, never was successful at anything, so that the support of the four children fell upon the slight little mother. But what a noble little woman she was, full of courage and cheer. She took into their home patients from the Sanitarium, often very queer people, and even adopted a little red headed girl whose mother had no way of caring for her. A great soul, from whom I learned many beautiful lessons.

Back of our house there was a large kitchen garden and beyond that a pasture field where our neighbors kept a fine herd of cows. In the field was a large hickory tree, under which we built a playhouse out of stones with a fireplace where we baked potatoes and apples, once burning a hole in a new gingham dress. One day while playing there we heard the bellowing of a bull and tearing over the top of the hill the whole herd was stampeding towards us. We had just time to run and scramble over the garden fence to safety.

Not far behind Mary's house was a lovely grove and a sand pit near by. Among the trees and in the moss around their roots we found exquisite arbutus and young winter greens. What a land for play we children had! I pity children who never have a chance to learn the lessons of real country life. Nature is so natural and refined in her teaching.

Mark Twain, his wife and three daughters, spent much of each summer at "Quarry Farm" with Mrs. Crane. They were most interesting neighbors. One day Mrs. Clemens and one of the daughters were driving down the hill when the horses became frightened and ran away. I saw them pass and in a few minutes, Mark Twain in his white suit ran after them as fast as he could. Fortunately my father was coming up the hill with a heavy load and when he saw the runaway turned his team across the road and so stopped the frightened team. When Mark Twain came up to them he cried out — "Oh Livy, I am so thankful you were not killed. I never could have taken time this week to attend your funeral."

My sister Ella was a great student. While she was attending the Academy there were floods every Spring when the bridge over the Chemung River would be partly submerged. Father said that many a time he took Ella to the Academy on horseback when the water over the bridge would be up to the horse's stomach. E. K., as we called her, was a member of quite a remarkable class. One of the young men, Sloat Facett, became a senator. Another, John Stanchfield, became a distinguished lawyer in N.Y. City. Della Gleason became a fine physician — and others attained distinction. Even with such competition Ella won the first prize at their graduation. Thos. K. Beecher said that she wrote the most interesting letters he received from any one. After she had graduated from the Academy, before going on with her education, she taught a country school for one winter. One day when the school was over and all the scholars had gone, as she was closing her desk, she happened to glance out of the window and there stood a man with a butcher knife in his hand looking in at her. Fortunately the door was on the other side of the building and she ran out just as some of the Asylum attendants, from which he had escaped, came looking for him.

Nan and I often wonder what would have become of us if it had not been for Ella; she was so ambitious for us and persevering in seeing that we should have educational advantages. She taught in Milwaukee College, Miss Dana's School in Morristown, N.J. and Miss Mittleberger's in Cleveland.

When I was twelve years old Father lost the farm and everything he had by signing notes for a man who proved to be dishonest. Then Ella undertook to finance our education. For a few years Nan and I went to public school, walking up and down the long East Hill road. I spent a year and a half in High School staying with an aunt in Elmira. Then Ella sent me, and later Nan, to Miss Dana's.

We were sad when we had to leave our beloved farm on East Hill, and, thereafter, live on rented property. Our first move was to Lattie Brook. It was an ideal place for us children—a comfortable white house, a large barn and the loveliest pool back of the house. One day when riding through it I let Fannie stop to drink, and there wiggling and squirming were three good-sized water moccasins.

Father had a herd of cows that fed in the hill pasture. It was very often my duty to go for them at milking time. One summer, cousin Francis Collingwood was living with us. He and I would go for the cows, riding bareback through the wooded roads, singing as loud as we could and calling "Co-boss! Co-boss!" We were all very fond of Francis. When he was ten or twelve years old, his mother being very ill and away from home in the sanitorium on the Hill, he ran away and, in trying to catch on to a freight train, fell under the wheels. One foot had to be amputated and from the other all of the toes were taken off.

From Lattie Brook we moved to Lowman. The house was a fine old place with great trees in the front yard. One day when I was out in front waiting for the family to come home, a young man drove up and, stopping in front of me, asked whether I knew any one who would like to teach school. Quick as a wink I said that I would like to if I could get a certificate. So he left with the understanding that I would try for a certificate and would let him know. I was but seventeen. Immediately I made inquiries about the school and found that several successive teachers had been turned out by the scholars. Notwithstanding this report, nothing daunted. When I received my certificate I took the school for one term. I was told later that the father of one of the little boys had told the people that he would shoot the teacher. Father drove me over the steep rough hills to the hill upon which the school was located. I was to board across the way from the school-house and was very fortunate in that I had a large well-lighted room and Mr. and Mrs. Reese were happy to have a young person in their home. The food was excellent and I still remember the buckwheat cakes, syrup, sausages and apples.

School began the following day. I crossed the road with fear and trembling, entered a large room with a great stove at one end, and rows of seats on either side filled with boys and girls. To my amazement some of the boys were much taller than I was, sixteen and seventeen years old. I stepped behind the desk, tapped the bell and, after the singing of two songs, started the lessons. There were most as many classes as scholars, as no two seemed to be studying the same lesson. I enjoyed much of the work, especially the Arithmetic classes. Some of the children were bright and did not mind hard work. My discipline was good, and everything went smoothly. Some of the parents sent word to whip their boys if they misbehaved. I never did this but once and that was when a youngster kicked a panel out of the door. How it made my heart ache!

The young trustee who had engaged me, and I, were very good friends, and I had a number of rides with him over the lovely country. It seemed that there was a feud between his people and the Cooper family. When one of the young Coopers asked me to take a drive with him and I refused, he boasted publicly that he would show that damn pretty, black-eyed teacher that she couldn't turn him down like that; that he would send the Superintendent of Schools and have me put out. It wasn't many days later that I saw a strange gentleman drive over the hill and stop in front of the school. I was almost petrified, but angry enough to rise to the ordeal. I said to the children: "Show the superintendent what you can do and I shall be proud of you." Then I told one of the boys to open the door, and as graciously as possible I invited the gentleman to be seated. Some of the children had beautiful voices and, after singing a couple of songs, we proceeded with our classes. The Superintendent listened for a couple of hours. When I asked him if he would like to question the scholars, he said he would. And now, after all these years, I say, "Bless you boys and girls!" for they were at their best in recitation and behavior. Then he complimented the scholars and departed.

Not long after the Trustee received word from the Superintendent that he had no fault to find, that the boys and girls seemed to be doing well in their studies and that they behaved unusually well.

I was so angry that any one could be so underhanded that, although I had taken the school for only one term, I immediately signed up for the second term; and I was not turned out. The boys related to the Cooper faction left school, taking the troublemakers with them, and I was happy. I loved those boys and girls.

With what I had earned Ella was able to send me to Miss Dana's, where I stayed for four years, enjoying the school to the fullest extent. One year I won the silver medal, which was the award for an average of over ninety-five for the year. One quarter Katherine Erdman and I tied for the first place. These were my only high lights, as in order to attain these standards I had to be a *grind*. I had proven that I could get top rating and so was content. I knew that when I graduated I must teach, so I decided to take all the fun I could as the time passed. The annual party (a great event) to which we looked forward. Nan and I always dressed as men and were in great demand as partners for we danced well and were taller than most of the girls. I always wore a Scotch Kilt.

I graduated in 1886. I first taught in a private school in Bergen Point, and then, for two years, in Miss Lewis' School in Brookline, Mass. Then in June 1890 I was married to Wm. H. Hudnut. He had taken a church in Port Jervis, N.Y., where, after our honeymoon in the Adirondacks, we lived in the brick parsonage next to the church.

[I append here a couple of paragraphs which I think should be included though they do not seem to have a place in the narrative as written.].

We always attended Church and Sunday School at the Park Church [of Elmira] of which Thomas K. Beecher was the minister. He was always called "Uncle Tom" though the relationship was a distant cousin. We had one of the finest Sunday Schools in the country of which Mrs. Beecher was the Superintendent. We received small booklets containing the lesson for each month. Mr. Beecher prepared his own lessons. (There were no quarterlies. There were weekly teacher meetings at which he taught the lesson.) Park Church was one of the earliest Institutional churches in the country. There was a large room called the *Romp Room*, where the young people gave theatrical plays and danced.

Mrs. Beecher, like her husband, was a remarkable person, related to the Websters and Woosters of Dictionary fame. The growth and program of the school were largely due to her. She was the first person I knew who made rag dolls out of silk underwear. All of the money which she received from their sale she gave for Missions. I remember the stuffed animals she made for our use in entertainments.

We were much interested in a beautiful lady who drove about in a small phaeton. Her lovely Shetland ponies were a delight to Nan and me. The lady was the wife of Brigham Young's oldest son. She always had her two small sons, Bobby and Briggy, with her. The father, a handsome man, came now and then to Elmira to visit his family. We heard later that he did not keep his anti-polygamous promise but married a second wife. The one we so much admired was crushed by his faithlessness and died soon afterwards, a broken-hearted woman.

Note by Will Hudnut:
"I persuaded Harriet to write this account of her early life. She began it shortly before her death and its imperfections and omissions are due to her serious illness at the time."

APPENDIX F

More About the Remarkable Fish House
Covered Bridge, and a Modern Addition
To Its History

For over a hundred years the covered bridge of the Sacandaga River was perhaps the prime landmark of the Fish House Village. Like so much of the place, it is gone now—and it is worth remembering. The Hudnut *Memoirs* mentioned it with all the pride that the true villagers felt for their bridge.

> This was the ancient river bridge that was built in 1818, and still stood as staunch as when its three supporting arches were hewn out of the original pine. I say three, but there were really twelve, for it was a two-way bridge, and each span had four arches. The curved sections of these arches were held in place by wrought iron bolts at whose ends were slots through which iron wedges were driven and then twisted. Generations of farmers had driven their cattle and their lumbering, heavy laden wagons through this causeway, and in summer its dark, cool passages were redolent of the pastures of new mown hay. There may have been larger wooden bridges, but I doubt there were any that were stauncher or showed finer engineering and workmanship.

Washington Frothingham, writing about Fish House in his *History of Fulton County*, says:

> One of the earliest and most marked public improvements was the building of the Fish House bridge across the Sacandaga in 1818. Prior to that time, the river was crossed by canoe and by ford, the old fording place beginning a few rods below where the south end of the bridge now is, and crossing to a short distance above the north end. At that time, the little village of Fish House had every prospect of becoming the center of trade for a rich agricultural and lumbering region and the fording place was much frequented. The spring and fall freshets each year greatly inconvenienced the people who had to cross the river at this point, and the inhabitants petitioned the legislature for, and received an appropriation of, $5,000 for the building of the bridge. To this was added $500 by local subscription. Daniel Stewart built the bridge, which is still standing (this was written in 1890) and probably is the best bridge in the state, a marvel

indeed in point of strength and age.

Every timber in the structure was hewn out of pine logs, some of the pieces being fully two feet square. When it is considered that the bridge is 280 feet in length, it will be seen what a wonderful task this must have been!

Mrs. Sleezer, our Fish House historian, has more to tell us, writing in the *Schenectady Union Star* on April 21, 1966:

Nearly thirty-six years ago, a storm swept the newly filled Sacandaga Reservoir, battering a century-old covered bridge, no longer useful with the coming of the reservoir.

For two nights and nearly three days, strong winds and six-foot high waves pounded the massive structure, until on April 23rd, 1930, the Fish House covered bridge was lifted from its piers to settle in the reservoir.

Today, hand-hewn wooden pegs used to hold the timbers together exist in the homes of many area residents. The pins were salvaged and sold as souvenirs by the Ladies Society of the Fish House Methodist Church to raise money.

Opened in 1818, the bridge was built by a young Saratoga engineer and his experienced crew, friendly Indians — and the efforts of Jacob Shew, son of the first Fish House settler, Godfrey Shew.

Daniel Stewart was called from Saratoga to estimate the cost. He chose the site, and set $5,500 to complete the 400 foot long, two-lane span.

Shew, a member of the State Legislature, won a state grant of $5,000 and the town raised the $500.

Stewart contracted Indian scouts to find a certain type of stone for the piers. Found near Maxon Ridge, the stone was cut from ledges and drawn by oxen to the bridge site.

The river was used to float logs from the Adirondacks to the Hudson River, and the piers on the west side were squared to prevent log jams, On the east side, the piers were slanted.

Timber came from Virgin Forest in the Fish House area and was hewn at the bridge site. Trees used for the lower chords of the bridge were reported to have reached 96 feet in length. Local blacksmiths supplied the hand forged strap irons that held the main chords together but no nails were used.

The wooden pegs, later varnished, lettered and dated in gold and sold by the church women, were used exclusively.

Several explanations exist for the heavy arched timbers but most logical is that extremely thick trees were hewn into curved lengths and then mortised to form the arch for each span of the bridge.

In the fall of 1929, the bridge was anchored by heavy cables to large tree stumps in the hope that it could be saved for a museum.

But the bridge could not withstand the storm the next spring when it settled in the reservoir, taking power and telephone lines to the Edinburg area with it.

The late Arthur Vandenburgh was the last man on the bridge and got off it shortly before it was lifted from the piers.

When it became apparent that the bridge could not be saved, men from Fish House salvaged whatever parts they could.

Our final story of the old covered bridge comes from Mrs. Jane Orton Moore (Jenny Orton of our story) who, with her daughter, Jacqueline, discovered the present whereabouts of many of the old arches and timbers of this icon of old Fish House. The detective work is an interesting story, and it shows the singular fondness that so many generations of Fish House people felt for it. These are excepts from Mrs. Moore's own account, sent to my father:

> In the summer of 1962, Jacqueline drove up to Old Sturbridge Village with some guests. They stopped at the Tavern, after visiting many of the exhibits. Now there were several dining areas in the Old Tavern; they went in to the part that serves cafeteria luncheon. Jackie was amazed to see that the room was made of arched timbers and many hand hewn beams. She had been only a little girl when the bridge at Fish House was allowed to break up, when the lake "came in." But with the Orton and Moore families being so familiar with—and proud of—the Big Bridge, she immediately surmised where these timbers had come from. The Hostess told her that all the timbers and beams had come out of a summer home, some 15 miles away from Sturbridge. That was all she knew about it.
>
> When Jackie arrived home in Greenwich, Connecticut, she phoned me immediately to tell me of her "find." She said that there were still parts of painted signs, or advertisements that could be seen on a few of the beams. For example: (Car)pets of M. E. Bank, Gloversv(ille) . . . and R. B. Poole, Drugs and Paints, Heath Block, N(orth)ville! She purposely didn't tell me any more, wanting me to see them for myself.
>
> I wrote to Old Sturbridge Village, merely asking where the timbers came from. I also said that if they were from where I surmised, I had pictures and data that I believed they would be interested in seeing.
>
> In just a few days I had a reply from Miss Catherine Fennelly,

Research Director at Old Sturbridge Village. She said that the timbers were in a summer home they had bought and moved to Sturbridge: that they knew very little about them, but had been told that they had come from some old bridge over the Sacandaga River!

In was 1964 when Mrs. Moore and her daughter finally got to go to Sturbridge together. When they did, they met with Miss Fennelly and an architect whom she had called in. They looked at all of Mrs. Moore's Fish House pictures and had copies made. And they explained that the owner of the summer home had been Mr. Wells, who had in turn bought the timbers from Mr. Law of Herkimer, New York. Doubtless, Mr. Law had bought the timbers from one of the Fish House residents who salvaged them from the wreckage of the storm — perhaps even from Percy Orton, Mrs. Moore's father. Finally Mrs. Moore described her visit to the Tavern at Old Sturbridge:

> I had not been told by Jackie how *many* timbers they actually had, so I was truly amazed. They had used the curved arch timbers to make the ceiling roof. Above the arches the actual roof was made of wide planks. The area was about 34 by 50 feet long — and there were actually twelve of the curved arch timbers in the ceiling! Big uprights from our bridge had become the uprights for the dining room. They had also used smaller beams as bracers, the same as in the bridge. At the top of the upright posts, they had used the huge stringers on both sides. The stringers were the largest timbers used in the entire bridge. Three, lashed together with wide hand-forged iron straps, used to rest on the abutments and piers. Another section of stringer timber was also used as a mantel for the Tavern's huge stone fireplace.

Mrs. Moore's father, Percy Orton, for many years considered the Fish House Historian, was the son of Dr. Darius Orton and brother of Zene. From her notes about Sturbridge, presumably via Percy Orton, we learn a few more facts about the interesting arches of the Fish House bridge. Some of the men who worked on the bridge, way back in 1818, had come from Rhode Island, from seafaring families. They had mastered the skill of steaming and bending arches through the construction of ship's hulls. She was told, at Sturbridge, that it sometimes took upwards of two years of continuous steaming and bending to get the desired arch.

The bridge is gone, as is so much of the old village of Fish House.

Only a historical marker remains to tell its tale. It is a happy thing to know that a bit of it has been put to what preservationists call "adaptive re-use."

APPENDIX G

Ouida Girard, on *Oregon in the Farming Years, Before Foxlair*

The Oregon tannery, erected in 1877 by Stephen Griffin, continued to operate until about 1890. Charles Bradt, age 85 in 1977, said that he remembered when he was eight years of age, visiting relatives in Oregon, and seeing the tannery operating about the year 1889. He said it was located at the head of the valley near where the caretaker's house was built years later by Richard Hudnut. He thinks it was by the river bank and that there was a dam there where water was obtained for running the tannery. He said that the tannery burned not long after it was closed down.

By this time the large lumber companies had done their work and moved out. There remained in Oregon only a few families: the Mc-Closkys, Browns, Greens, the Alban Harrington and the Jim Harrington families. Alban's and Jim's farms were adjoining and were located beyond the schoolhouse on the road toward Griffin. They made their living off their farms, and with long rifles and hound dogs kept a supply of venison in the pot.

The Browns did some lumbering of softwood and drew the logs in winter eight miles to the flow behind the flood dam in Griffin. They unloaded them on the ice, and in spring when the ice melted, the dam was "tripped" and the logs started their voyage down the Sacandaga to a paper mill on the Hudson River.

Alban Harrington was married at the age of 16, and his bride, Eliza Morehouse of Bakers Mills was but 13. The wedding took place at her home and the local minister came there to perform the ceremony. They had ten children, two of whom died in childhood. They raised five sons: Charles, Fred, Ben, Ed and Seth, and three daughters: Mary, Viola, and Emeline, all comely girls. Eliza, the mother, died at the early age of 39. The children are all dead by now, but there are many grandchildren and great-grandchildren.

Times were hard and men out of work passed through Oregon look-ing for work or a hand-out. A schoolteacher told the story of the time

Eliza Harrington was at home alone and a strange man came to the door and asked for food. She was frightened and reached behind the door for the rifle. Then she slammed the door shut in his face. She was taking no chances. The famous corduroy road through the "Oregon Woods" to Griffin was now breaking up from neglect and disuse, and few Surries, and Buckboards went through; travel was a mere trickle.

The nearest church and post office were in Bakers Mills six miles distant. The Oregon schoolhouse, sitting on a wayside knoll, played an important part in the cultural and social lives of the children. Nellie Northrup of Griffin taught there about 1901; Nellie Cassidy of East Poultney, Vermont in 1903, and Effie Bradt, a niece of Mrs. Alban Harrington in 1904. Their education had taken them through the eighth grade and the County Superintendent of Schools had issued them permits to teach. They were good disciplinarians and commanded the respect of their pupils. They did not supervise the recesses or noon hour, however, and intervened mostly when blood flowed. The favorite games were "Tag," "Hide-and-Seek," and handball, not to mention wrestling. Every boy got to be an expert at that.

At the time when Jim Harrington was trustee, the teacher's salary was probably about $7.00 a week, and board about $2.00 or $2.50. There was always some rivalry to be trustee and get the teacher to board. The janitor work was done either by the teacher or an older boy for about $8.00 a year. This included building a fire in the big box stove each morning, carrying in the wood, and sweeping the floor every Friday afternoon. The teacher usually cajoled the big girls to sweep, and as they whisked the broom, clouds of dust from the knotty and splintered floor would roll up and choke the children.

It was considered a privilege to be permitted to ring the bell or go for a pail of water to the nearest spring. Whoever asked "Teacher" first, got it. Then everyone had a drink from the dipper. It was considered poor etiquette to lean over the pail while drinking.

Once a year the County Superintendent would come unannounced and make an inspection and sign the Register. If a child chanced to spy his horse and buggy coming down the road, in time, there was a great burst of activity as all helped to pick up the scrap paper that littered the floor and tidy things up. By the time he was at the entry, the room was spick and span and all heads were bent studiously over open books.

There was no organ and no pitchpipe for the singing. Songbooks were few and Nellie Cassidy would write all her old favorites, including "The Battle of Gettysburg" from memory on the blackboard. They copied them with pencil into tablets, and she taught them by rote. Ed Harrington was one of her best singers so she often asked him to give the pitch. His voice was changing so she had to say several times, "Take it up a little bit higher, Ed." Finally he would make it.

When Ben Harrington was a boy, he saw his first bicycle as it was being peddled over the stony, rutted road of Oregon. His family still laugh at how excited he was, and how he shouted, "Here comes the devil and his imps!"

Ed Harrington's widow, Elsie Harrington (DeMun) recalls that he told her he was fifteen when all the residents of Oregon sold their farms to Richard Hudnut. Alban's family moved into Hamilton County and settled on the "Windfall" near Wells in the spring of 1906. Elsie said she was just a few months old at that time.

Written c. 1977
by Ouida Girard, Wells, New York

Note: Griffin was a lumber and tannery community south of Oregon and close to Wells. In its prime it was a large and productive community, far more thriving than Oregon ever was. The Girards kept the hotel at Griffin, and after the industries moved out, they stayed on in the old homestead. The last living member of that strong Adirondack family was Miss Ouida, as I called her. She and her brother, Frank, and her sister, Miss Beatrice, drove up to visit me at Windover several times in the 1970s. During that time, Miss Ouida collected these notes about Oregon for me from the many friends she had who had lived there and remembered its last days.

In 1980 Ouida Girard sent me a copy of her own Adirondack memories, *Griffin: Ghost Town in the Adirondacks and Other Tales*. It is a wonderful picture of life in an isolated territory similar to Oregon.

APPENDIX H

Hiking Through Foxlair's Past—Today

From Barbara McMartin's excellent guide "Discover the Adirondacks, I":

> When the State of New York acquired the Hudnut estate, Foxlair, it made accessible one of the most beautiful locations on the East Branch of the Sacandaga. The ruins of the estate, which was lavishly landscaped, spread across a small hill beside the river. The flagpole promontory beside the foundation of the main house commands a view north-northeast along the East Branch valley. Black, Big Hopkins, Little Hopkins, Square Falls, and Eleventh mountains are framed by a row of planted evergreens that border the sweeping drive.
>
> If decaying ruins disturb your view of the wilderness take heart, the wilderness has almost overcome. Tangled roots and rank new growth are interwoven across the sweeping staircases and garden walls. Young hemlock and spruce fill the untended gardens. Before long, all will be as overgrown as the other treasure beside the riverbank.
>
> Foxlair was also the site of the Oregon Tannery, one of the Adirondacks' largest tanneries. It now lies partially concealed by jungle-like thickets of brambles. As overgrown as the foundations are, it is remarkably easy to discern the outline of the long tannery shed, the sluice for water, and the leaching house where all that remains of the huge leaching vats are their long iron straps.
>
> The DEC, which has responsibility for Foxlair, does not permit camping here but there are a variety of other ways to enjoy the site, which is accessible from either end of a road that passes through the estate grounds roughly parallel to Route 8. You can park at the southwestern end, off Route 8, 1 and ⅔ miles east of the Shanty Brook parking area, or at the northern end ⅔ mile farther along Route 8. This intersection is 2 and ⅔ miles west of the Siamese Ponds trailhead and leads into fields the state has reforested. The estate road makes a lovely short walk. Do not try to drive it, however, even though there are no barriers. The bridges are in need of repair.
>
> Near the southern end of the estate, the East Branch flows through

a small gorge with a deep swimming hole. There are trout in the river and many places to picnic along it. . . . A tour around [Foxlair] whatever the season is an exploration into the Adirondack past.

The tannery site is between the river and the estate road at the southwestern end of the property. Walk 100 yards in on the road and around a small hill toward the East Branch. The westernmost foundations belonged to the old springhouse. The foundations for two long sheds range northeast along the river, and other walls indicate at least three more buildings. . . .

Northeast of the tannery site stairs lead from the old road to a picnic spot overlooking a smooth, rock-lined gorge. Nearby can be found the ruins of an old bridge that served the farm communities north along Cook Brook. The principle buildings and gardens of the Hudnut estate were on the hill above, midway between the estate road and Route 8.

As Barbara McMartin noted in her acknowledgements, she saw my materials on Foxlair some years ago for whatever help they might provide. I admire her work immensely, and particularly enjoyed reading her description of what today's hiker and nature lover will find at Foxlair. She ended this section on a perfect note: "The hillside where the main house stood is as beautiful as ever. Enjoy a picnic there and be entertained, not by dancing pigeons, but by hawks soaring in the north over Black Mountain."

Bibliography

Aber, Ted and King, Stella, *The History of Hamilton County*, Great Wilderness Books, Lake Pleasant, NY, 1965.

_____, *Tales from and Adirondack County*, c. Speculator, NY, c. 1970.

Boos, John, *The Sacandaga Valley*, published by author, Albany, NY, 1962.

Carmer, Carl, (ed.) *The Tavern Lamps are Burning*, David McKay, New York, 1964.

Chambers, Robert W., *The Little Red Foot*, A.L. Burt Co., New York, 1921.

Dailey, W.N.P., The History of Montgomery Classis, (Mohawk Valley History & Old RCA Church Records) Recorder Press, Amsterdam, NY, c. 1900

Dunham, Harvey L., *Adirondack French Louie*, published by author, Utica, NY, printed by T. Griffiths, Utica, NY, 1953.

Flexner, James Thomas, *Lord of the Mohawks, A Biography of Sir William Johnson*, Little, Brown, Boston, MA, Revised ed., 1979.

Frothingham, Washington, *History of Fulton County*, Syracuse, NY, 1892.

Girard, Ouida, *Griffin, Ghost Town in the Adirondacks & Other Tales*, by author, Speculator, NY, 1980.

Hart, Larry, *The Sacandaga Story, A Valley of Yesteryear*, Riedinger & Riedinger, Schenectady, NY, 1967.

Headley, J.T., *The Adirondack, or Life in the Woods*, Baker & Scribner, New York, 1849.

Jamieson, Paul F., ed. *The Adirondack Reader*, MacMillan, New York, 1964.

McMartin, Barbara, *Discover the Adirondacks* (from Indian Lake to the Hudson River), New Hampshire Publishing Co., 1979.

Moore, Sophie Dunham, *Descendants and Ancestors of Jacob Dunham and Stephen Shew with Historical Accounts of the Shews, etc.*, compiled by Moore. Mimeograph copy, also privately printed by Edward Bothers at Ann Arbor, 1963. (Johnstown Library)

Morris, Michael, *Madam Valentino: The Many Lives of Natacha Rambova*, Abbeville Press, New York, 1991.

Murray, William H.H., *Adventures in the Wilderness*, William K. Verner, (ed.), introduction and notes by Warder Cadbury, Syracuse University Press, 1970.

Oberfirst, Robert, *Rudolph Valentino: The Man Behind the Myth*, Citadel, New York, 1962.

Rambova, Natacha, *Rudy*, London, 1926.

Sawyer, Donald J., *They Came to Sacandaga, The Story of Godfrey Shew: Fish House Patriot*, Prospect Books, Prospect, NY, 1976.

Shulman, Irving, *Valentino*, Trident, Simon & Shuster, New York, 1967.

Simms, Jeptha, *Trappers of New York*, J. Munsell, Albany, NY, 1871. Also 1980 Facsimile Reprint, with publisher's preface, Harbor Hill Books, Harrison, NY

_____, *The Frontiersmen of New York* (2 vols.), George Riggs, Albany, NY, 1882.

Sleicher, C. A., *The Adirondacks, American Playground*, Exposition Press, New York, 1960.

Stanyon, Mabel, *The Quiet Years*, Speculator or Lake Pleasant, NY, c. 1965.

Tibbitts, George F., *The Mystery of Kunjamuk Cave*, Cornwall Press, Cornwall, NY, 1928.

Vrooman, John J., *Clarissa Putman of Tribes Hill*, Baronet Litho, Johnstown, NY, 1950.

Wessels, William L., *Adirondack Profiles*, Adirondack Resorts Press, Lake George, NY, 1961.

White, William Chapman, *Adirondack Country*, Duell, Sloane & Pearce, New York, 1954.

New York Times articles, 1922-1928, on microfische re. Hudnuts and Valentinos.

Hudnut Family records, journals, letters and papers.

Perkins Family materials, given by Rose Perkins Gallup.

Girard Family memoirs.

Willett Randall memoirs.

Materials on the Shews and Sir William Johnson from the Johnstown Public Library.

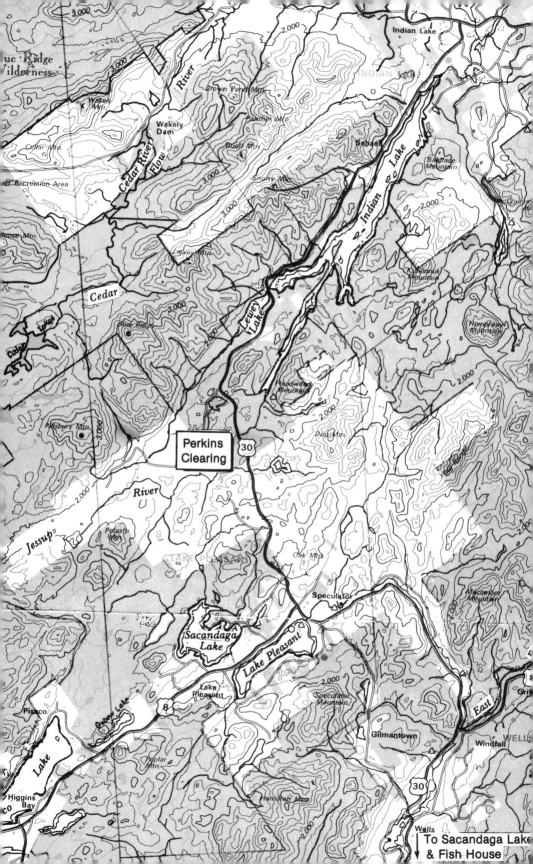